AF339217

Hindu
Gods and Goddesses

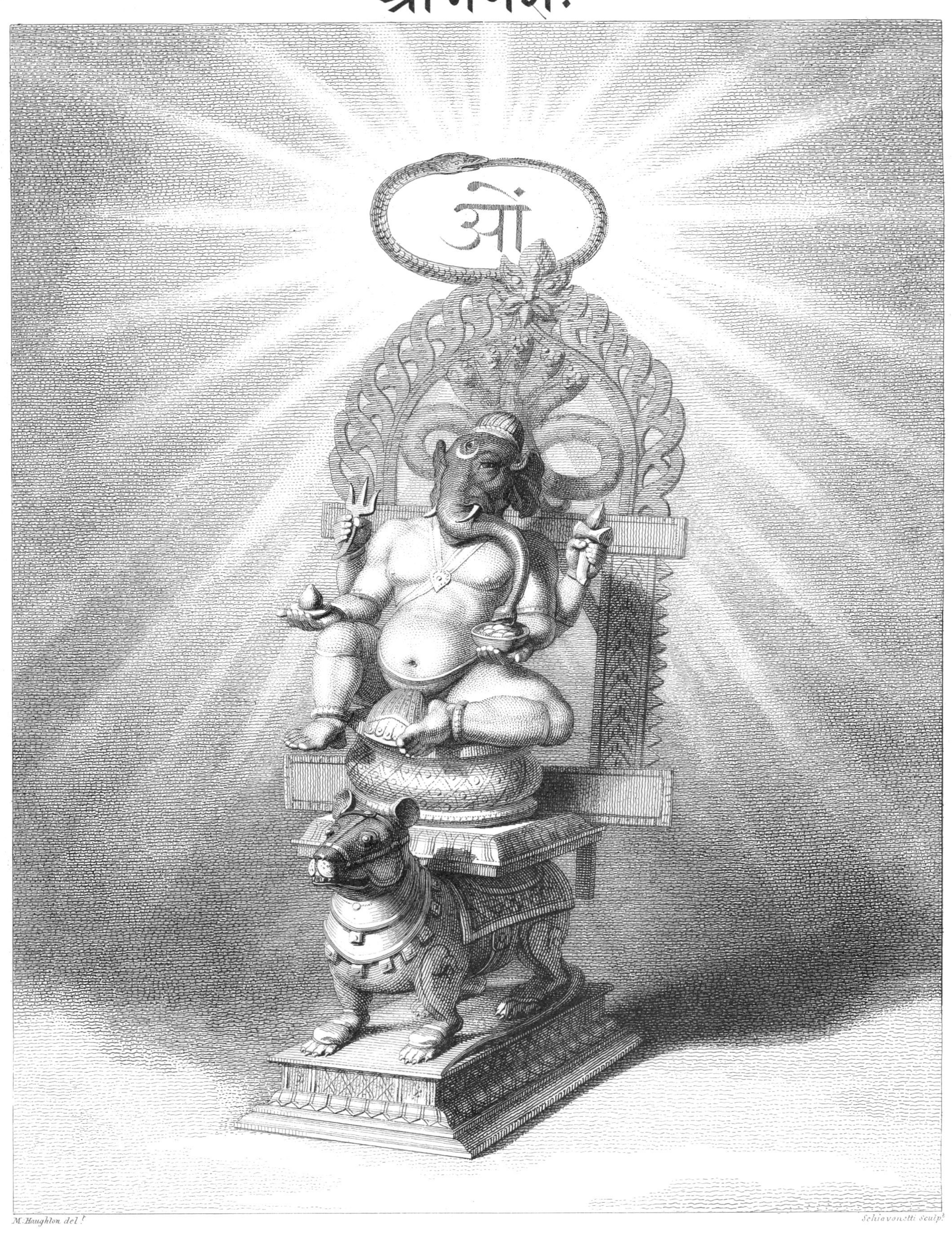

GANESA.

Hindu
Gods and Goddesses

300 Illustrations from
"The Hindu Pantheon"

Edward Moor

Dover Publications, Inc., Mineola, New York

Bibliographical Note

This Dover edition, first published in 2006, is an unabridged republication of the work originally published in 1861 by Williams and Norgate, London under the title, *Plates Illustrating the Hindu Pantheon, Reprinted from the Work of Major Edward Moor, F.R.S.* The volume was edited with a brief Descriptive Index by Allen Page Moor.

International Standard Book Number: 0-486-45131-3

Manufactured in the United States of America
Dover Publications, Inc., 31 East 2nd Street, Mineola, N.Y. 11501

DESCRIPTIVE INDEX.

Pʟ. 1. Fʀᴏɴᴛɪsᴘɪᴇᴄᴇ. *(From a cast in brass.)* Gᴀɴêçᴀ, son of Çiva and Pârvatî; the God of Prudence and Policy, invoked by Hindus at the commencement of any important undertaking. He is frequently represented, as in this cast, riding upon a rat, as an emblem of wisdom and foresight. Above his head is placed the mystic syllable of the Brahmans, from the pen of **Mr. Wilkins**, as are also the Sanskrit words, Çʀî Gᴀɴêçᴀ, in the upper margin.

Pʟ. 2. Sᴇᴄᴛᴀʀɪᴀʟ Mᴀʀᴋs, ᴇᴛᴄ. The marks contained in the three upper rows distinguish, generally, Vishnu, or deities closely connected with him, and his Avatârs; they are therefore borne especially by the Vaishnavas, or devotees of the Vishnu sect. The important element in these marks is the perpendicular stroke. 27 and 28 are very rarely found, and may represent the Chakra of Vishnu. 29—33 are of doubtful meaning and authority. 34—37 mark generally, though not exclusively, Çiva, Pârvatî, and their votaries. 38 is seen on Kâlî, a form of Dêvî, in Pʟ. 27. 39 is thought to represent the Linga. The triangle, with the apex upwards, as in 40 and others, belongs to Çiva, as representing fire; the inverted triangle, in 41 and others, is Vishnu's symbol, representing water. 47 and the following, containing horizontal lines, belong to Çiva, Pârvatî, and their kindred deities, and their adherents. In Pʟ. 18 many of these sectarial marks are well seen on the foreheads of the different figures. 71—74 are rare, and, as well as 84, belong rather to certain great families than to religious sects. 75—83; the crescent seems to belong exclusively to Mahâdêva and his family. 85—88 are found on some of the Avatârs of Vishnu. 89 "is taken from a stout piece of copper of the same size, rising, layer over layer, as the circles lessen upwards," and containing a mystic emblem in the centre. The characters are ancient Sanskrit.

Pʟ. 3. *(From a modern cast, ten inches high, designed by Wilkins, under the direction of learned Pandits.)* Bʀᴀʜᴍâ, in his usual form, has four faces and four arms; in the hands he holds a portion of the Veda, a spoon for lustral ablutions, a rosary, and a vessel of lustral water. He bears on the forehead the mark of

Çiva; he is sometimes found with the mark of Vishnu; sometimes with both combined, as partaking of the character of both deities.

Pl. 4.   *(From a coloured drawing.)*   Brahmâ, officiating as a Brahman.   His consort, or Çakti, Saraswatî, is attending upon him.

Pl. 5.   *Above: (From an outline sketch.)*   The three grand attributes of the Deity—Creation, Preservation, Destruction—personified in Brahmâ, Vishnu, Çiva. Brahmâ holds the same instruments as in Pl. 3.   Vishnu holds in his extended right hand the *Chakra*, a missile weapon, like a quoit, in this figure emitting flames from its edge; in his left extended hand the *Çankh*, a sea-shell of the genus Buccinum.   This shell is the attribute which more certainly distinguishes the figures of Vishnu.   These are seen more simply represented in Vishnu's right pair of hands, in Pl. 13.

Çiva holds a warlike weapon, and an antelope, generally given to *Chandra*, the moon, as in Pl. 89.   Çiva, here, as in the figure below, has his loins wrapped in a tiger's skin.   The face in his head-piece is that of the river-goddess *Gangâ*, as in Pl. 19.

Below: (From an outline sketch.)   Çiva or Mahâdêva, as above, with his consort Pârvatî.   The small figure between them is unexplained.

Pl. 6.   (1) Vishnu, from a cast about twelve inches high.

(2) Vishnu, in his Avatâr of Varaha, or the Boar; with his consort Lakshmî; in this character called Vârâhî.

(3, 4) Probably Lakshmî; unless the cup in the inferior left hand distinguish the figure as Dêvî, the consort of Çiva.

(5) Lakshmî.

Pl. 7.   *Above: (From a tinted picture.)*   Vishnu, under this form called *Nârâyana*, "moving on the waters" (Manu, I. 10), reposing on the serpent Çesha, (called also *Ananta*,) contemplating and willing the creation of the world. The creative power, Brahmâ, is seen springing forth upon a lotus to the surface of the ocean.   The figure chafing Vishnu's feet is Lakshmî.

Below: (From a tinted picture.)   Çiva and Pârvatî conjoined, under this form called *Arddhanâri*.   The same combination is seen in figs. 1 and 2 of Pl. 24.

Pl. 8.   (1) *(From a bronze cast.)*   Vishnu, with his wives Lakshmî and Satyavâmâ; Brahmâ, as in Pl. 7, springing forth upon a lotus.

(2, 3, 4) Lakshmî; under this form called Kamalâ, as bearing the lotus.

Pl. 9.   *(All the figures are from bronze casts.)*   (1) Vishnu.

(2, 3) Lakshmî, or Kamalâ.   The infant may represent Kâma.

(4—7) Dêvî, or Bhavânî (a form of Pârvatî); when, as in these figures, bearing the ladle, called Annapûrnâ.

PL. 10. *Above: (From a picture.)* MAHÂKÂLA (represented as MAHÂPRALAYA, "grand consummation of all things"), devouring the universe. Around him are seen Brahmâ, Vishnu, and Çiva, all awaiting the inevitable doom.
Below: VISHNU, with LAKSHMÎ, on Garuda.

PL. 11. (1, 2, 3) VISHNU, with LAKSHMÎ. Each cast is about the size of the engraving; fig. 3 is of gilt brass, the eyes formed of rubies, with which the figures are otherwise ornamented.
(4, 5) VISHNU, in a subordinate Avatâr, called, by Western pandits, BALLAJI; and Lakshmî.
(6, 7) VISHNU, in a subordinate Avatâr, called Wittoba; and Lakshmî.

PL. 12. *Left-hand figure: (From a cast in silver; the central figure gilt.)* VISHNU, in his Avatâr called Ballaji; with his wives Lakshmî and Satyavâmâ.
Right-hand figure. The attributes in the hands indicate Vishnu; those on the pedestal, Mahâdêva or Çiva. The figure is described as BHAIRAVA, an Avatâr of the latter deity.

PL. 13. ÇIVA and VISHNU, from modern casts, executed at Benares, under the direction of Wilkins and learned Brahmans. The small figure above is KRISHNA.

PL. 14. *(From a bronze cast, twenty-four inches high.)* ÇIVA destroying the demon TRIPURÂSURA.

PL. 15. ÇIVA, from a modern cast designed by Wilkins. Under this form Çiva is known as MAHÂDÊVA PANCHAMUKHÎ, or the *five-faced.*

PL. 16. (1, 2) Back and front views of a bronze image of the size of the engraving of MAHÂDÊVA PANCHAMUKHÎ.
(3) ÇIVA or MAHÂDÊVA, with PÂRVATÎ. In bronze, about ten inches high.

PL. 17. *(From a highly finished and elaborately coloured native painting.)* MAHÂDÊVA and PÂRVATÎ.

PL. 18. *(From a large coloured picture.)* MAHÂDÊVA and PÂRVATÎ, in Kailâsa, the terrestrial Paradise. The mythological figures on the right are their sons, Ganêça and Kârtikêya; on the left, Brahmâ and Vishnu.

PL. 19. *(From pictures.)* *Above:* MAHÂDÊVA PANCHAMUKHÎ, with PÂRVATÎ, nursing the infant GANÊÇA. The attendant on the right wears his hair after the fashion of Mahâdêva.
Below: MAHÂDÊVA, mounted on his bull, carrying his wife PÂRVATÎ, and his sons Kârtikêya and Ganêça.

PL. 20. *Above:* MAHÂDÊVA, attended by PÂRVATÎ and GANÊÇA.
Below: VISHNU, under the form NÂRÂYANA, as in PL. 7.

Pl. 21. *Above:* Mahâdêva, springing from his symbol, the *Linga*, slaying a demon, or *Daitya.*

Below: Mahâdêva and Pârvatî, on their respective *vahans* or vehicles.

Pl. 22. *(From a highly finished painting.)* A female devotee performing the ceremony called *Lingapújâ*, in honour of Mahâdêva.

Pl. 23. *(From pictures.)* *Above:* A group representing the three personified powers of the Deity (comp. Pl. 5); each with his *Çakti*, or consort; namely, Vishnu with Lakshmî; Çiva and Pârvatî; Brahmâ and Saraswatî, or Brahmî. Vishnu and Brahmâ are seated on expanded lotus-flowers.

Below: Mahâdêva and Pârvatî, in the Avatâr in which, according to some local legends of Western Hindustan, they bear the names of Kanda Rao and Mâlsârâ.

Pl. 24. *(From pictures).* (1, 2) Mahâdêva and Pârvatî conjoined; in this form called Arddhanârî.

(3) Bhairava, an Avatâr of Mahâdêva.

(4) Saraswatî, consort of Brahmâ, on her *vahan*.

Pl. 25. *(From an embossed brass shield.)* Probably Vîrabhadra, either a son, or an Avatâr of Mahâdêva. The side figures may represent Daksha, slain by Vîrabhadra, and his wife, Çrîdêvî.

Pl. 26. *(From casts in brass.)*

(1) Vishnu and Lakshmî.

(2) Mahâdêva and Pârvatî.

(3) The same subject as Pl. 25.

Pl. 27. *(From a cast, eighteen inches high.)* Kâlî, a form of Pârvatî, as an impersonation of Vengeance.

Pl. 28. *(From a bronze cast, twelve inches high.)* Kâlî, in this form called Bhadrakâlî.

Pl. 29. *(From an ink sketch.)* Kâlî, with Brahmans and other attendants. The peacocks, seen above, generally belong to her son Kârtikêya, or to Saraswatî. The Lingas, in the temples above, right and left, mark her as the consort of Mahâdêva.

Pl. 30. *(From a well-executed marble, about two feet high.)* Dêvî, a form of Pârvatî.

Pl. 31. *(From a drawing by a native artist, under the direction of a learned pandit.)* A mythological composition, introducing the chief deities. Above is Dêvî; then in descending order on the left, Çiva, Vishnu, Brahmâ; on the right, Agni, Indra, and an attendant, or worshipper. The figures in the upper corners are Sûrya and Chandra, the Sun and Moon. On the lower part of the mountain are seen devotees in various postures of penance.

Pl. 32. Dêvî, with attendant deities, named below.

Pl. 33. *Above:* Dêvî, with elephants above, as in Pl. 30.
Below: Durgâ (Dêvî, or Pârvatî, personifying Active Virtue) slaying an impersonation of Vice, generally named Mahishâsura.

Pl. 34. (1) The same subject as in the lower half of Pl. 33.
(2) From a small and very rude cast in brass, made, probably, to invoke a happy calving-season, with reference to Surabhî, the Cow of Plenty.
(3) From a thin piece of embossed copper. Saptâpsarâ, or the seven Apsaras, or inferior deities, who presided over wells and fountains. The accompanying buffalo is an animal that delights in water, and is often used in raising it for purposes of irrigation.

Pl. 35. The same subject as in Pl. 34, 1.

Pl. 36, 37, 38, 39. Dêvî, under various forms. The casts are all about the same size as the figures. (2) of Pl. 38, and (1), (2), (6), of Pl. 39, represent the avenging character of the goddess. In (3) and (4) of Pl. 39 are seen the elephants, as before in Pl. 30 and 33.

Pl. 40. (*From thin stamped plates of copper, the size of the figures*).
(1) Bhavânî; when sitting, as here, on a litter, called Palyanka.
(2) A local deity or saint, named Yenkuba, with Ganêça, here called Ganapati.
(3) Dêvî, mounted on a tiger; under this form called Vyâghrayâyî.
(4) Hanumân.
(5) Dêvî, under the form called Rudrânî.
(6) Garuda.
(7) Dêvî, on a buffalo; under this form called Mahishaçâyî.
(8) Unexplained by the author. The names in the Plate probably given on the authority of Pandits.
(9) A form of Bhavânî.

Pl. 41. (1) Dêvî, marked by the trident and cup.
(2) Dêvî.
(3) From a very old and rude cast, said to be Bhairava.
(4) Doubtful; the Çankh and Chakra seem to indicate Vishnu, or Lakshmî.
(5) Dêvî, under the form called Satvadêvî.

Pl. 42. (1), (3), (4). Dêvî, with various attributes, some rather rare.
(2) Probably Çiva and Pârvatî.

Pl. 43. *Upper figures:* Marked in Plate Bhairava. Some of the attributes of the left hand figure are those of Dêvî; as is also the Linga in the hand of the figure on the right.

Below : VISHNU and LAKSHMÎ; ÇIVA and PÂRVATÎ, or else BHAIRAVA and his consort.

PL. 44. (*From casts about the size represented.*)   GAṆÊÇA, the God of Wisdom and Prudence, under various forms.

PL. 45. (*From pictures.*)   *Above :* GAṆÊÇA, seated on an expanded lotus, with SARASWATÎ, consort of Brahmâ, on a peacock.
Below : SARASWATÎ, as before, with an attendant.

PL. 46. (*From pictures.*)   *Above :* KÂRTIKÊYA, with his reputed parents, ÇIVA and PÂRVATÎ.
The subject of the lower picture is doubtful.

PL. 47. *Above :* Marked BHAIRAVA in the Plate.   It is doubtful whether the picture represents a mythological subject at all.
Below : BHAIRAVA (see PL. 24, 3), with worshipper and attendant.

PL. 48. (*From zinc casts after designs by Wilkins.*)   The first three Avatârs of Vishnu; the MATSYÂVATÂRA, the KÛRMÂVATÂRA, and the VARÂHÂVATÂRA : or the *Fish-*, *Tortoise-*, and *Boar-incarnations.*

PL. 49. The churning of the ocean, during the second incarnation of Vishnu, for the recovery of the Amrita, or elixir of immortality, and other valuable gifts, lost to man by the Deluge.   In the picture Vishnu appears thrice : as the tortoise, as seated on the mountain *Mandara*, and in his place among the chief deities on the left.   The mountain served as an axle, the serpent *Vâsuki* as a rope, and the *Asurâs*, or powers of evil, as the counter-power.   Below are seen the gifts that were thus recovered, some of them endowed with preternatural virtues.

PL. 50. (*From a cast designed by Wilkins.*)   Vishnu, in his fourth incarnation, as the Narasinha, or man-lion ; here represented as bursting forth from a rent pillar to avenge the impiety of Hiranyakaçipu, who, denying in an argument the omnipresence of the Deity, had pointed to a pillar, and derisively asked, "Is, then, the Deity here ?"

PL. 51. (*From the set of casts by Wilkins.*)   (1) Vishnu, in his incarnation as KRISHNA.
(2), (3), (4). The incarnations known as Halâyudharâma, Râmachandra, Paraçu-râma; (or Plough-armed Râma, Moon- or bow-armed Râma, and Axe-armed Râma).   Of Vishnu's incarnation, as VÂMANA, the dwarf, the author has given no illustration.

PL. 52. (*This Plate, together with the five following, is taken from drawings illustrating the Râmâyana.*)   The contention between Râma and Râvana for the possession of the beautiful Sîtâ (an incarnation of Lakshmî).

Above : Is the discomfiture of the many-headed Râvana in his attempt to bend the bow Dhanush, witnessed by Râma and others.

Below : Râma is performing the difficult condition of victory, to shoot with the bow Dhanush through the left eye a fish, while revolving on a pole, without seeing the fish, but only its reflection in a pan of oil.

PL. 53. HANUMÂN, assisted by SUGRÎVA and his associates, building Râma's bridge from the Continent to Ceylon, in order to attack Râvana, and rescue Sîtâ. The rocks with which it was constructed, being marked RÂ, MA, adapted themselves by the magic potency of these syllables, to the precise spot destined for them, Hanumân having merely to receive and place them.

PL. 54. (*From pictures representing legends in the Râmâyana.*) *Above :* HANUMÂN, five-headed, as son of Çiva (see PL. 19), supporting on his arms Râma and Sîtâ.

Below : HANUMÂN, having an audience with the ten-headed and twenty-handed Râvana, tyrant of Ceylon. On this occasion, it is related, Hanumân's tail, on which he was seated, spontaneously lengthened itself, and, by its repeated folds, raised his head above that of Râvana.

PL. 55. *Below :* SÎTÂ learning from RÂMA the necessity of her undergoing the fire-ordeal, to satisfy the world of her chaste escape from the power of Râvana.

Above : SÎTÂ is seen in the flames, comforted by the presence of AGNI, the God of Fire.

PL. 56. In continuation of the subject of the preceding Plate, the triumphant issue of the ordeal is rapturously hailed by the associates of Hanumân, who communicates to Rama the joyful tidings.

PL. 57. RÂMA re-united to SÎTÂ, round whose neck he throws the chaplet of marriage. From above, the *Pushpavrishṭi*, or *flower-rain*, is seen falling upon the happy pair.

PL. 58. KRISHNA, after his birth from DÊVAKÎ, conveyed across the river Yamunâ by his reputed father VASUDÊVA, under the protection of the serpent ÇÊSHA. He thus escapes from his uncle Kansa, and is placed under the charge of his foster-mother Yaçodhâ.

PL. 59. KRISHNA nursed by his mother DÊVAKÎ, or by his foster-mother Yaçodhâ.

PL. 60. (*From casts, except fig. 9, which is from a picture.*) (1)—(6). BÂLAKRISHNA, or Krishna as a boy. The ball in the hand is said by some to represent the world, by others to be a plaything. In (7), while yet a boy, he is destroying the serpent *Kâliya.* In (8), he is seen in his character of *Muralidhar,* "the Tuneful." (9) seems to combine both characters ; identifying him with Apollo, the slayer of the serpent Pytho, and the deity presiding over music.

PL. 61. KRISHNA uplifting the mountain Gôvardhana, to shelter his worshippers from the wrath of Indra, the Jupiter Pluvius of the Hindu Pantheon, who is attempting to destroy the world by the deluge of rain seen falling above.

PL. 62. Described by the author, with some doubt, as representing "Krishna about to destroy the serpent Kâliya."

PL. 63. RÂSAMANDALA, a circular dance in honour of Krishna. The following legend is related in order to account for the multiplied appearance of Krishna :—A number of virgins having assembled to celebrate the descent of Krishna, the deity himself appeared among them, and proposed a dance, and, to supply the deficiency of partners, he divided himself into as many portions as there were damsels.

PL. 64. *Above :* The marriage of KRISHNA with a bear.
Below : A miracle attributed to KRISHNA. "Being on one occasion in great jeopardy from the wrath of some of his numerous enemies, he produced an immense snake, which received and sheltered in his capacious stomach his flocks, herds, himself, and fellow-shepherds."

PL. 65 and 66. Whimsical combinations of KRISHNA and his attendant Gôpîs.

PL. 67. KRISHNA, with his chief wife RÂDHÂ, and attendants.

PL. 68. (*From a statue of black marble of life size.*) BUDDHA. The rings in the ears are probably given, by a mistake of the engravers, for the elongated ears common in the statues of Buddha (see PL. 73).

PL. 69. (*From a statue in white stone.*) BUDDHA, represented with seven faces. The author is inclined to consider this an unauthorized innovation on the part of the sculptor, never having seen Buddha thus represented elsewhere.

PL. 70. (1), (2), (3), (4) (*From metal casts of the size given.*) Possibly Buddhas, but in rare and exceptional forms.

(5) BUDDHA, from a fine cast in brass, gilt. The peculiar mark on the forehead may represent the lock of hair mentioned as one of the special beauties of Buddha.

(6), (7), (8) From small casts in *lak*, dug up at Buddhagaya.

PL. 71. (1) BUDDHA, from Wilkins' set of Avatârs, cast at Benares: it is of zinc, six inches high. "The position of the hands and feet, and the woolly head, are in the usual style ; but being a Brahminical Buddha, we here see long hair braided in a neat knot on the top of the head ; and he has not the pendent ears common to the Buddhas of Ava, the Dekkan, and Ceylon."

(2) A BUDDHA, from China ; of alabaster, delicately sculptured, about six inches high.

(3) A Buddha, from Ava; of silver, eleven inches high.

Pl. 72. Buddha, from a sculpture in the rock temple at Karlee, between Bombay and Poonah.

Pl. 73. (1) Colossal statue of Gomatîçvara, or Gomata Râya, seventy feet high, at Sravana Belgula, a village in the Mysore, in which the Jain tenets still continue to be prevalent. The statue is of one solid block, and is supposed to have been formed by hewing away the original mass of rock, until the statue alone remained.

(2) A similar statue of the same at Einûru, in Canara.

Pl. 74. "The sketch from which Pl. 74 is taken, I must, I think, have obtained from the same source as that of fig. 1 of the last plate; but having omitted to mark it, I am not certain."—*Hindu Pantheon*, p. 254.

Pl. 75. (1) Vishnu, gorgeously attired and decorated, with his usual attributes, standing upon an expanded lotus. The canopy is formed by Çesha doubled; a very rare form.

(2) Mythological group representing the union of the three sacred rivers, Ganga, Yamuna, and Saraswatî, personified respectively by Pârvatî, Lakshmî, and Saraswatî. This figure is called Trivênî, or "three plaited locks," and forms a female Triad.

(3) Buddha, as a Brahminical Avatâr.

Pl. 76. *Above:* Ballaji (a form of Vishnu), with two wives.

Below: Fac-simile of a sketch by Mr. Salt, from a ruined temple at Çiva Samudra, an island in the river Caverî. Possibly Buddha.

Pl. 77. Elevation and view of a pillar of granite, 52 feet in height, facing a Jain temple at Mudubidery, near Mangalore, in Canara.

Pl. 78. A wooden pillar from a palace at the same place.

Pl. 79. Indra, the god of the firmament or atmosphere. The upper half of his body is covered with eyes. In the upper figure he is mounted on his elephant Airâvata, coloured in this picture white, with a crimson outline.

Pl. 80. *Above:* Agni, the god of Fire; coloured, as he generally is, deep red. His *vahan* is a ram.

Below, to the right: Agni, seated. *To the left:* Probably Pâvana, holding the infant Hanumân.

Pl. 81. Trimûrti, the Hindu Triad. From a bust in granite, about two feet high, dug from the ruins of a temple in the island of Bombay, and deposited by Major Moor in the Museum of the India House.

Pl. 82. The Trimûrti, represented at full length, very rare. The original is about two feet high and broad, and one foot thick; the back unhewn. It was found in the same place as the preceding.

The small figure in the upper corner is from the rock temple of Salsette, "representing an individual of one of the many celestial bands introduced among the epic machinery of the Hindus."

Pl. 83. (1) A complicated form of *Linga*, from an ancient and rude cast in brass of the size of the figure.

(2) From a very old cast of the same size, apparently representing a tiger bound to a stake, with a *Linga* and *Nandi* beside it; possibly a votive offering of gratitude, in allusion to some personal escape.

(3) A subject similar to fig. 1, carved in hard black wood, of the size of the figure.

(4) An expanded lotus-flower, borne on the back of a tiger, forming a lamp.

(5) A group in brass, about three inches square. At the back is *Ganêça*, and in front a *Linga* and *Nandi*.

Pl. 84. (1) From a brass cast. *Nandi* kneeling before a Linga.

(2), (3) The same, with the addition of the serpent *Nâga*, with a hood expanded over the Linga. The five balls in fig. 2, appearing again in Pl. 85 (1), are said to refer mystically to Ganêça, Dêvî, Sûrya, and Vishnu, with Mahâdêva resting upon them.

(4) A lotus borne by Garuda, from a cast in copper, of the size represented.

Pl. 85. (1), (3) Groups composed of the same elements as fig. 2 of Pl. 84; the Nâga in fig. 1 being five-headed.

(2) A five-wicked lamp, used in pûjâ to Çiva.

(4), (6) Spoons for laving images with holy water. The usual Sanskrit name for them is Sruva.

(5) A Kamala, or lotus, closed; borne by a tortoise (Kûrma); used, when expanded by screwing down the confining circle round the base, for holding flowers in pûjâ to Vishnu in the Kûrmâvatâra.

Pl. 86. (1), (2) Two sacrificial spoons richly ornamented.

In (1) Ganêça is above the bowl; then Krishna, with his usual attendants; the handle being formed by a head crowned with the Linga, overshadowed by a five-headed Nâga.

In (2) the handle is formed by Ganêça holding the Linga in his lap, overshadowed by Nâga.

(3), (4) Two boat- or Linga-shaped sacrificial vessels.

Pl. 87. Sûrya, the Sun ; from a cast executed at Benares, under the superintendence of Wilkins, from a sculpture in the temple of Viçvêçvara (Çiva).

Pl. 88. (*From a picture.*) The Hindu Zodiac, called Râçichakra. In the centre is (1) Sûraj, the Sun; surrounded by (2) Vrihaspati (Jupiter); (3) Kêtu (the descending node); (4) Râhu (the ascending node); (5) Budha (Mercury); (6) Mangala (Mars); (7) Chandra (the Moon); (8) Çanîchar (Saturn); (9) Çukra (Venus). The names are here given in their Hindi forms.

Pl. 89. (*From tinted pictures.*) Sûrya, the Sun; and Chandra, the Moon; each bearing the Çankh and Chandra of Vishnu, and his sectarial mark. Both figures are copper-coloured; their cars and banners are alike: the banners deep red; the only difference in colour is in the scarfs, Sûrya's being yellow, Chandra's blue fringed with yellow. Sûrya's car is drawn by his seven-headed horse, driven by the legless Arun; his glory is white, with golden rays. Chandra is drawn by a pied antelope, and has a silver crescent.

Pl. 90. *Above:* Hanumân struggling with Garuda.

Below: Garuda bearing Vishnu in an uplifted argha, the deity being about to reveal himself to Viçvamitra, the Guru, or spiritual guide of Râma.

Pl. 91. (1) (*From a fine cast in brass, of the size represented.*) Hanumân. The ground of the circle surrounding the figure is perforated, giving the effect of filigree work. The figure at the top is Krishna, seated upon and overshadowed by the five-headed serpent. On the sides of the rim are seen the Çankh and Chakra of Vishnu. The small prostrate figure on the rim below may allude to some warlike exploit of the hero.

The figures in the four corners of the plate are from casts of the same size, representing Hanumân; and (6), a cast of a monkey, may have some reference to him.

Pl. 92. (1) Possibly Hanumân, surmounted by Nâga; cast separately, for the purpose of being inserted behind casts similar to (5) of this plate, and (1) of Pl. 91.

(2) A small bell, the handle formed by a figure of Hanumân.

(3) Hanumân and Garuda, back to back, forming the handle (apparently) of a bell.

(4), (6) Garuda, known by his beaked nose and wings.

(5) The same subject as (1) of the preceding plate.

Pl. 93. *Above:* Hanumân "appears on this occasion full-gifted. He bears the *triçúla* (trident) of his reputed father Çiva; the sword of *Kâli*, and a corpse emblematical of death; the *gadâ* (club) of Vishnu; the *pâça* (cord) of Varuna; the shield of Lakshman; the *ankuça* (hook) of Ganêça; the *pârijâta* (tree of

Paradise) of Indra; and the sacrificial vase of Brahmâ." The figure may represent an epitome of Hanumân's character and actions.

Below: The meaning of this figure is very doubtful. The author describes it as a Hippogriff appearing to Lakshmî, and gives it the name Virâtarûpâ, "Universal-monarch-form." The peacock's head is devouring a city (compare Mahâpralaya, in PL. 10); the uplifted man's hand holds the gadâ of Vishnu; the other fore-foot is that of an elephant; one hind foot corresponds to the body, which is that of a tiger; the nearer hind-quarters and remaining hind-foot are those of a horse; a serpent forms the tail (comp. Rev. ix. 19).

PL. 94. Four casts representing the Avatâr of Çiva known as Kanda Rao. Of these (1) and (2) are very old and rudely executed. In (4) the dog is added, as in PL. 23. The sun and moon on the pedestal of fig. 2 should be noticed. See PL. 25, and PL. 26, fig. 3.

PL. 95. Figures from stamped plates of metal, generally copper, similar to those given in PL. 40. (1) and (3) represent the same subject as the preceding plate.

 (2) Bhairava; a son, sometimes spoken of as an Avatâr, of Çiva; with whom also (4) and (5) must, from the accompanying attributes, be in some way connected; unless the bow and arrows, in the case of (5), mark this figure as Paraçurâma.

PL. 96. From a picture representing a miracle performed near Poonah, by Nânêçvara, a local Avatâr of Vishnu. The story is briefly as follows:—Nânêçvara, with his brothers and sister, was seated on a wall, when a holy man, named Changa Dêva, was known to be approaching to visit him. Nânêçvara caused the wall to move forward and convey him and his companions to the presence of the visitor, who appeared mounted on a tiger, with a cobra for a whip. The picture exhibits a *double action:* the two principal personages having also met, Nânêçvara being in the act of raising the prostrate worshipper. The miraculous wall is said to be still shewn at Alundy, a few miles from Poonah.

PL. 97. (*From a modern cast in brass.*) BALLAJI (an Avatâr of Vishnu) with his wives (see PL. 76).

PL. 98, 99, 100. (*Chiefly from old and very rude casts in brass.*) The connection of many of these figures with the Hindu Pantheon might seem very doubtful, except when marked by the Linga, five balls, sun or crescent, or other distinctive sign. They probably occupy the position of Penates, of obscure and almost undefined character.

PL. 101. (*From a fine four-sided cast in brass.*) The four figures in order are, probably, GANÊÇA, VISHNU, ÇIVA (MAHÂDÊVA), and PÂRVATÎ. Of the second and last of these, the attributes are not distinctly given in the cast.

PL. 102. (*From a very old and rude four-sided cast in brass.*) This very complicated subject may, from the tortoise being the leading figure, be considered to have some reference to the Kûrmâvatâra, or tortoise-incarnation of Vishnu. The chief difference noticeable between the four several sides consists in the groups of figures on the lowest tier. These are, in the order shewn in the Plate, 1. GAṆÊÇA; on his right, a sword and human figure in posture of adoration; on his left, a tree and some quadruped. 2. GARUDA; on his right, a shell, a quadruped, and a bird; on his left, a head and a human figure. 3. HANUMÂN; at the feet of the animal on his right, a bow and arrow; of that on the left, a sword. 4. BHAHMÂ, four-faced; on his right, a bird and a vase; on his left, a bird and a boat-shaped argha; in front, a sceptre. As to the exact reference of the pair of feet on the back of the tortoise, overshadowed by Nâga, the author can give no satisfactory explanation.

PL. 103. Gold coins, of the size represented, from the collection of Tippoo Sahib.

PL. 104. A sacrificial vase of gilt copper, of elaborate workmanship. The handle is formed by Nâga, with Garuda behind, and a figure holding a Çankh in front. In the place of a spout is a lamp, supported by a monster; on its sides are two kneeling figures, armed with sword and shield, attendants, perhaps, of Durgâ, who is in the act of spearing the personification of Vice.

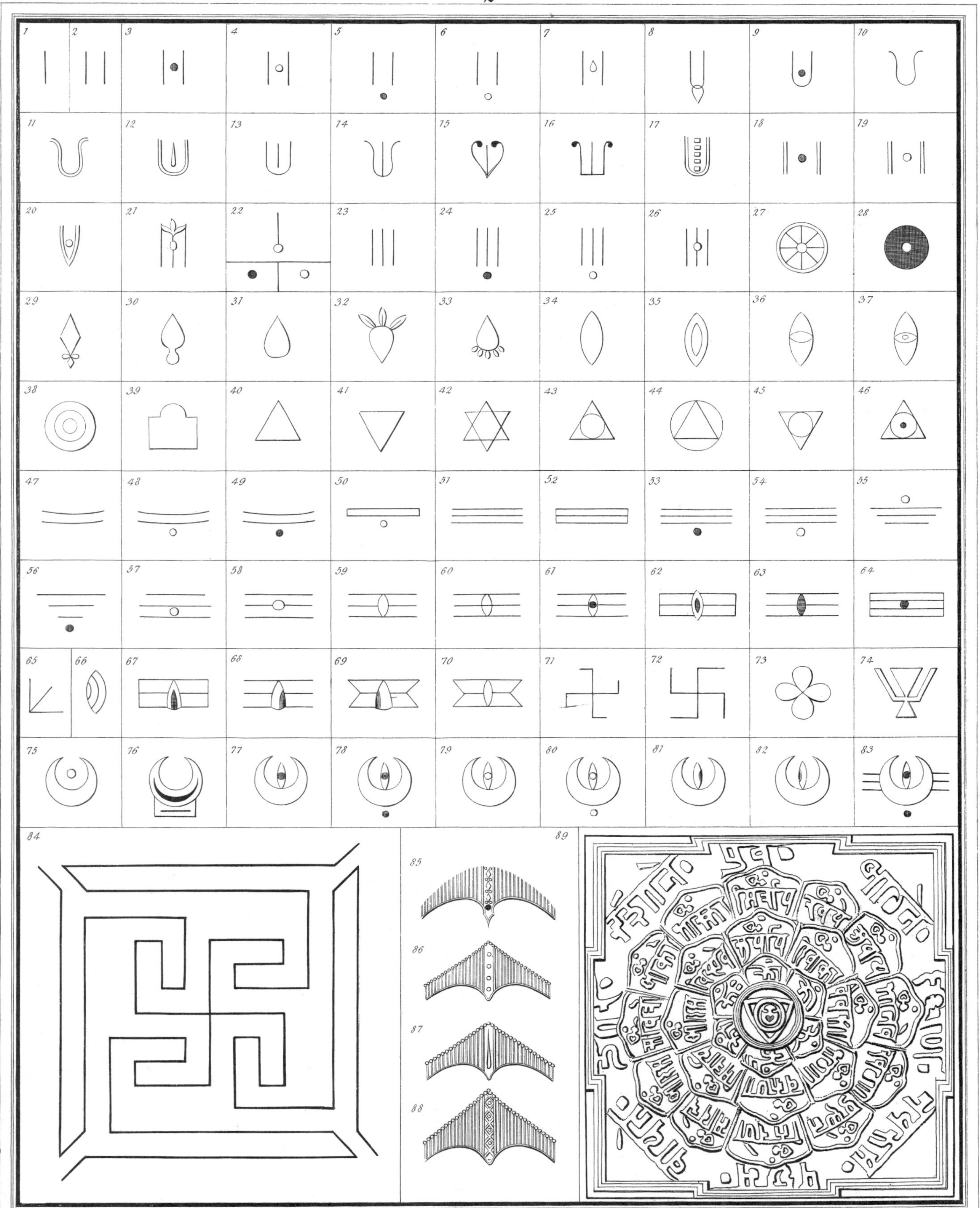

Sectarial Marks or Symbols &c.

Swaine del et. Sc.

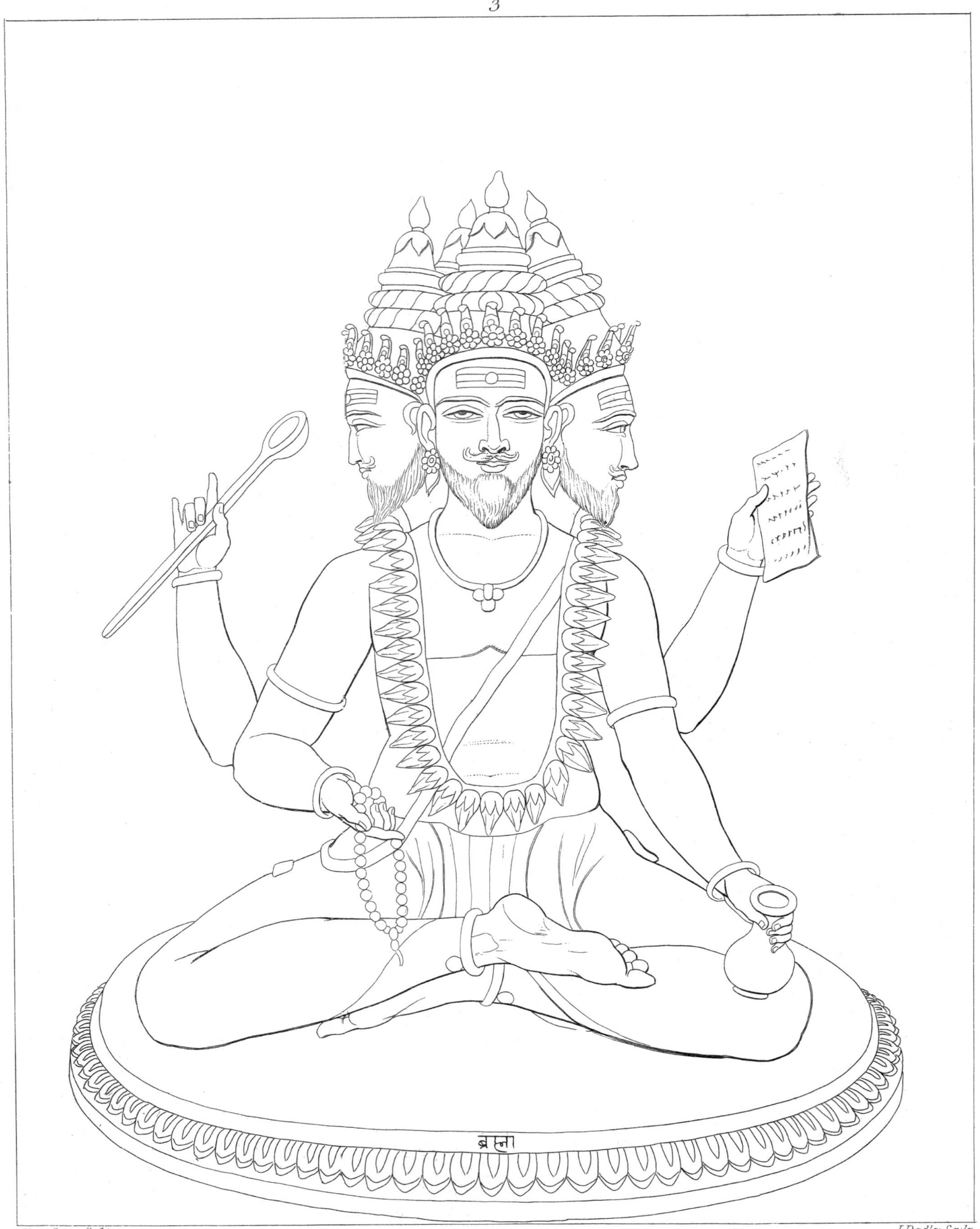

BRAHMĀ.

From a Zinc Statue in the Museum at the East India House.

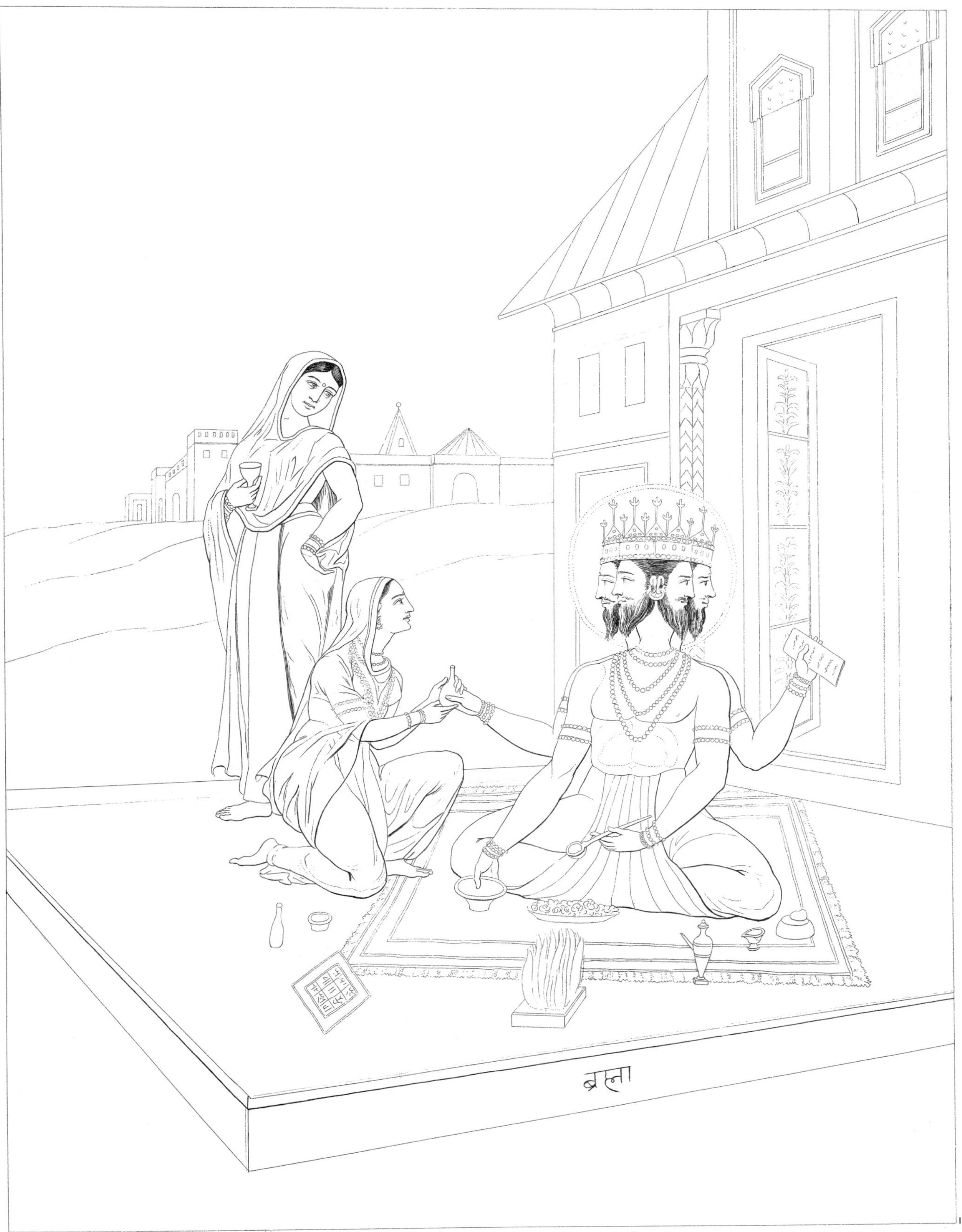

BRAHMĀ.

From a painting in the collection of Colonel Stuart.

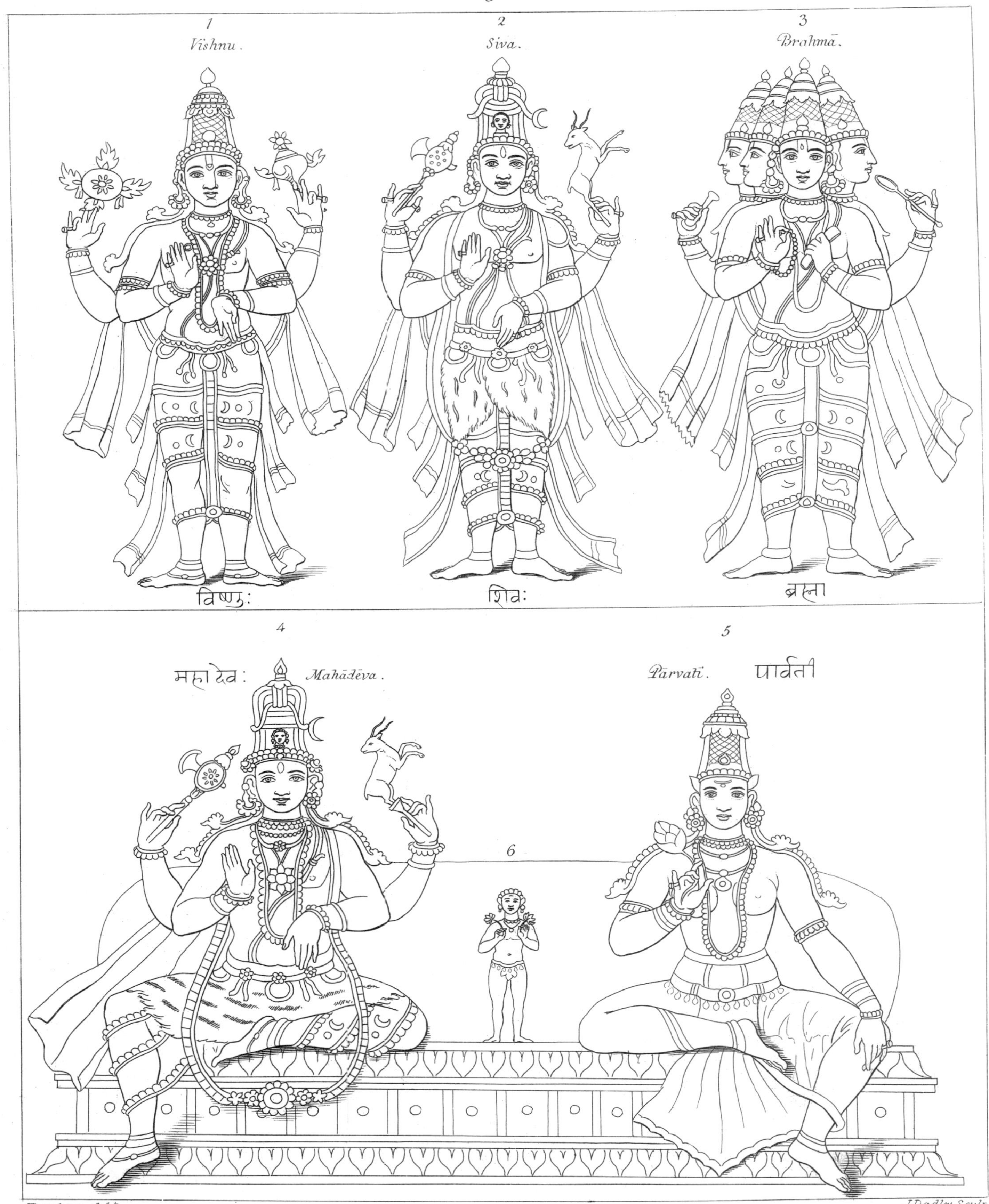

Houghton delt.

J. Dadley Sculp.

From sketches of unknown Originals.

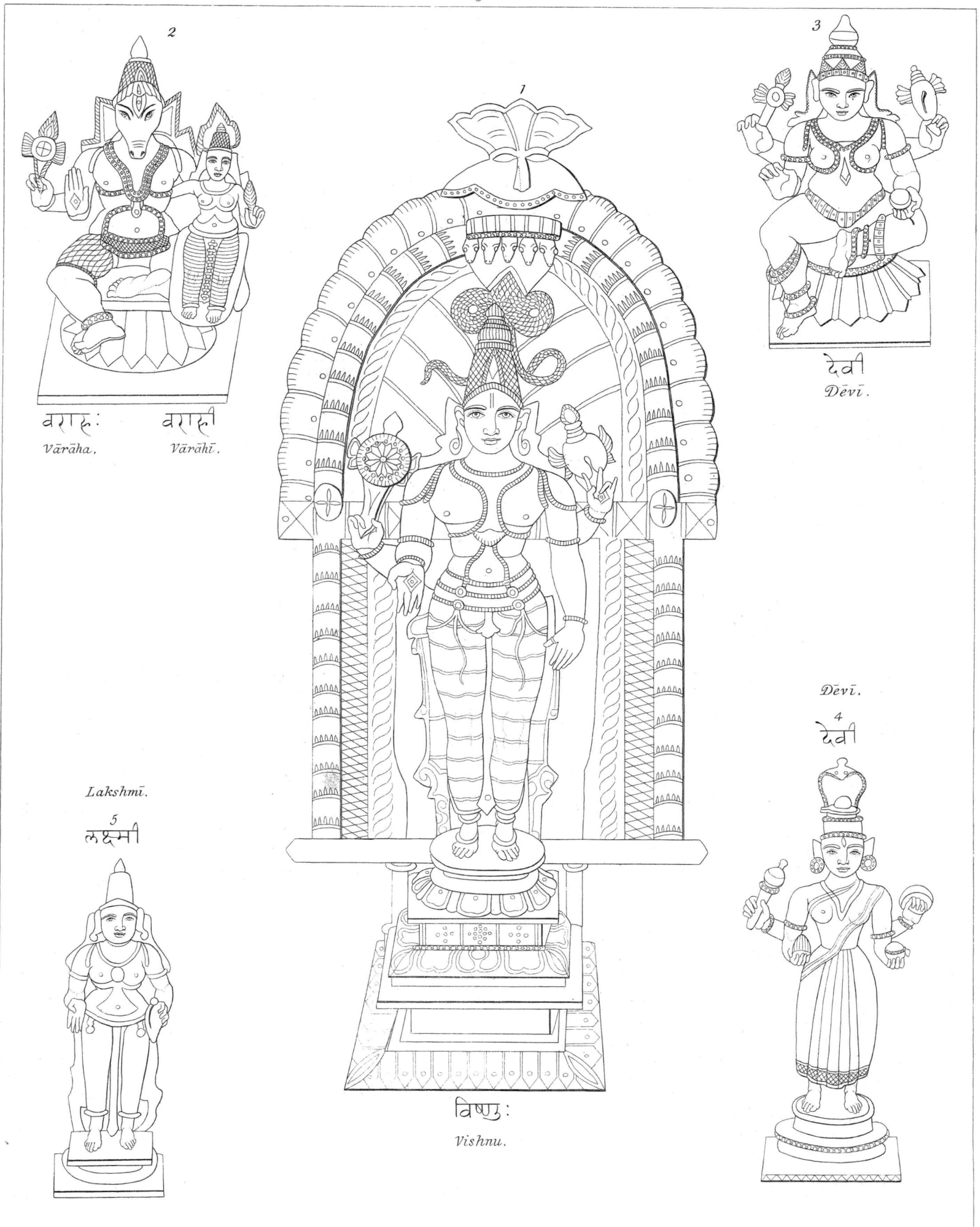

From casts in Bronze &c.

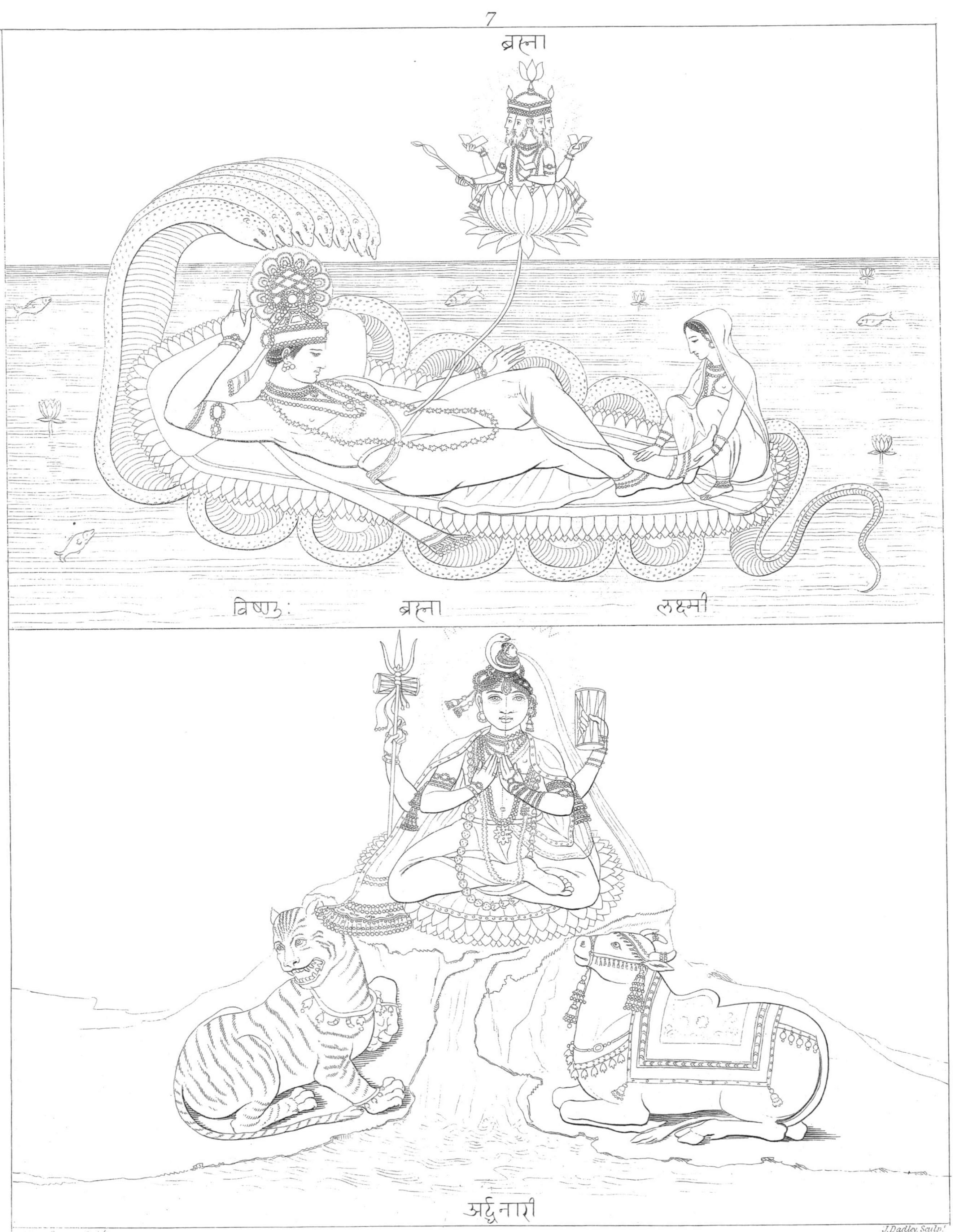

VISHNU & LAKSHMI on *SESHA* or *ANANTA* contemplating the Creation,
with BRAHMĀ springing on a lotos from his Navel to perform it.
Below, SIVA & PĀRVATĪ conjoined, called them *ARDDHA-NĀRĪ*.

From pictures in the collection of Colonel Stuart.

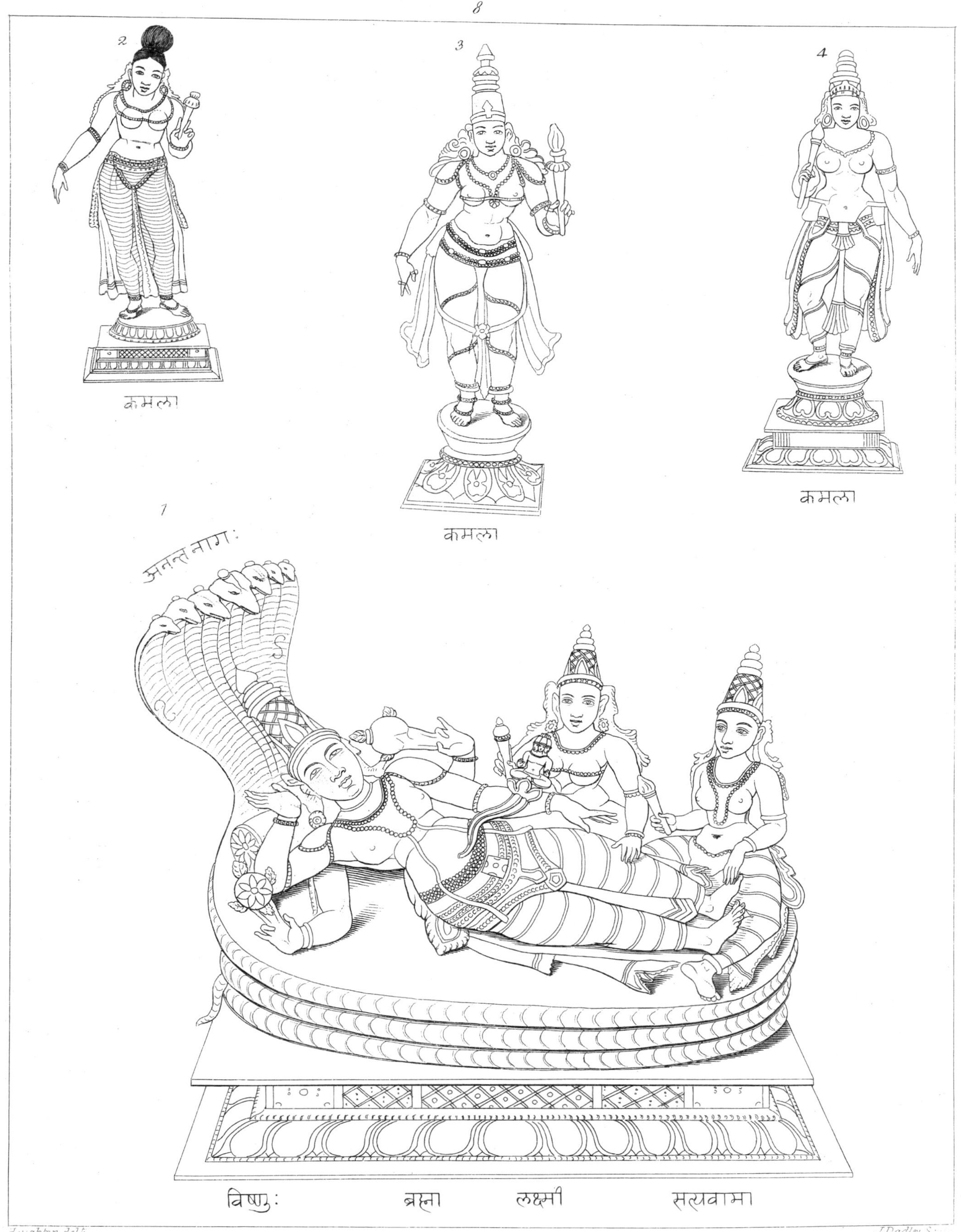

Lughton del.?   J. Dadley. S.

1. VISHNU with LAKSHMĪ & SATYAVĀMĀ on ÁNANTA NÁGA, (eternity.)

2. 3. 4. LAKSHMĪ or CAMALĀ.

1. From a bronze cast in the collection of the Right Hon. Viscount Valentia. 2. 3. 4. From bronze images.

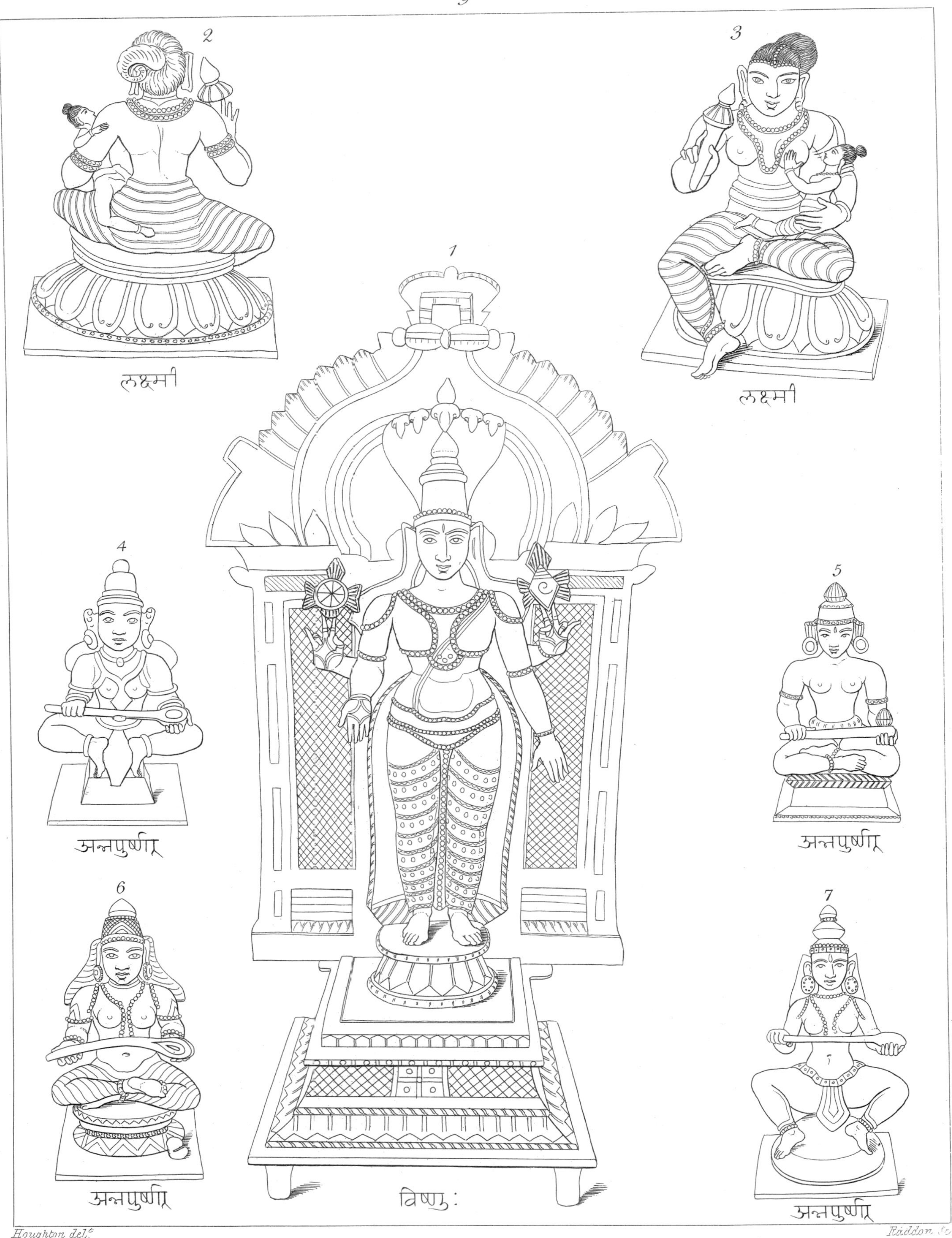

1. VISHNU. 2, 3. LAKSHMĪ. 4, 5, 6, 7. ANNA PURNĀ DĒVĪ.

From images in Bronze &c.

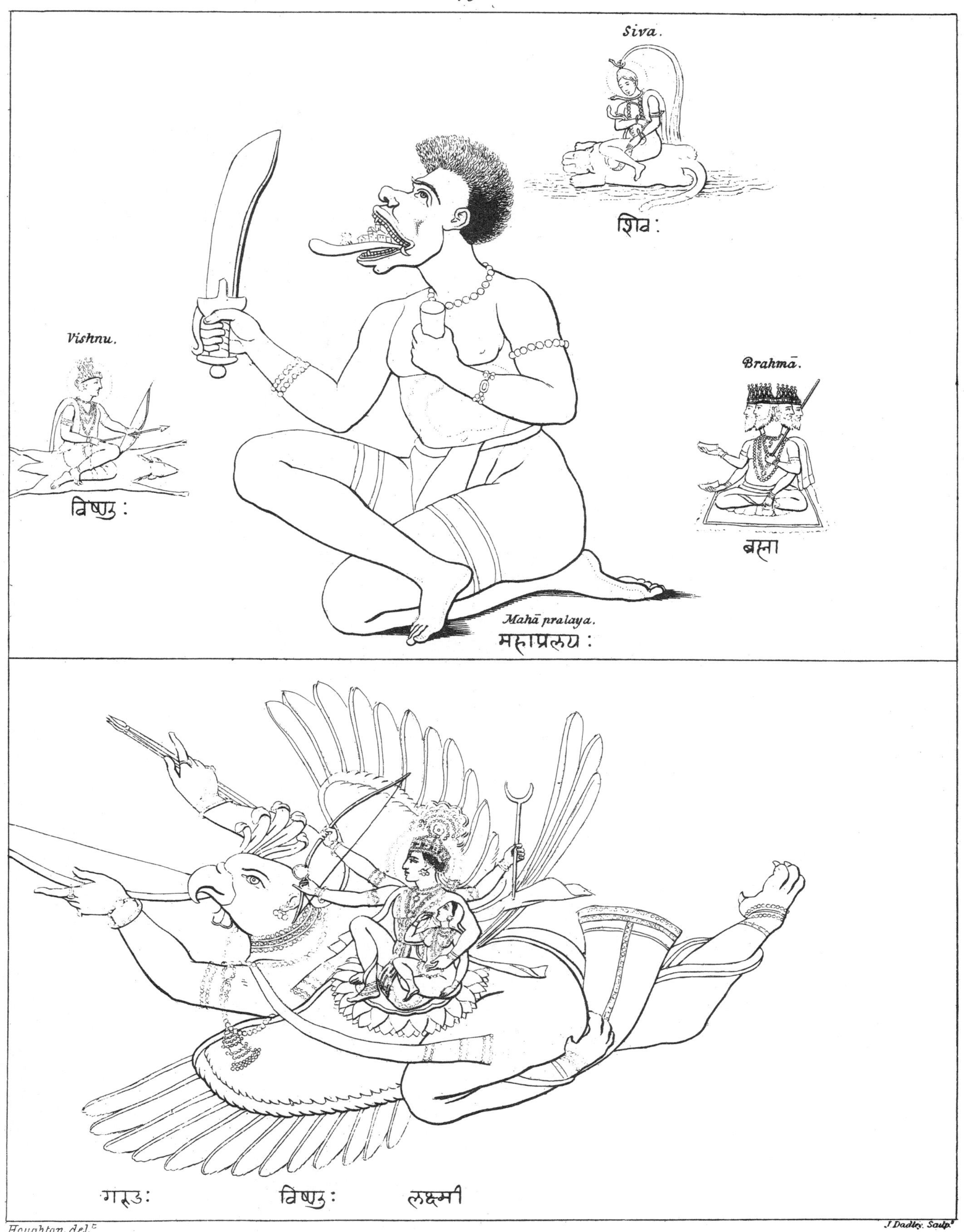

VISHNU and LAKSHMĪ on GARUDA; and MAHĀ-PRALAYA.

From pictures in the collection of Col. Stuart.

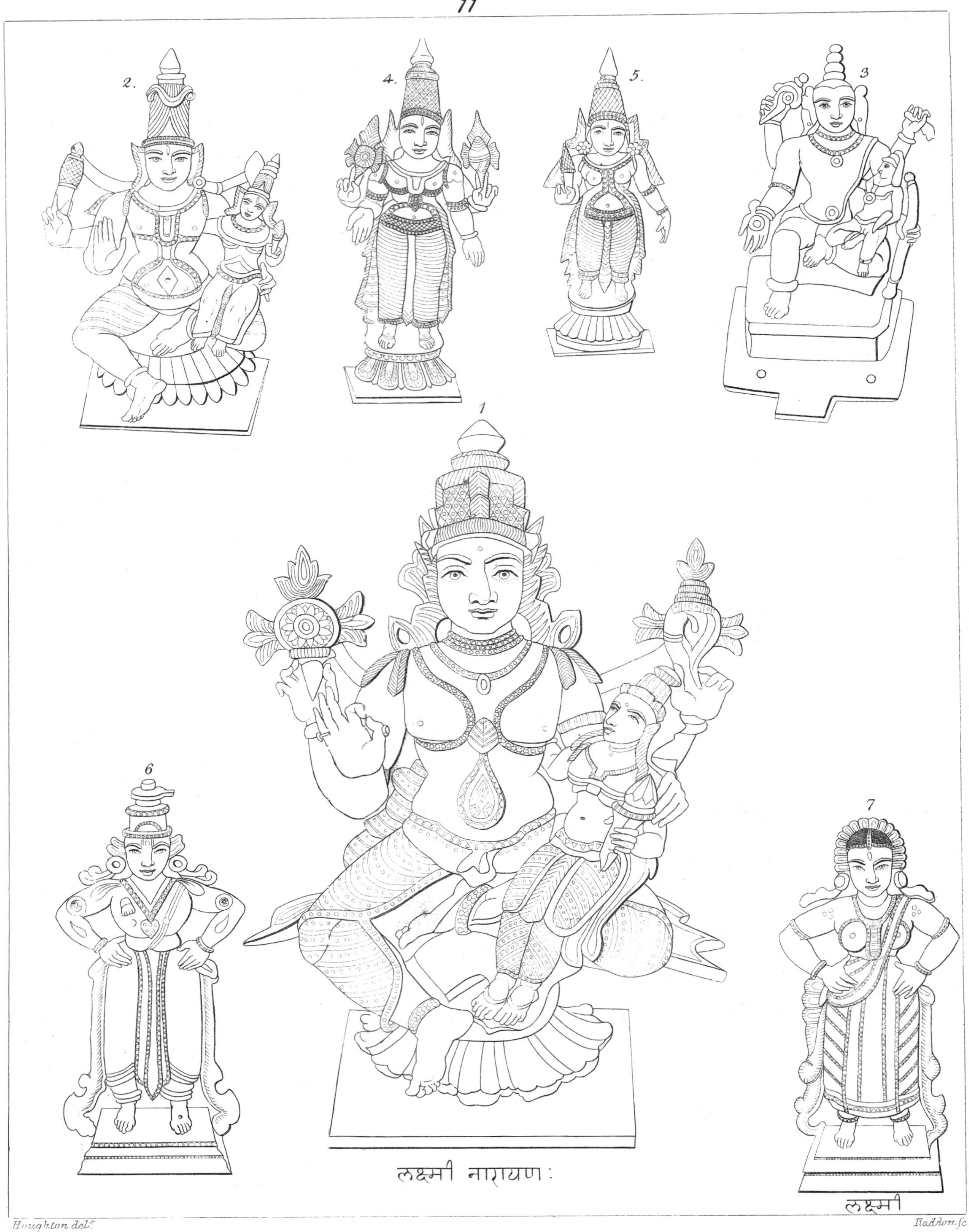

1, 2, 3, LAKSHMĪ NARAYAN. 4, 5, BALLAJI & *WIFE* 6, 7, WITTOBA & *WIFE*.

From images in Bronze, Copper and gilt Brass.

BALLAJI and his wives LAKSHMĪ & SATYAVĀMĀ.

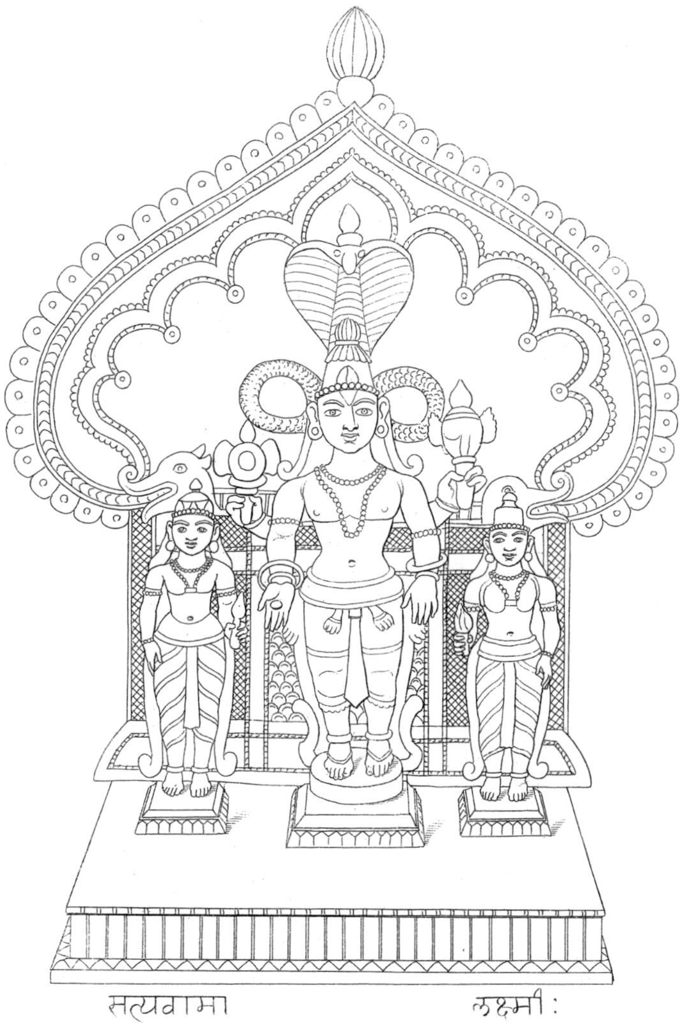

From a statue in Silver.

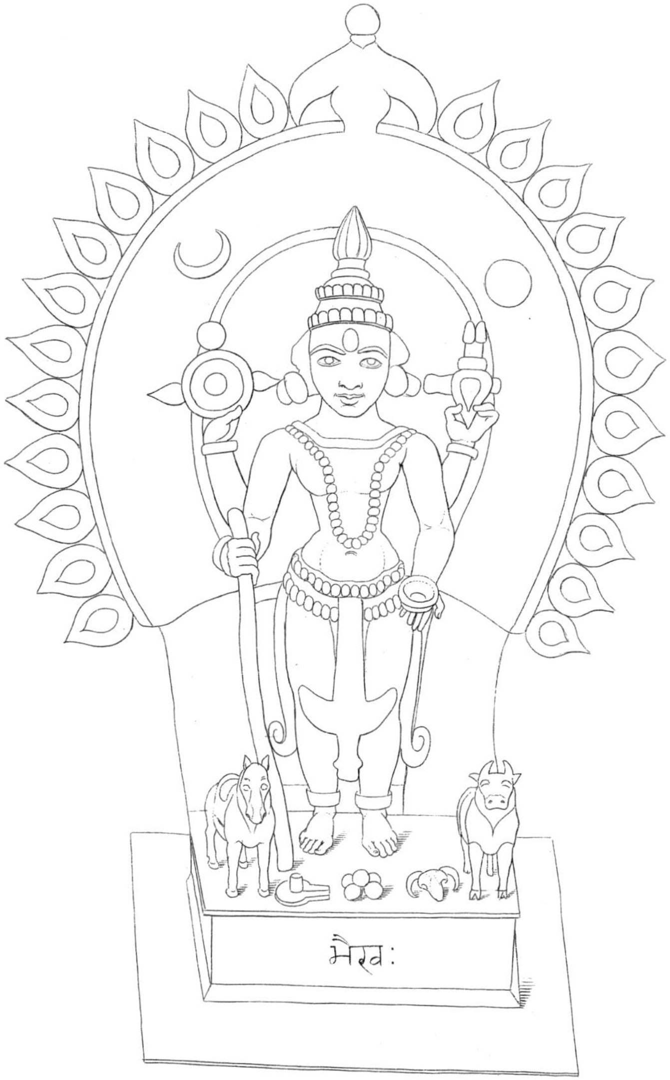

BHAIRAVA an AVATĀRA of MAHA-DĒVA.

From a cast in Brass.

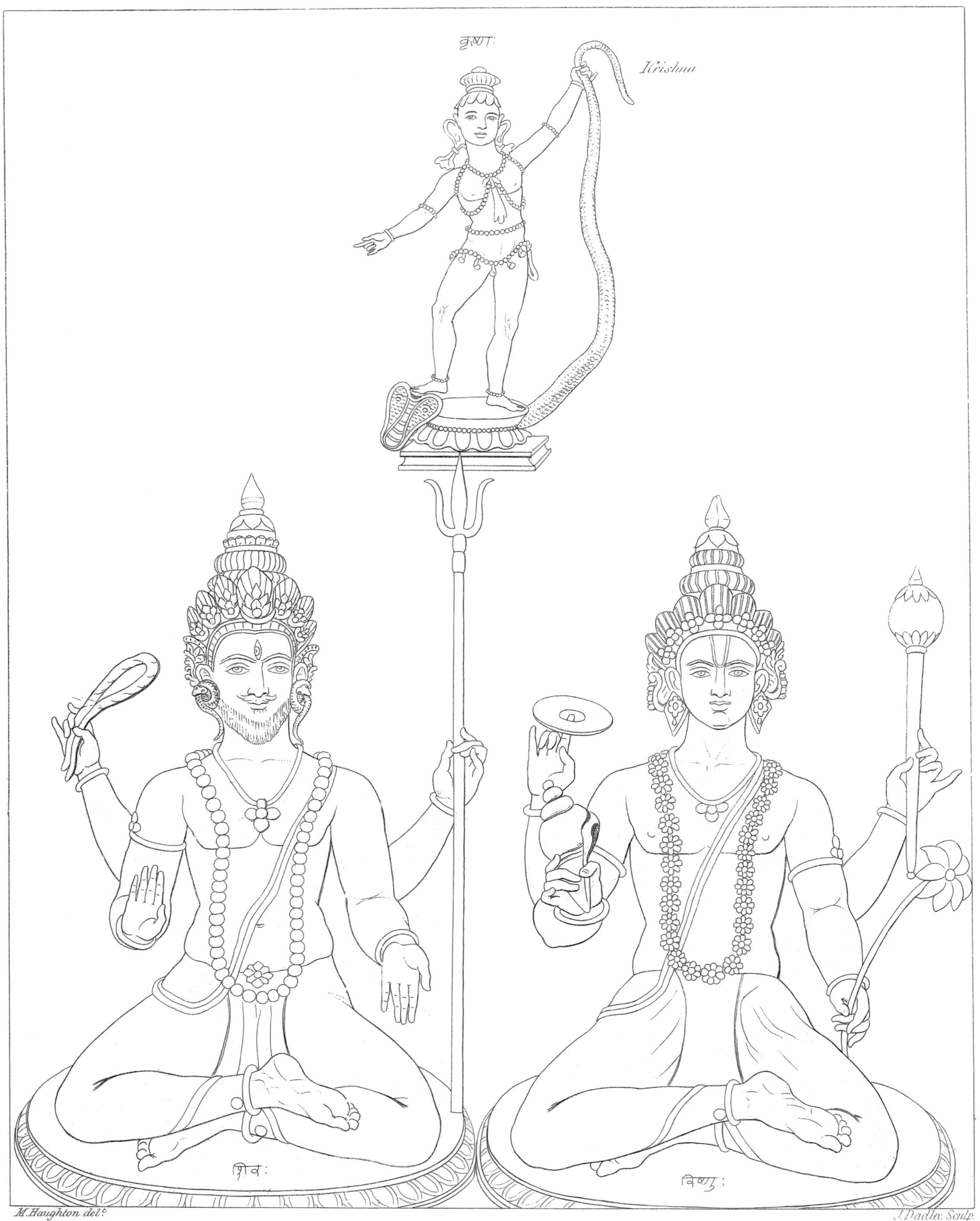

M. Haughton del.

SIVA

VISHNU

J. Dadley. Sculp.

From Zinc Images in the Museum at the East India House

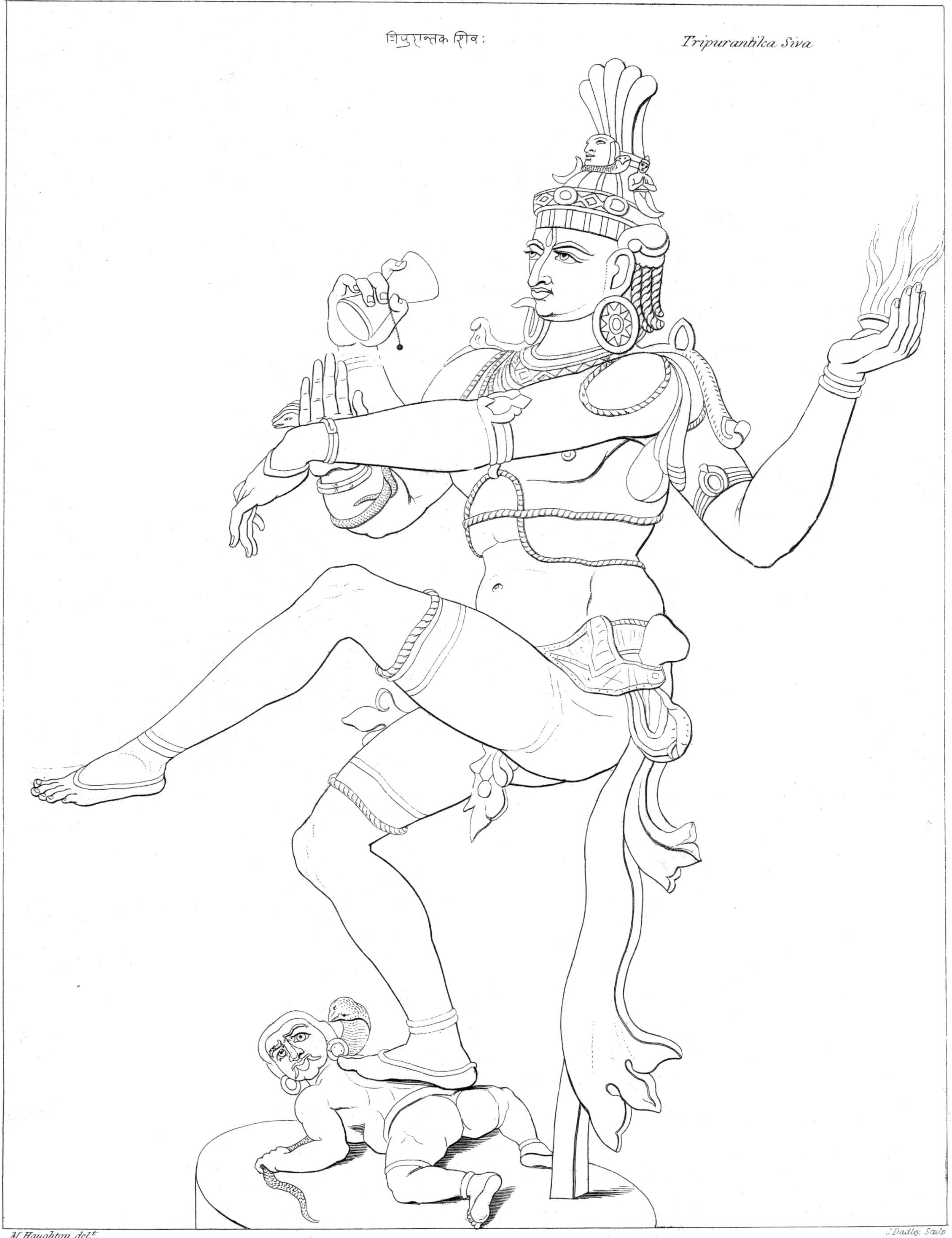

MAHĀDĒVA *destroying* **TRIPURĀSURA**

from a Bronze Statue in the Museum at the India House.

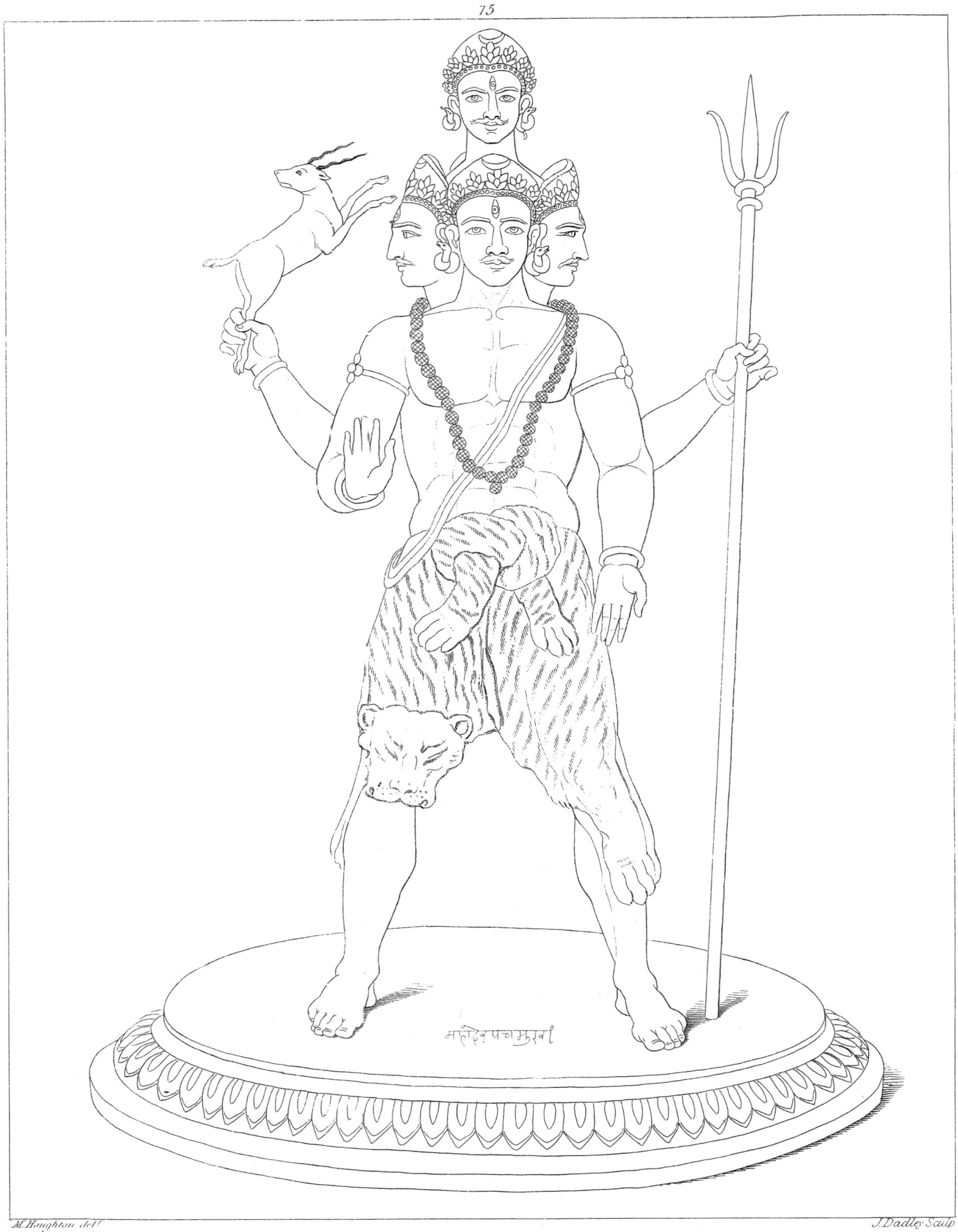

MAHĀDĒVA - *PANCHAMUKHĪ*.

from a Zinc Image in the Museum at the India House.

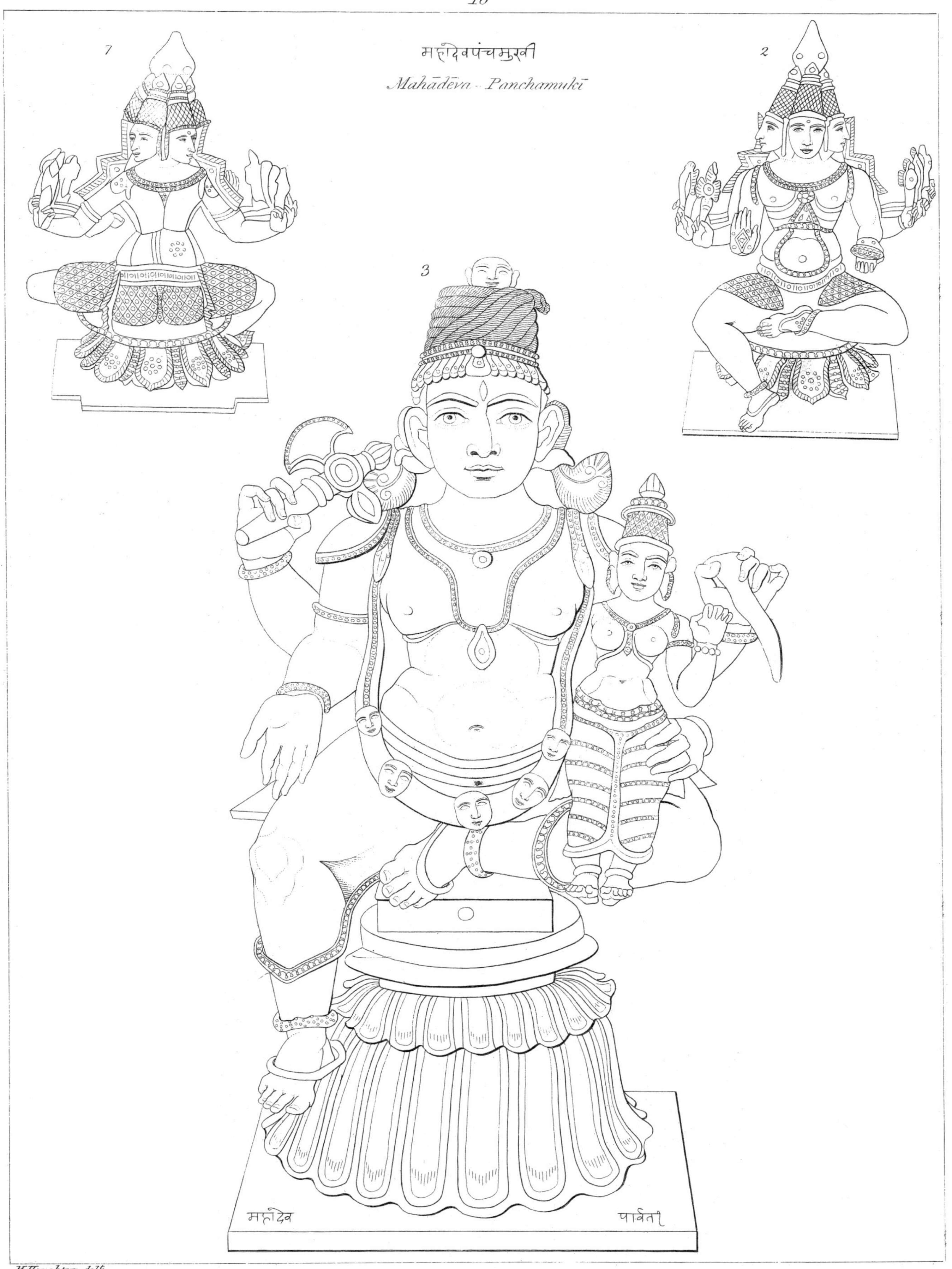

M.Haughton delt.

MAHĀDĒVA and PĀRVATĪ

From Statues in Bronze & Brass.

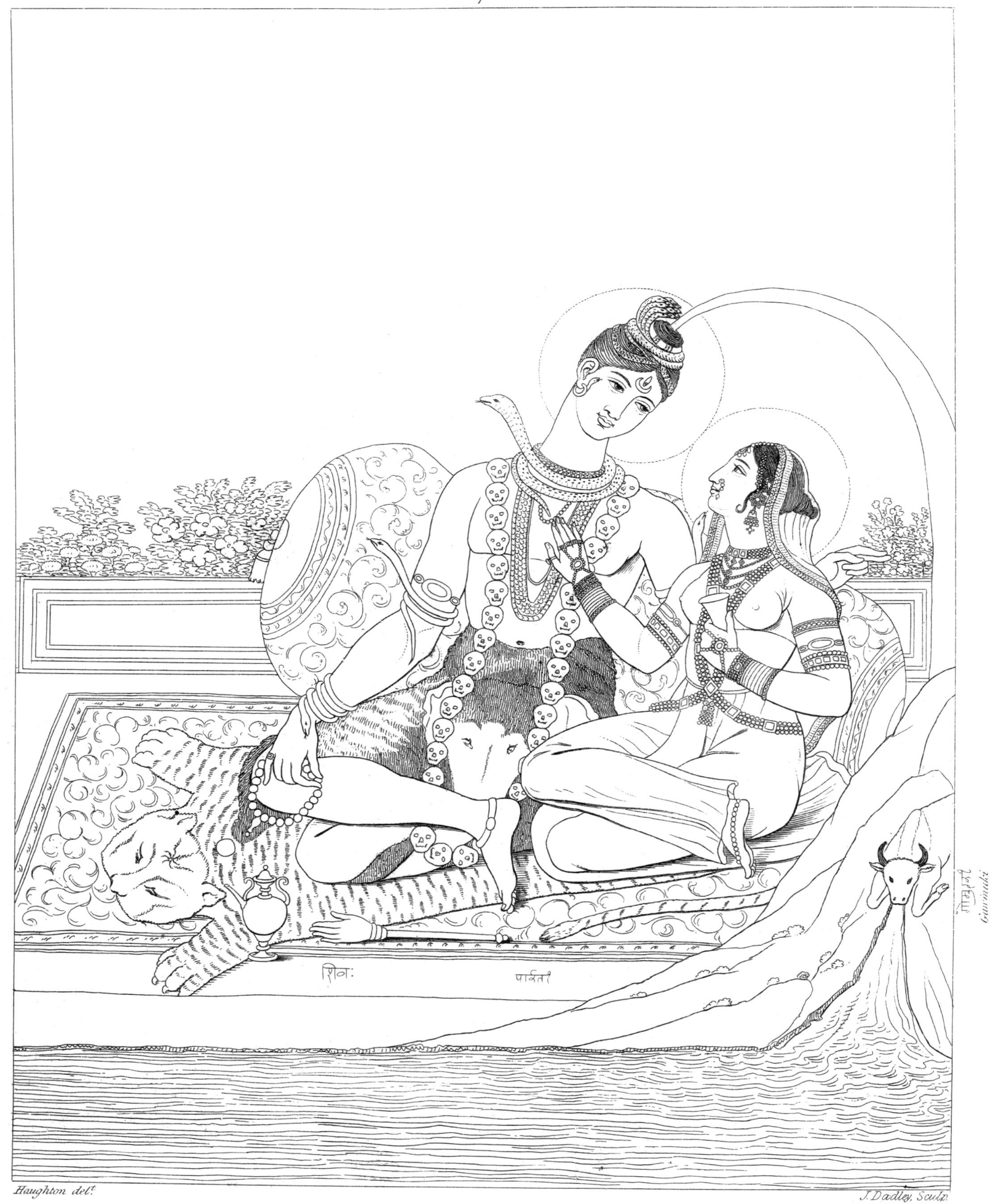

MAHĀDĒVA and PARVATĪ.

from a highly finished Painting.

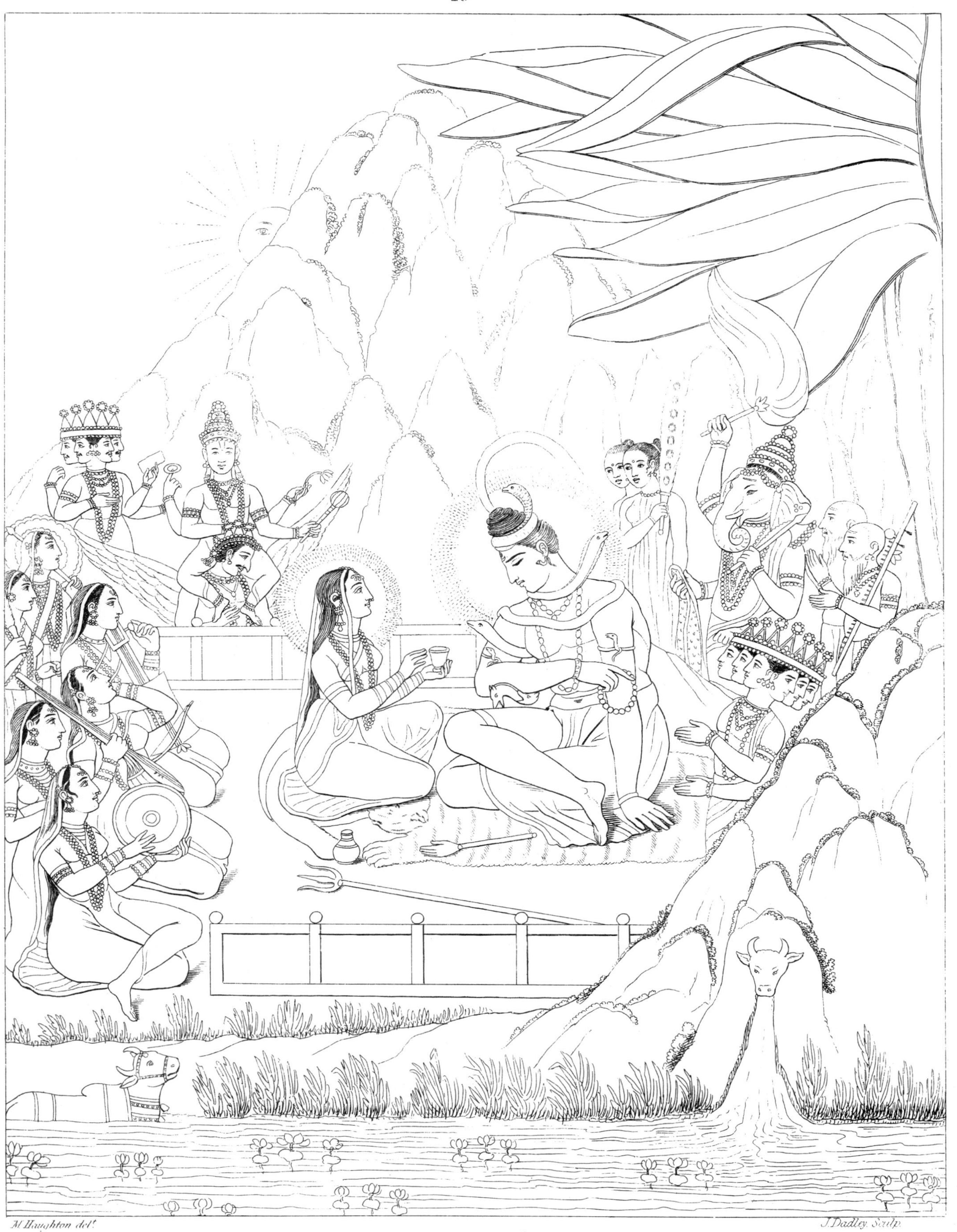

MAHĀDĒVA *and* PĀRVATĪ *on* KAILĀS'A, *the* HINDU OLYMPUS:

BRAHMĀ, VISHNU *on* GARUDA GANĒSA *and* KĀRTIKYA;

with celestial choristers (gandharvas) and others in attendance.

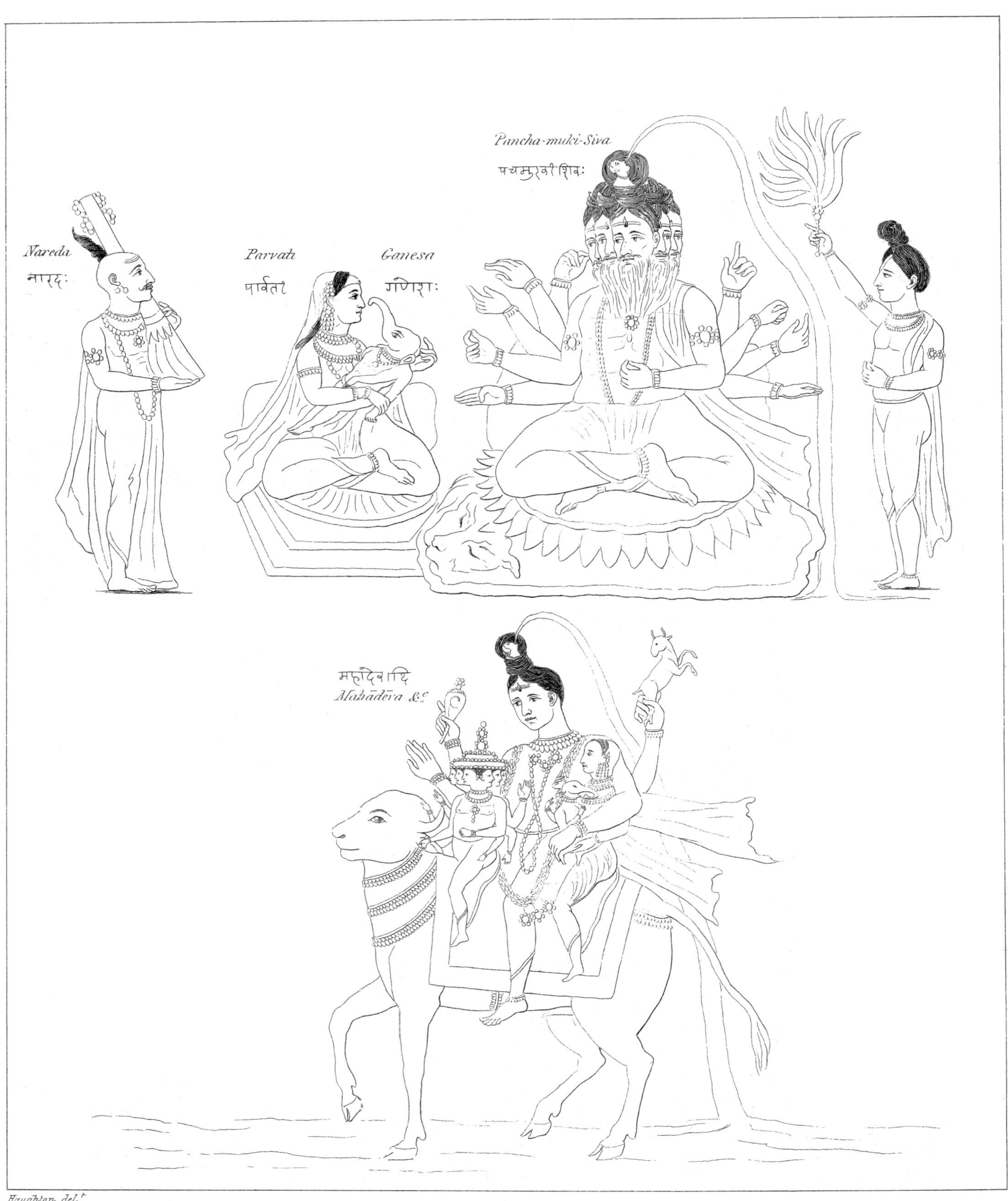

MAHĀDEVA-PĀRVATĪ-GANĒSA *and* KARTIKIYA.

from Pictures.

Haughton del.

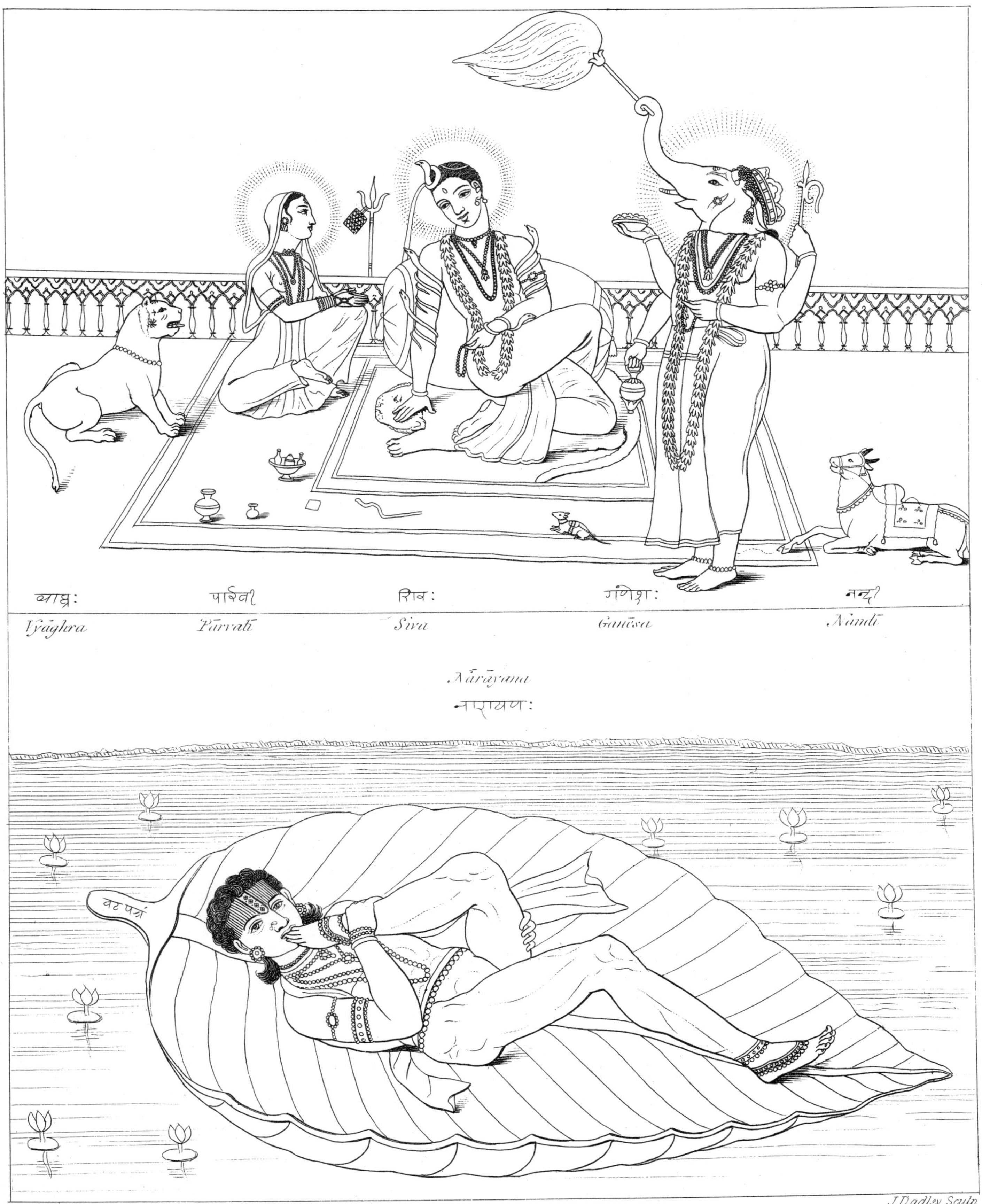

Narayana

M. Haughton delt.

J. Dadley Sculp.

from Pictures

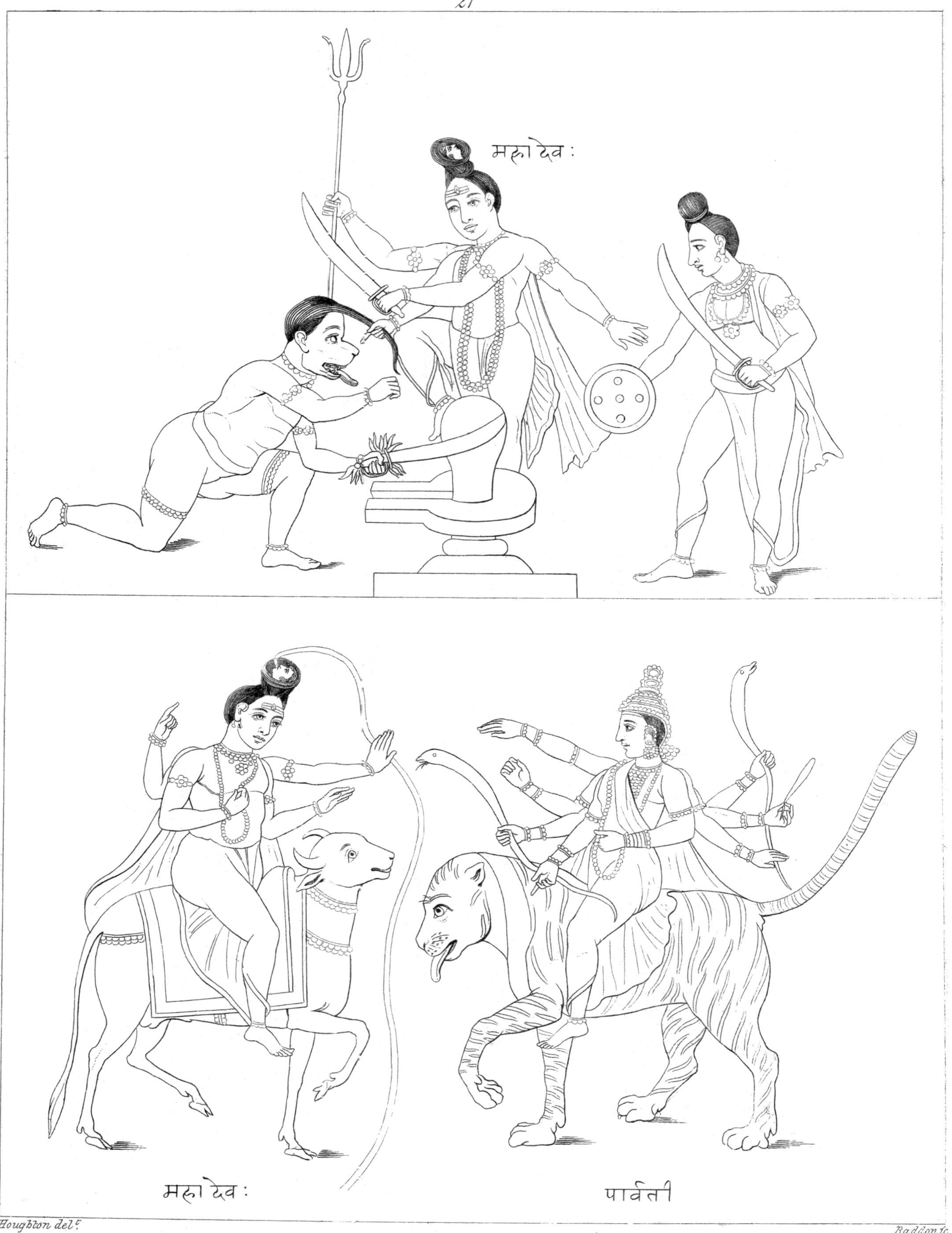

Houghton del.t   Raddon fc.

MAHĀDĒVA & PĀRVATĪ.

From Pictures

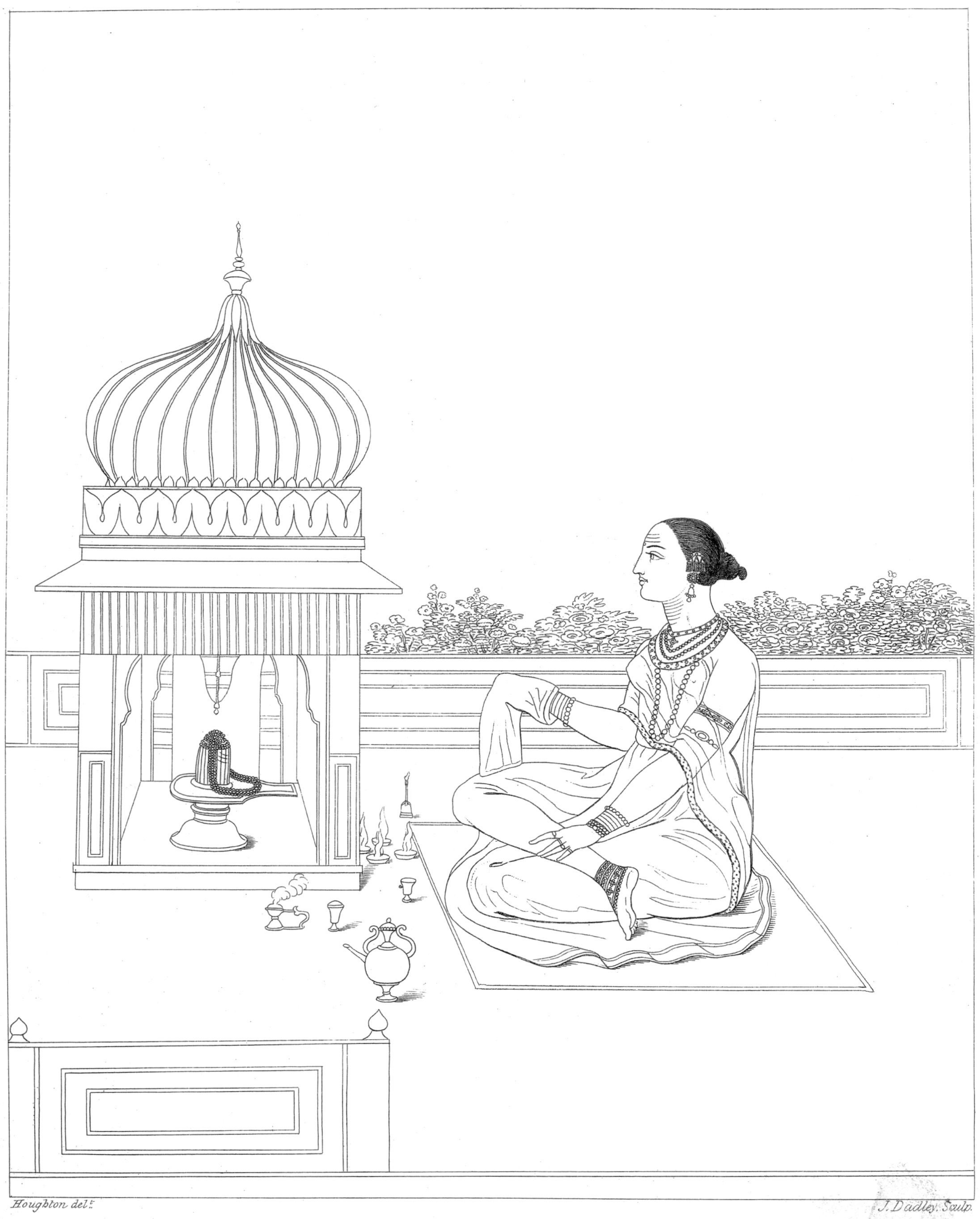

PĀRVATĪ or some holy female at the ceremony of *LINGA PŪJĀ* in honor of MAHĀDĒVA.

From a highly finished Picture.

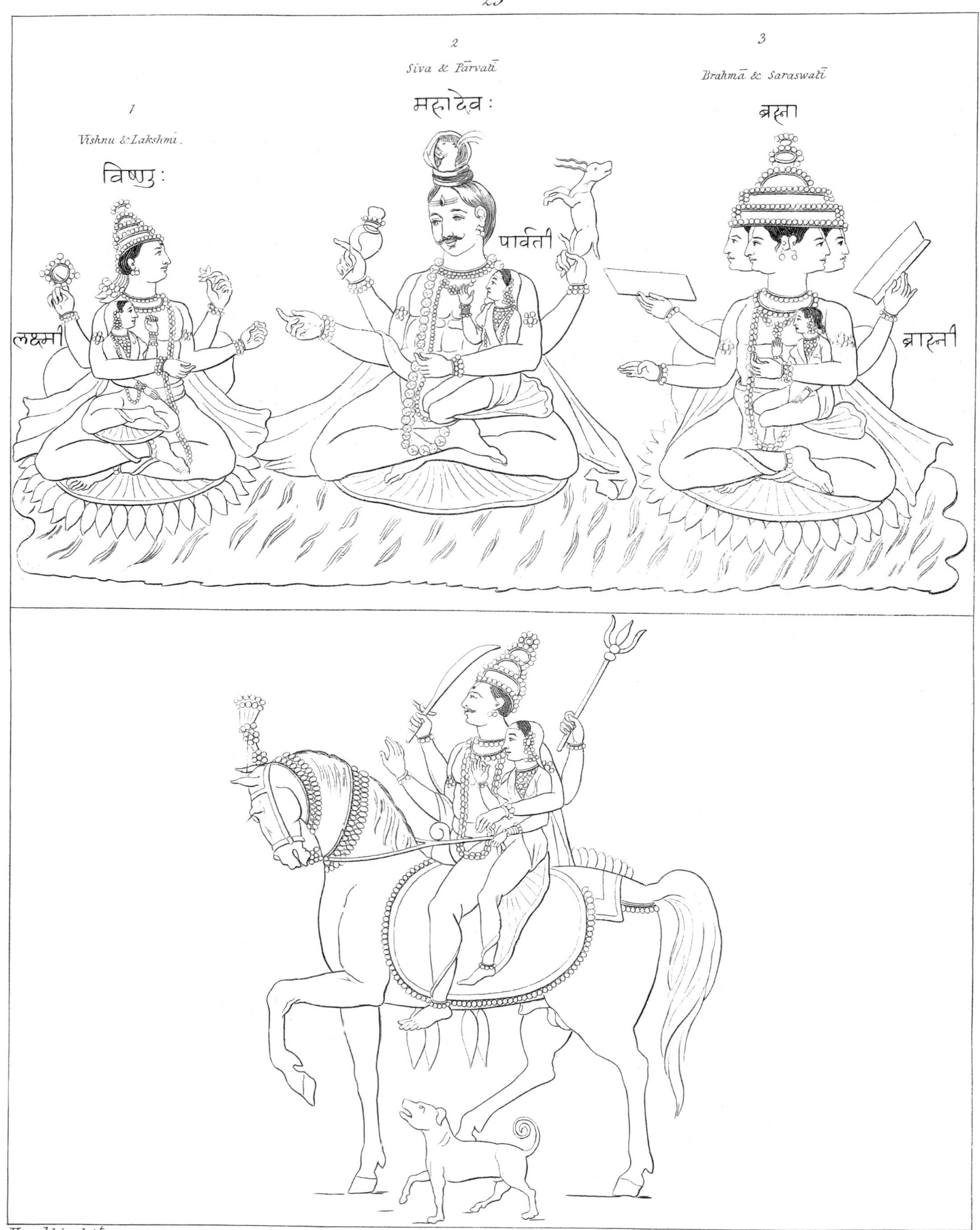

Houghton delt.

Skelton fc.

KANDEH RAO & MALSARA.

From Pictures.

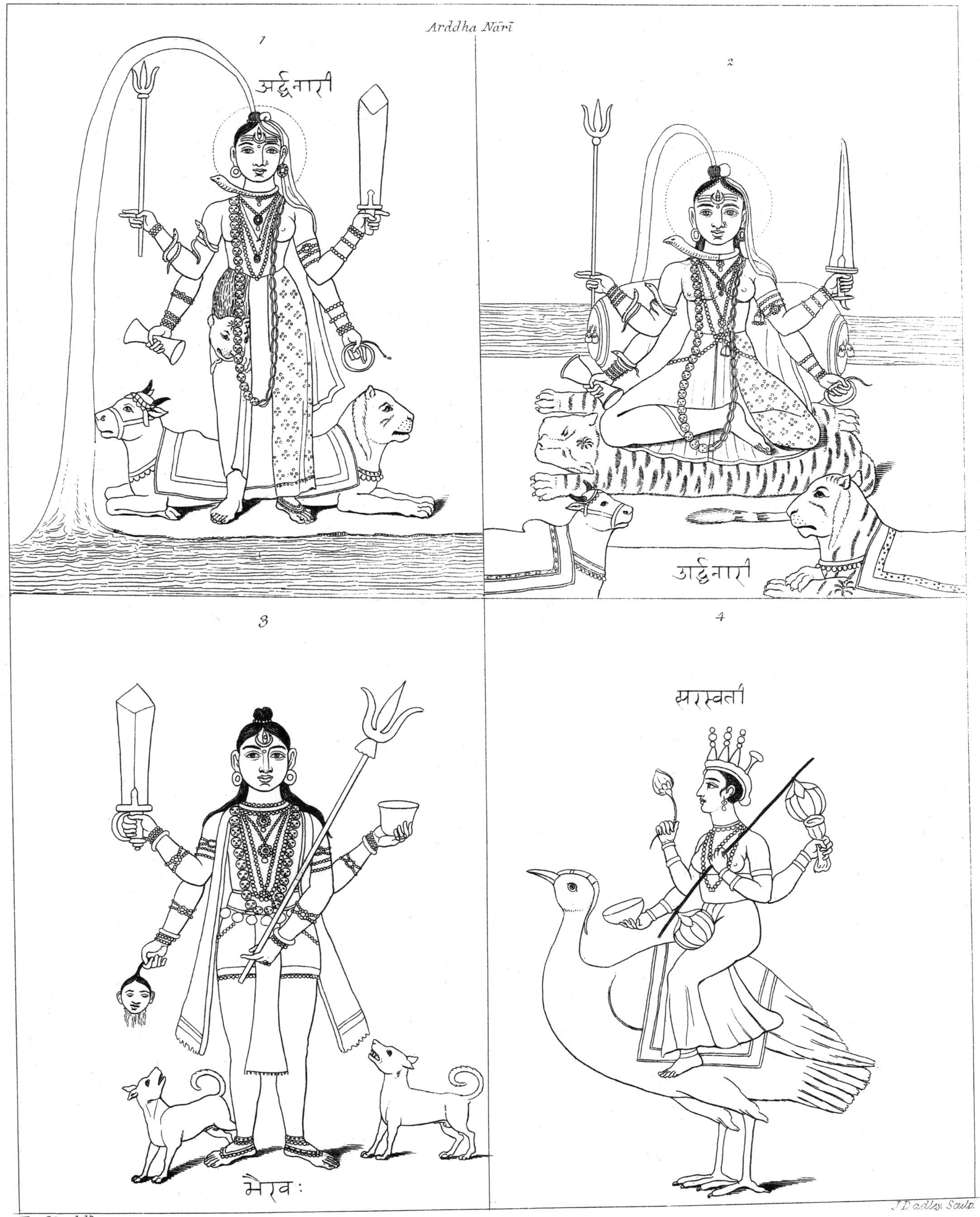

BHAIRAVA.

SARASWATI.

From Pictures.

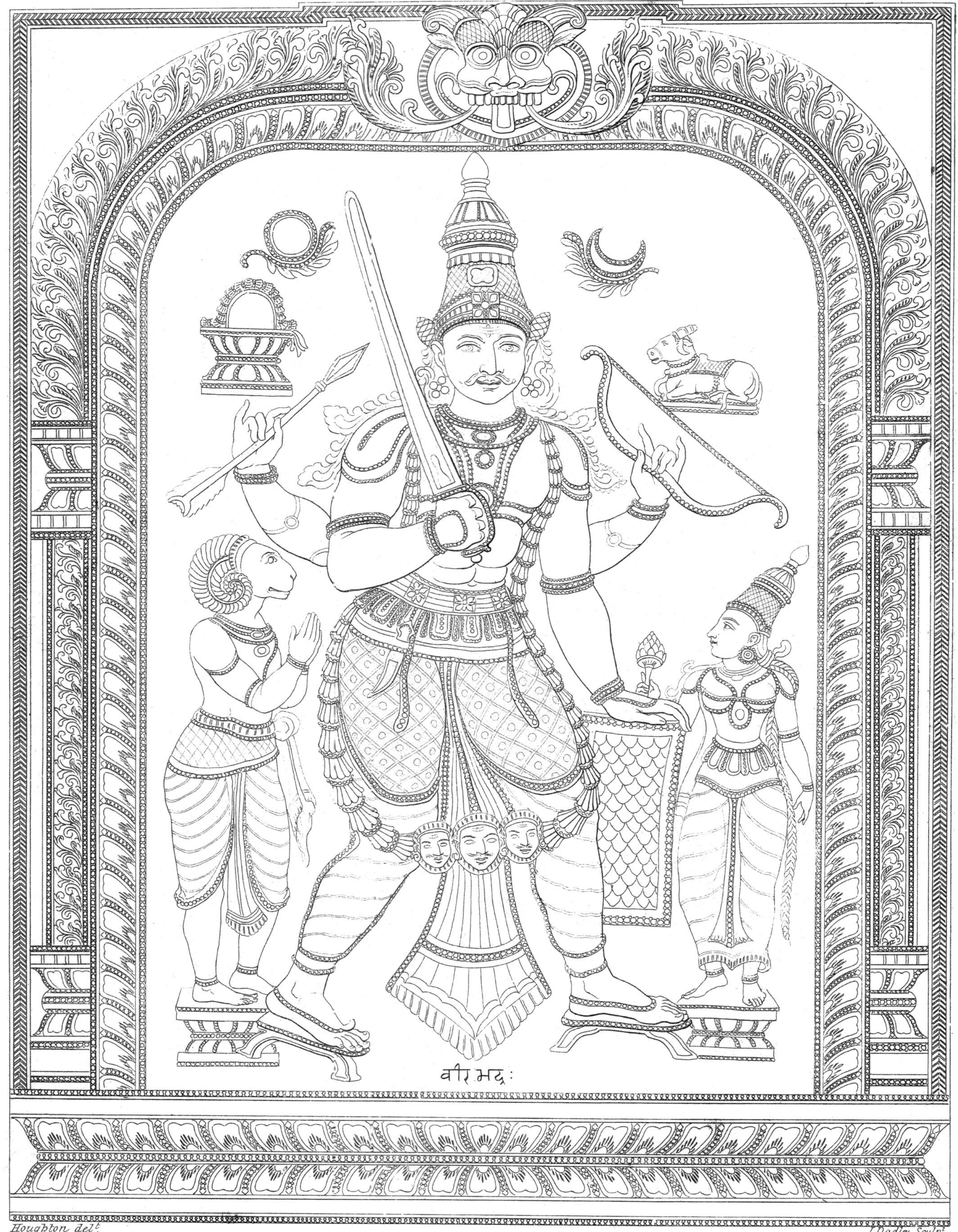

VĪRA BHADRA an _AVATĀRA_ of MAHĀDĒVA.

From an embossed brass shield in the collection of the Right Hon. Viscount Valentia.

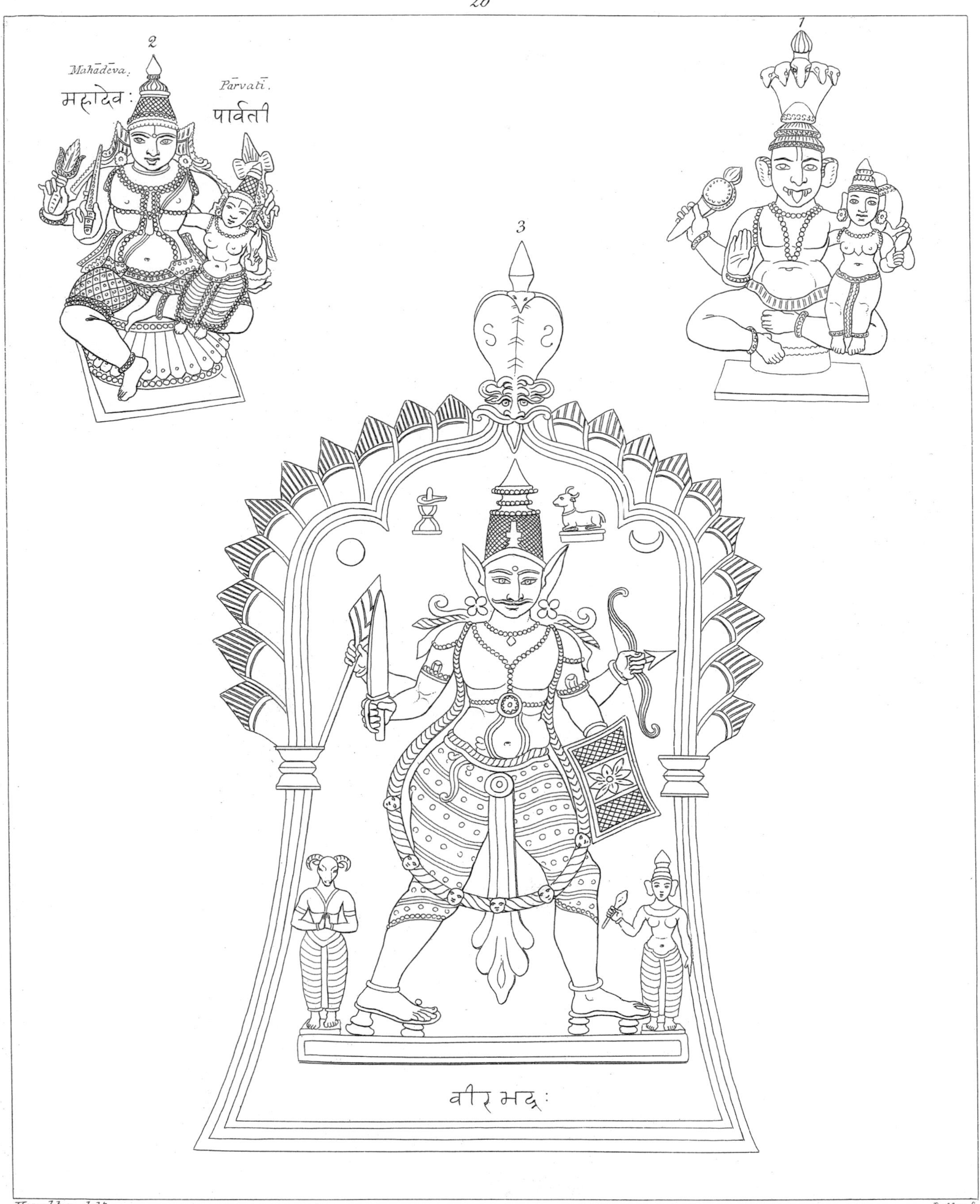

Houghton delt.

Ruddon Sc.

VĪRA BHADRA &c.

From Subjects in brass.

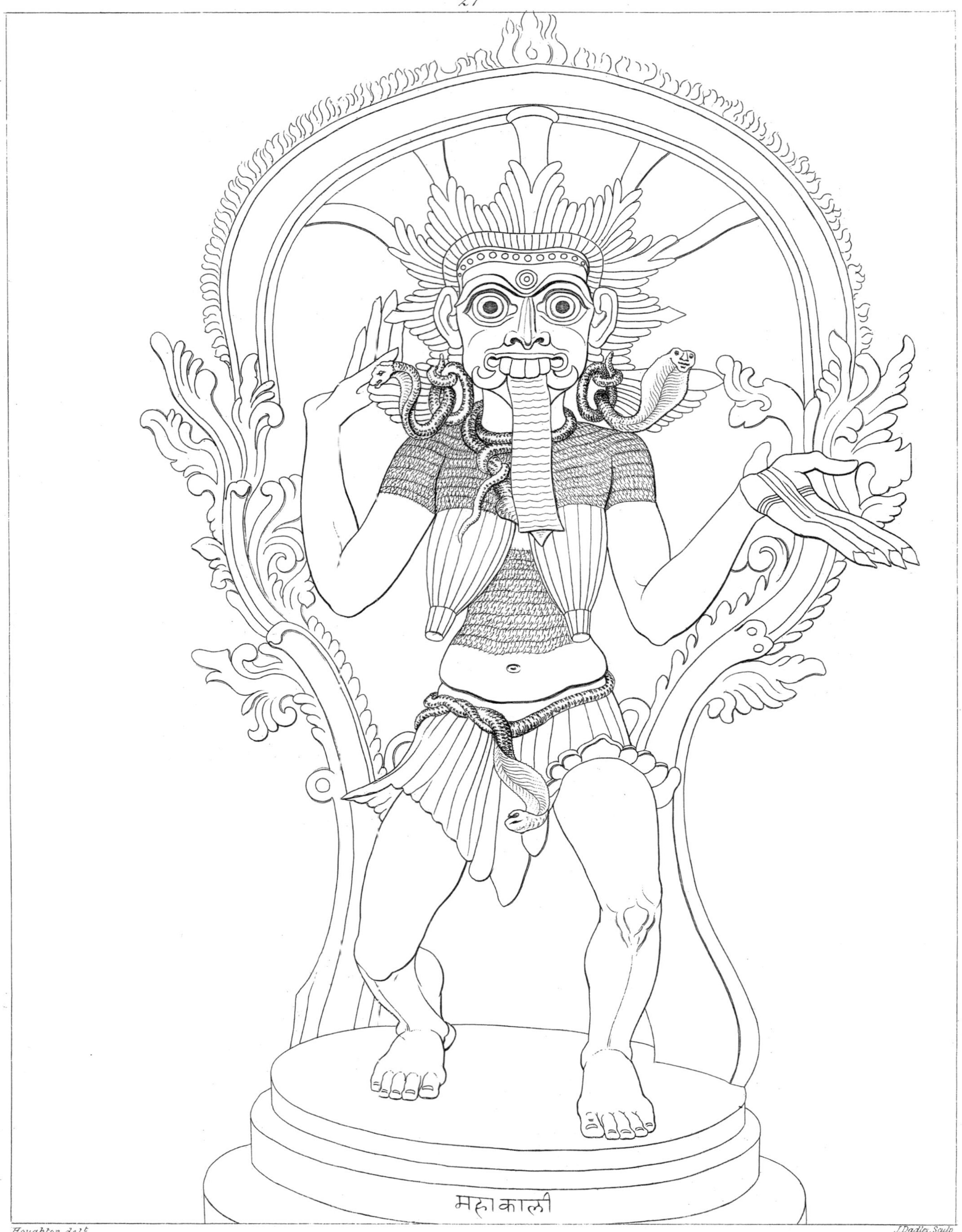

KĀLĪ, BHAWĀNĪ, PĀRVATĪ, or DURGĀ, consort of SIVA.

From a Brafs Statue in the Museum at the India House.

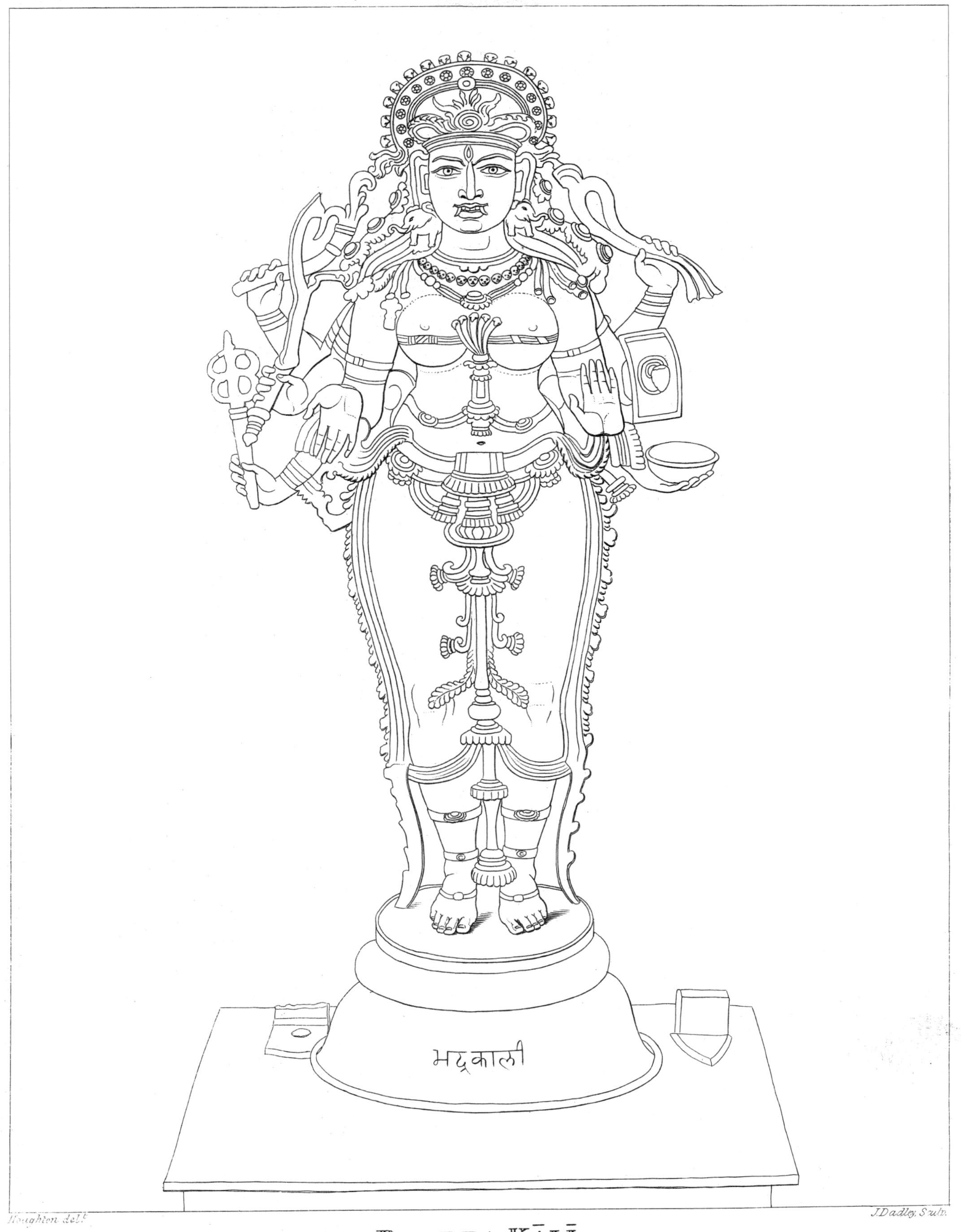

BHADRA KĀLĪ.

From a Bronze Statue.

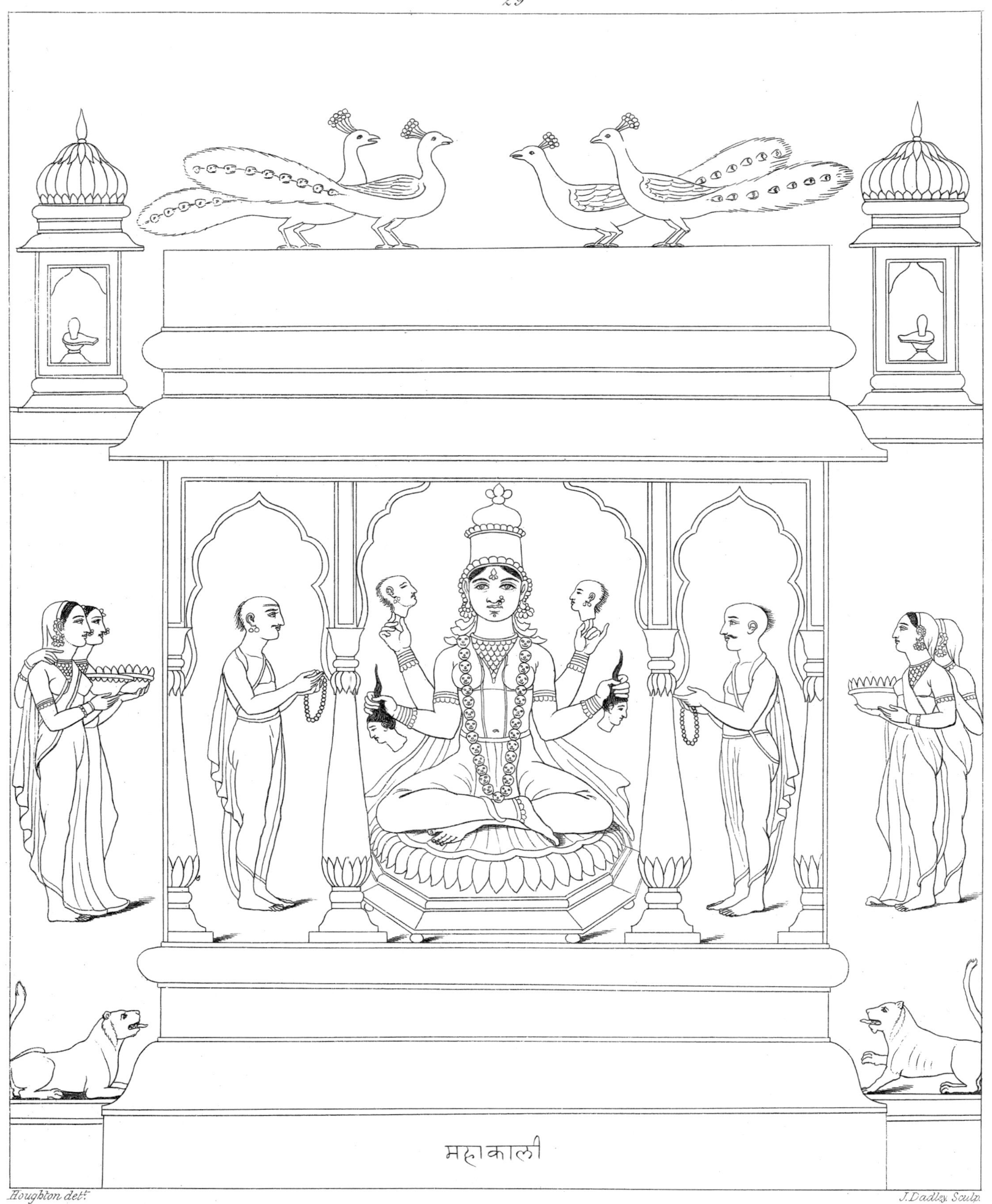

MAHĀ KĀLĪ.

From a Picture

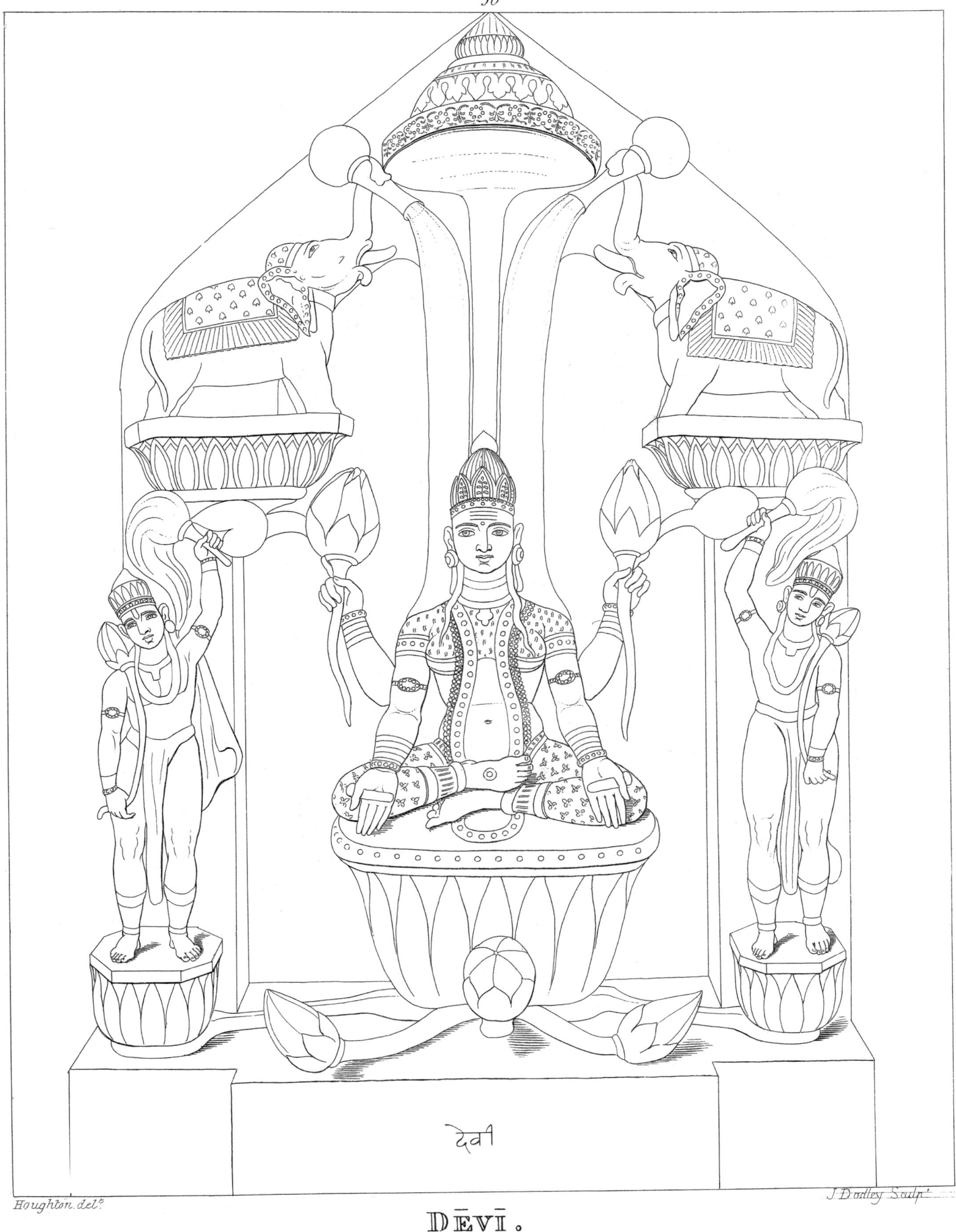

DĒVĪ.

From a subject in Marble brought from INDORE the capital of HOLKAR.

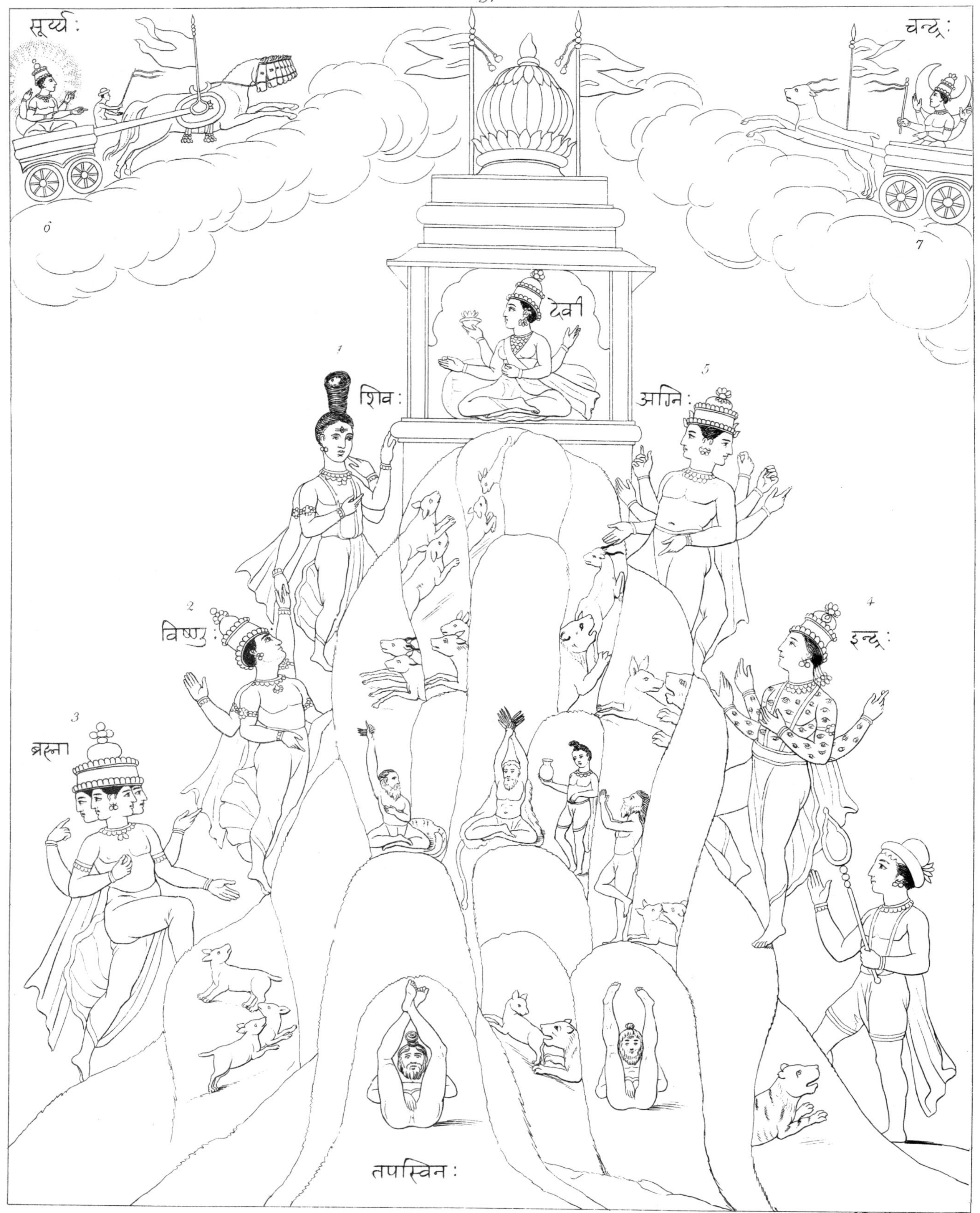

DEVI or PARVATI, Propitiated by 1. SIVA, 2. VISHNU, 3. BRAHMĀ, 4. INDRA, 5 AGNI, 6. SŪRYA,

7. CHANDRA. and devotees in several postures of penance & austerity.

From a Picture

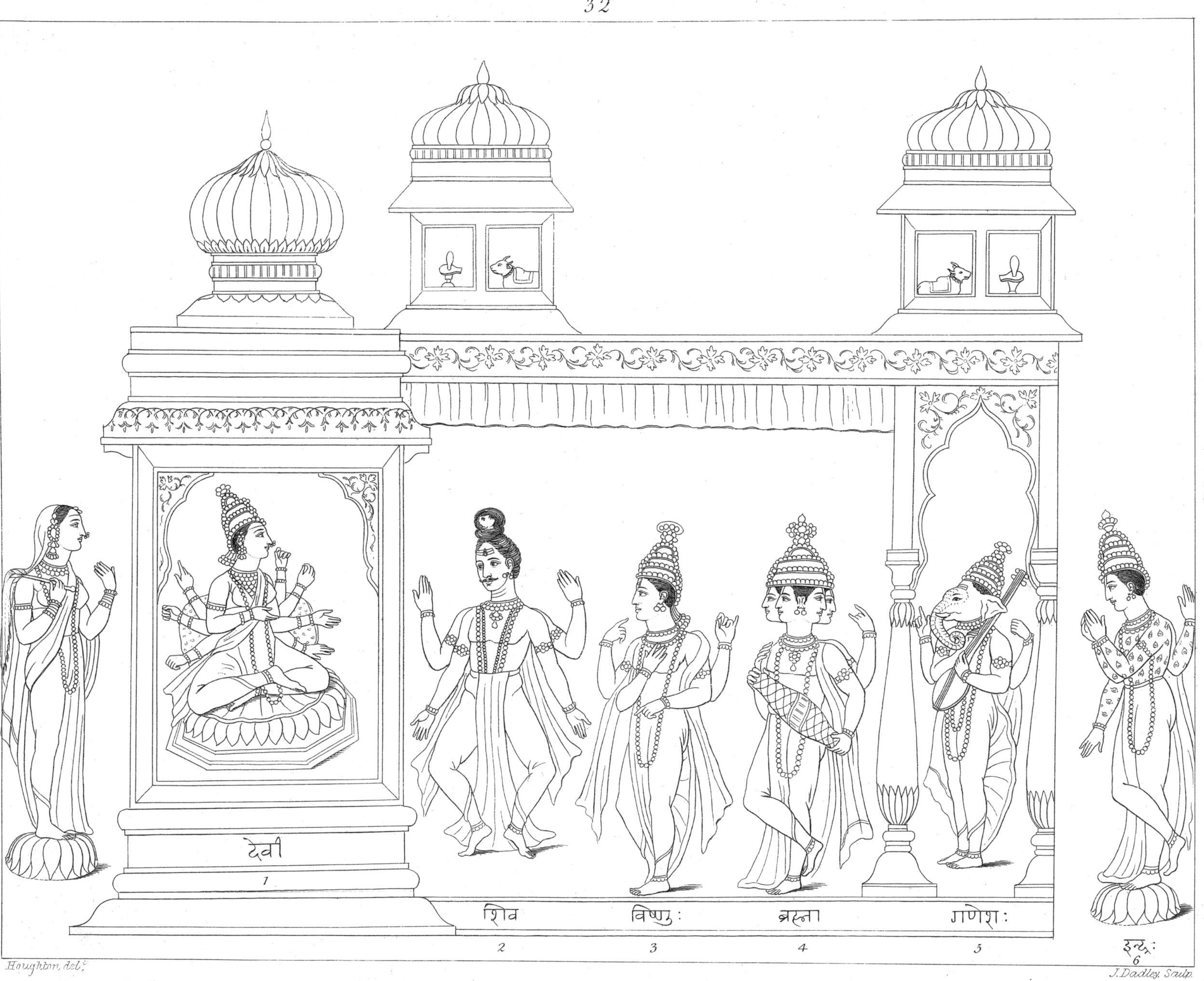

1. DĒVĪ, or BHAVĀNĪ honored by 2. MAHĀDĒVA, 3. VISHNU, 4. BRAHMĀ, 5. GANĒSA and 6. INDRA.

From a picture.

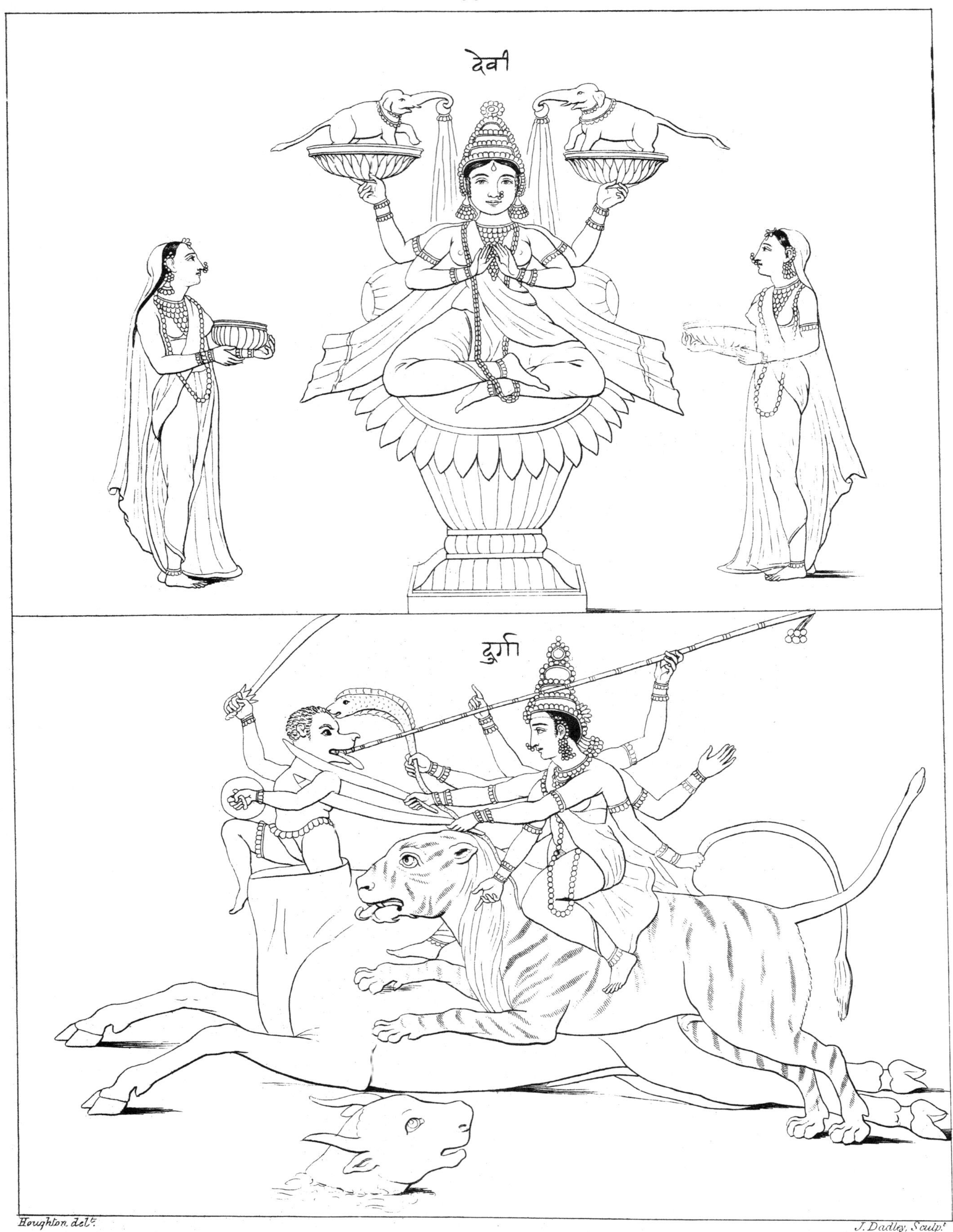

DURGĀ or *ACTIVE VIRTUE* slaying **MAHISHĀSURA** a personification of *VICE*.

Above is DĒVĪ.

From pictures.

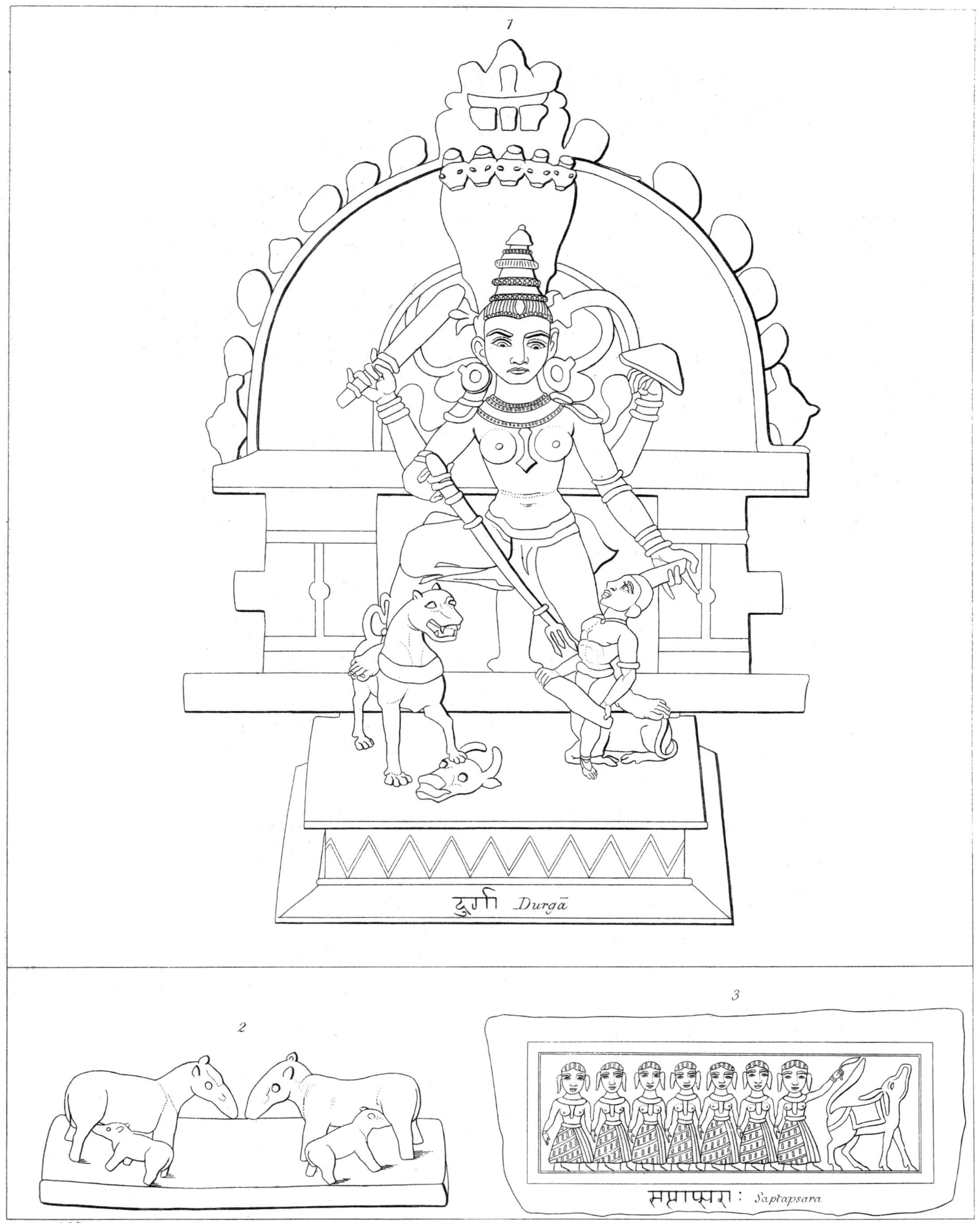

From casts in brass.

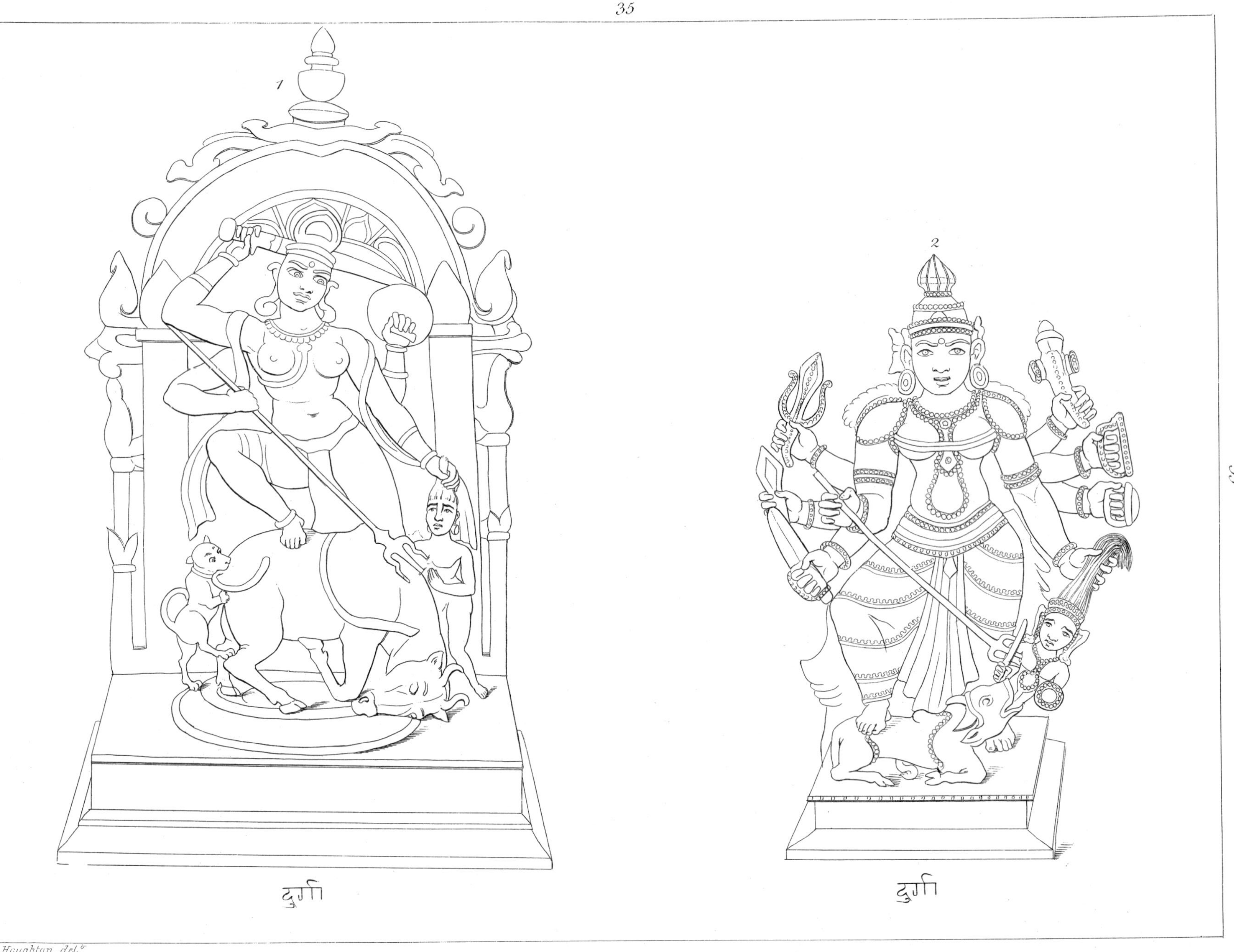

DURGĀ, or *ACTIVE VIRTUE*, slaying the monster MAHISHĀSURA, or *VICE* personified.

From subjects in brafs.

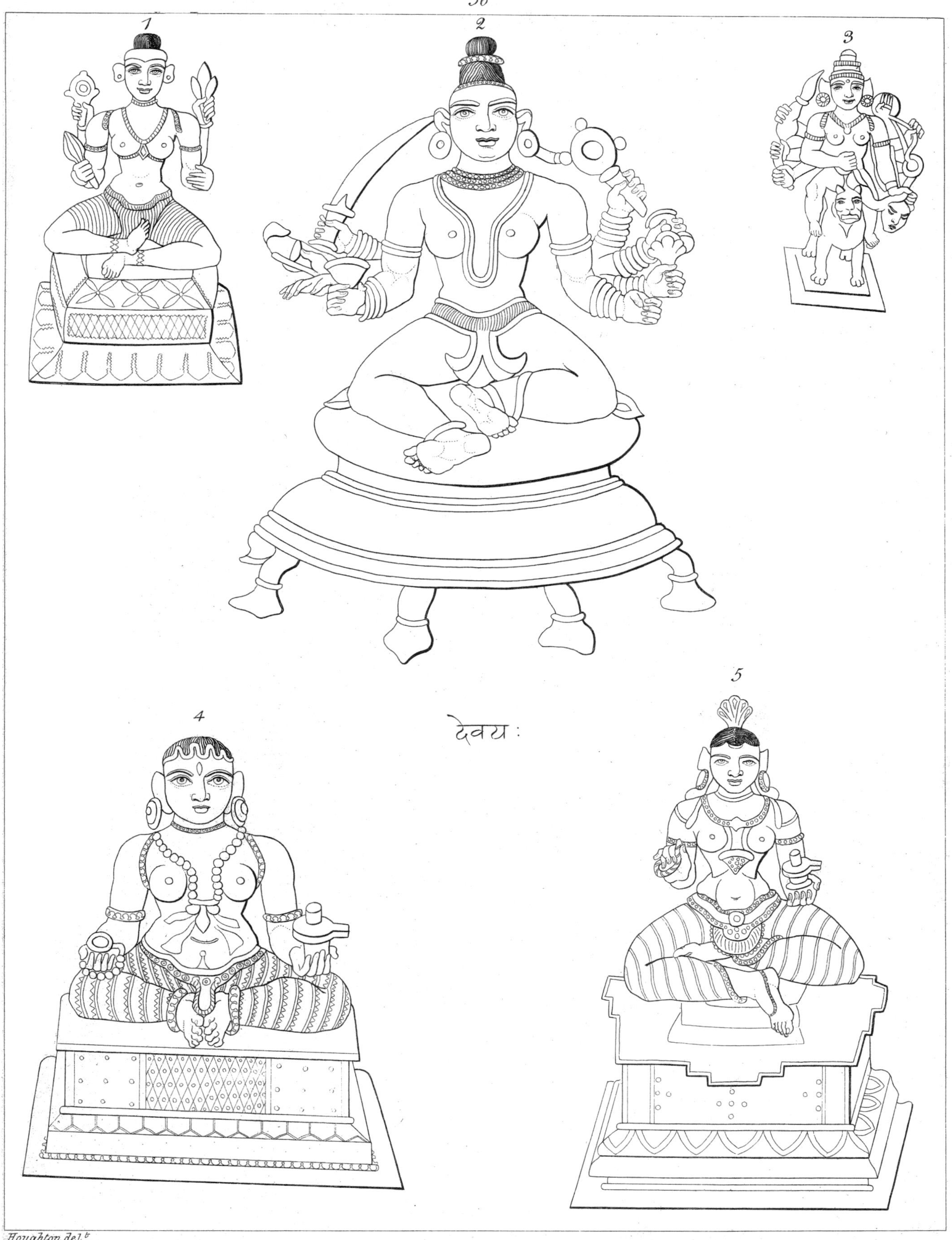

देवयः

DĒVĪ or BHAVĀNĪ in different characters.

From images in brass &c.

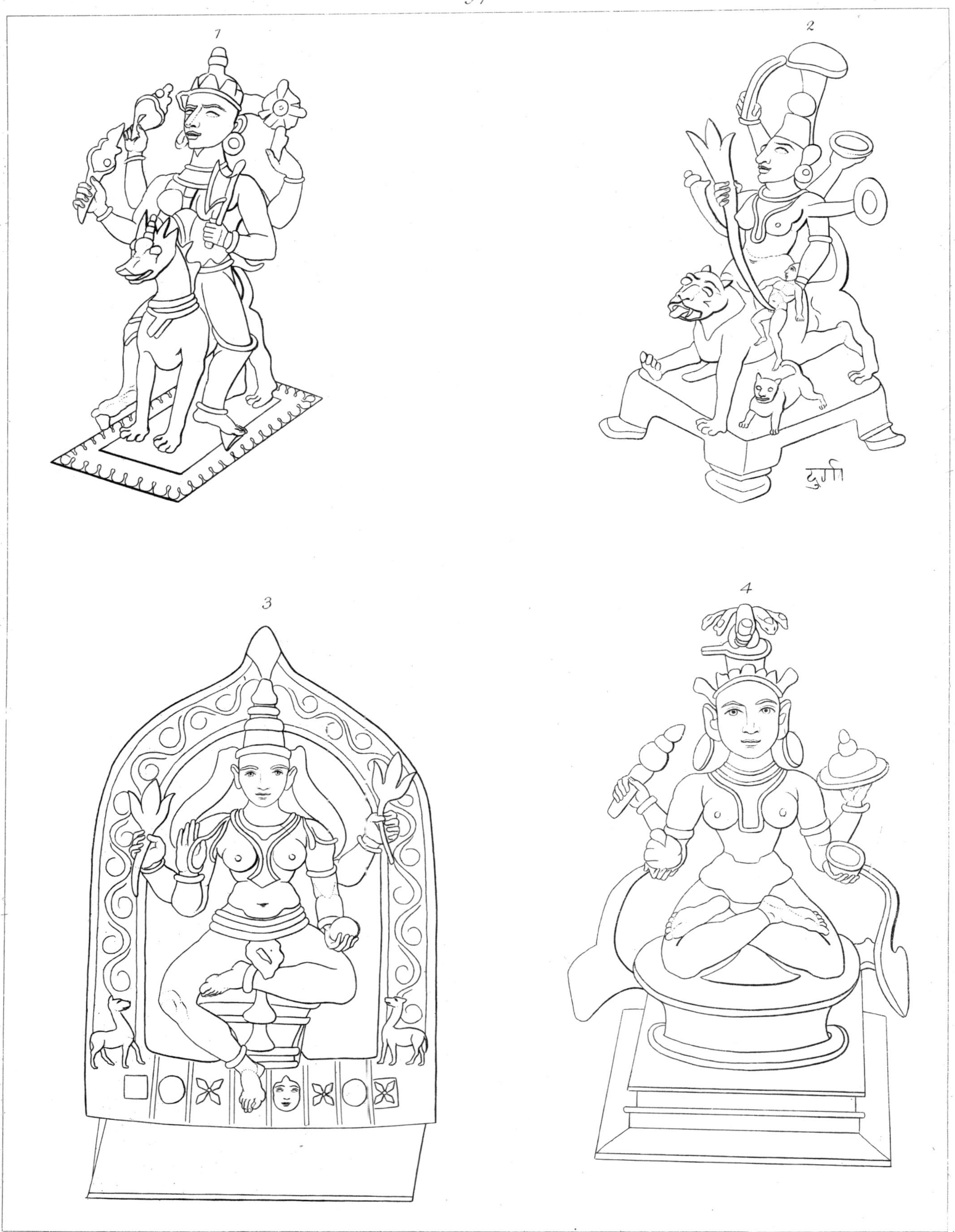

DURGĀ, DĒVĪ, or BHAVĀNĪ, in different forms.

From images in brass &c.

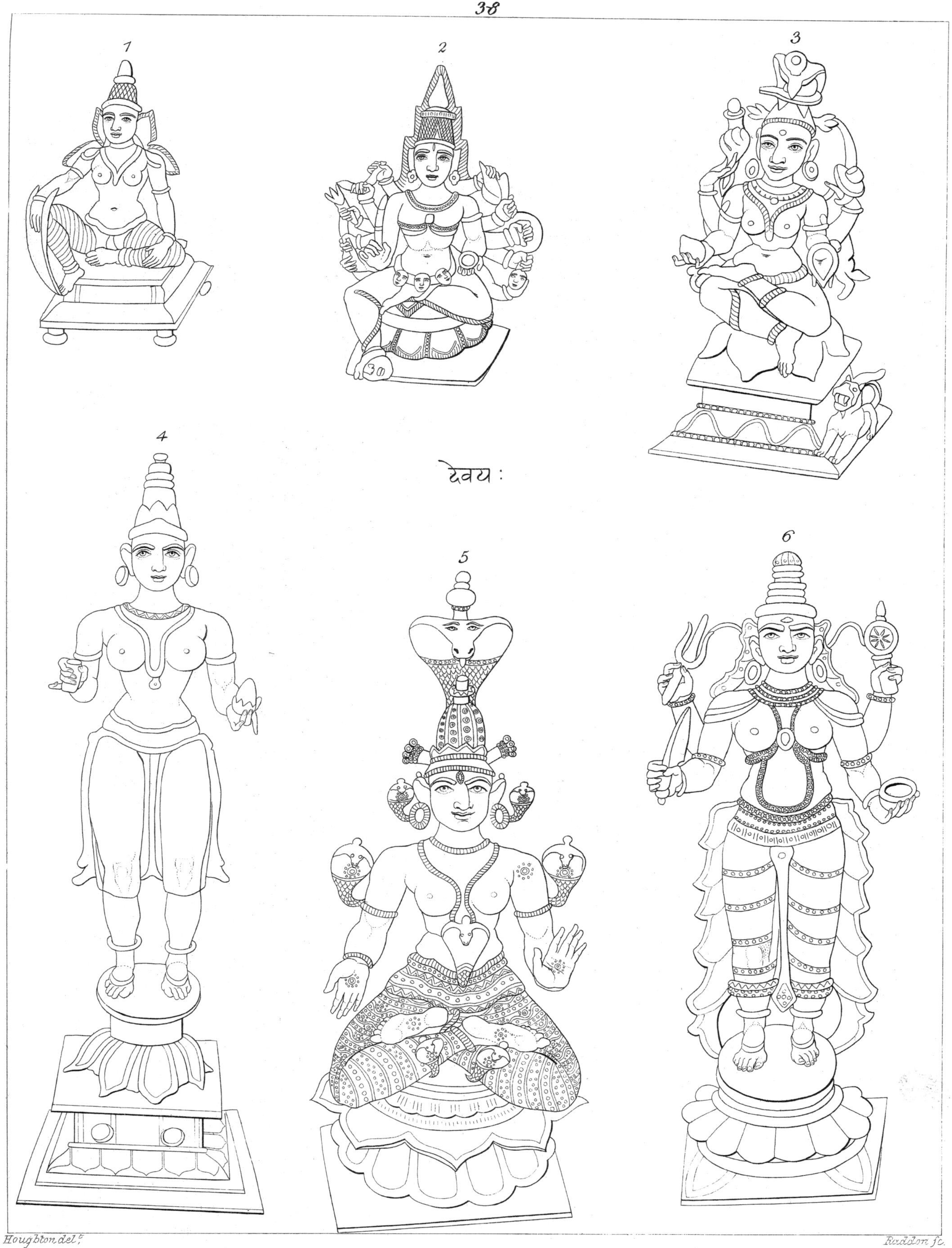

DĒVĪ, or the *GODDESS*, consort of SIVA, in different forms.

From casts in bronze and brass.

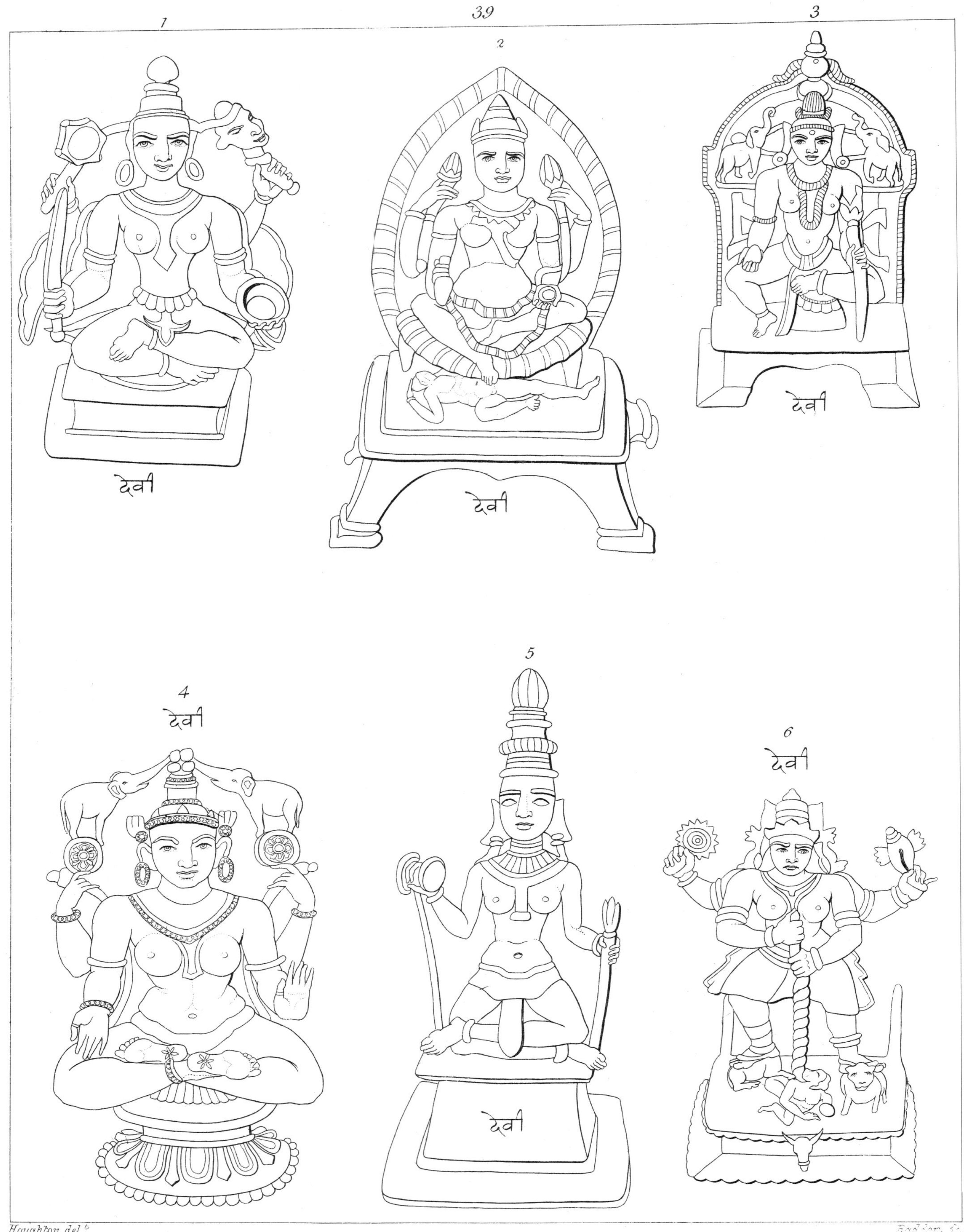

DĒVĪ or the *GODDESS*, in different characters.

From Casts in bronze and brass.

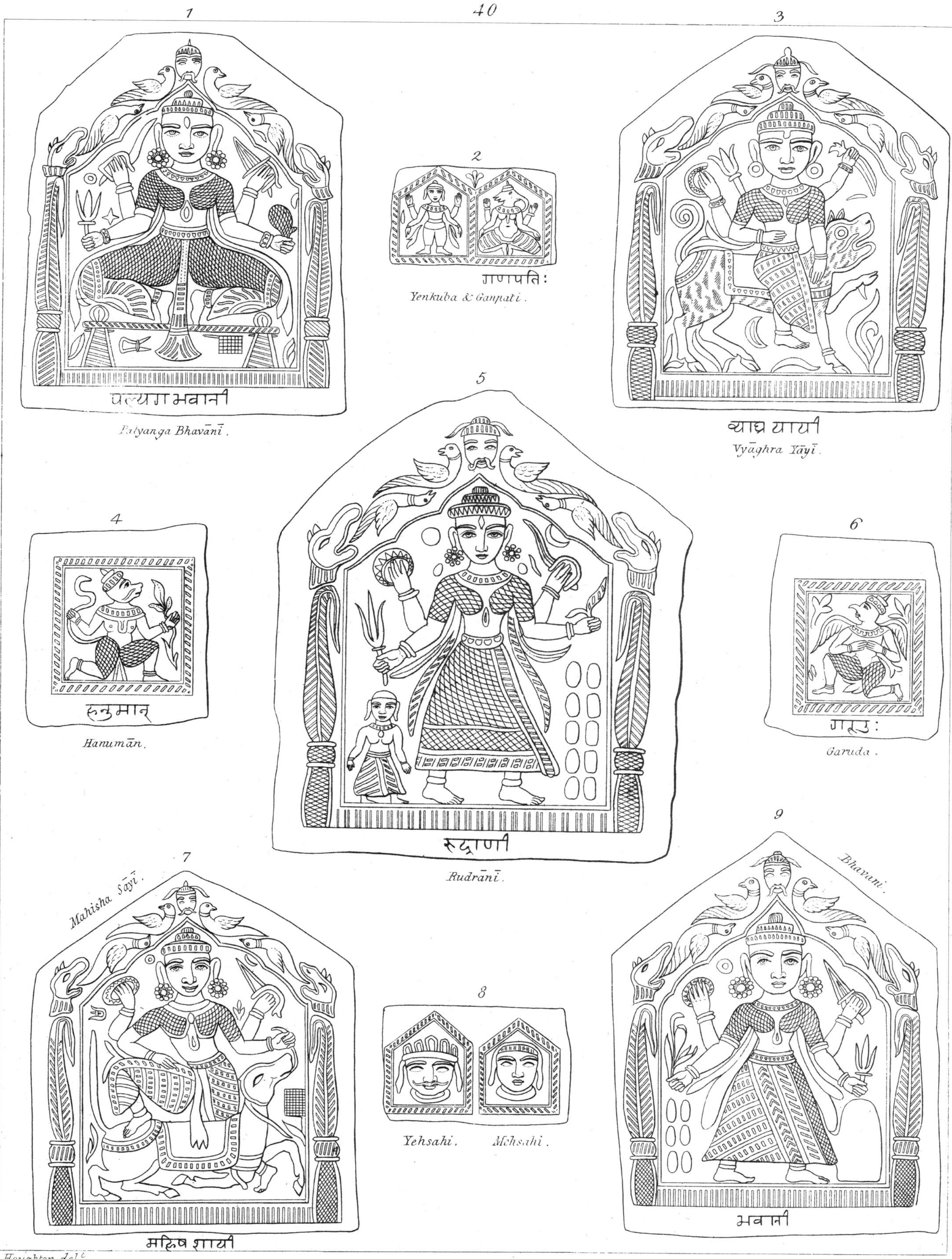

From embofsed plates of thin copper.

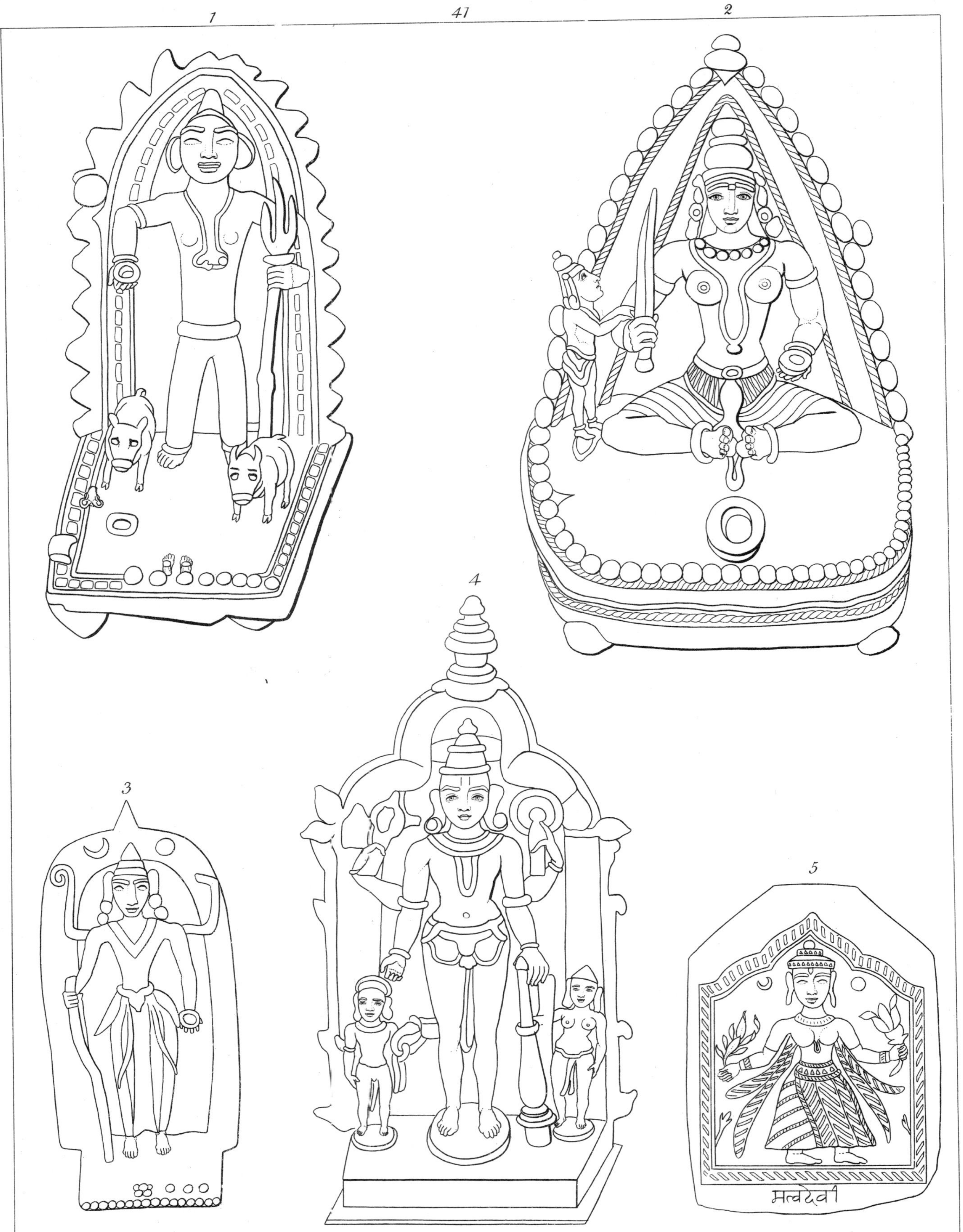

DĒVĪ or the *GODDESS*, consórt of SIVA.

From subjects in brafs &c.

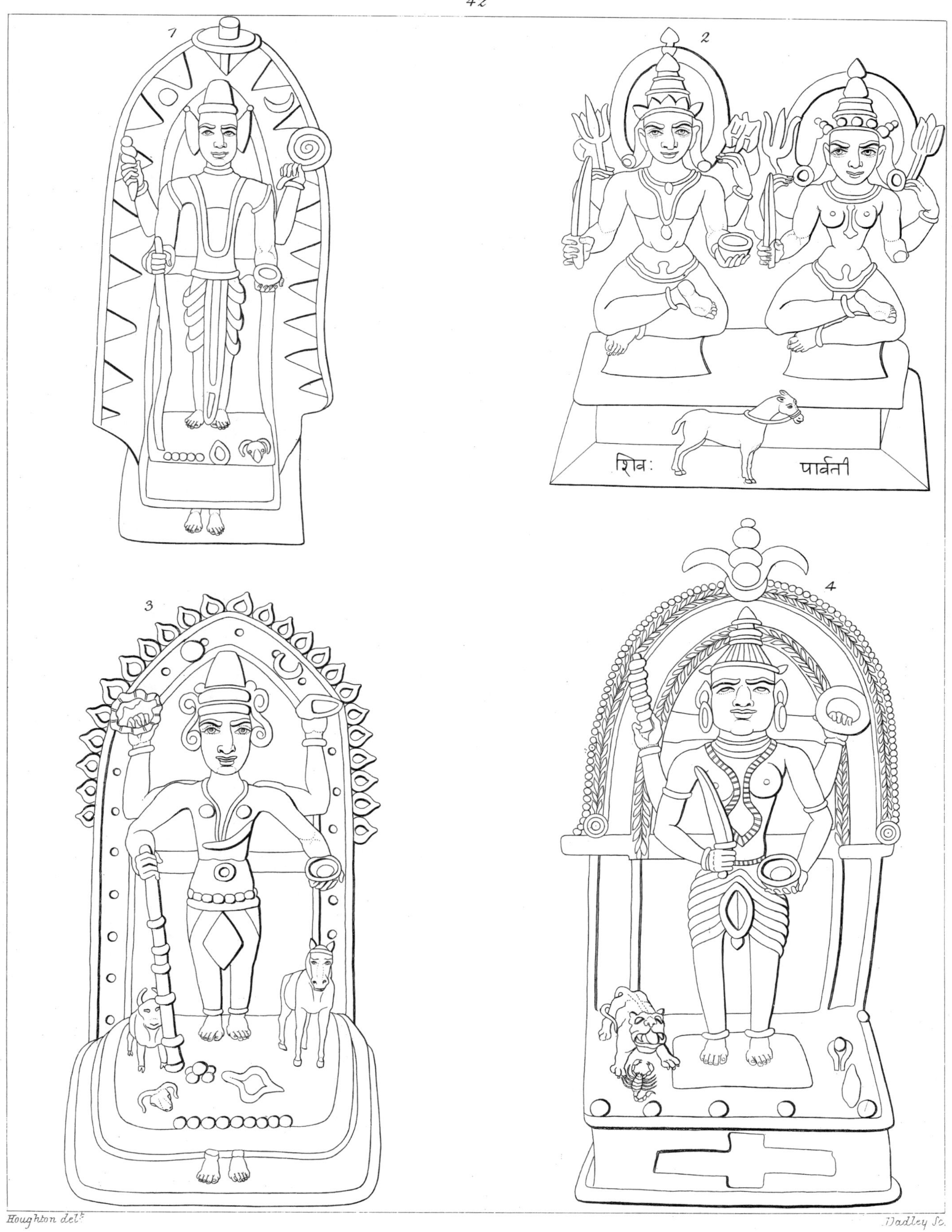

DĒVĪ *or the* GODDESS *the* SACT'I *or* ENERGY *of* SIVA.

And other subjects, From casts in brass.

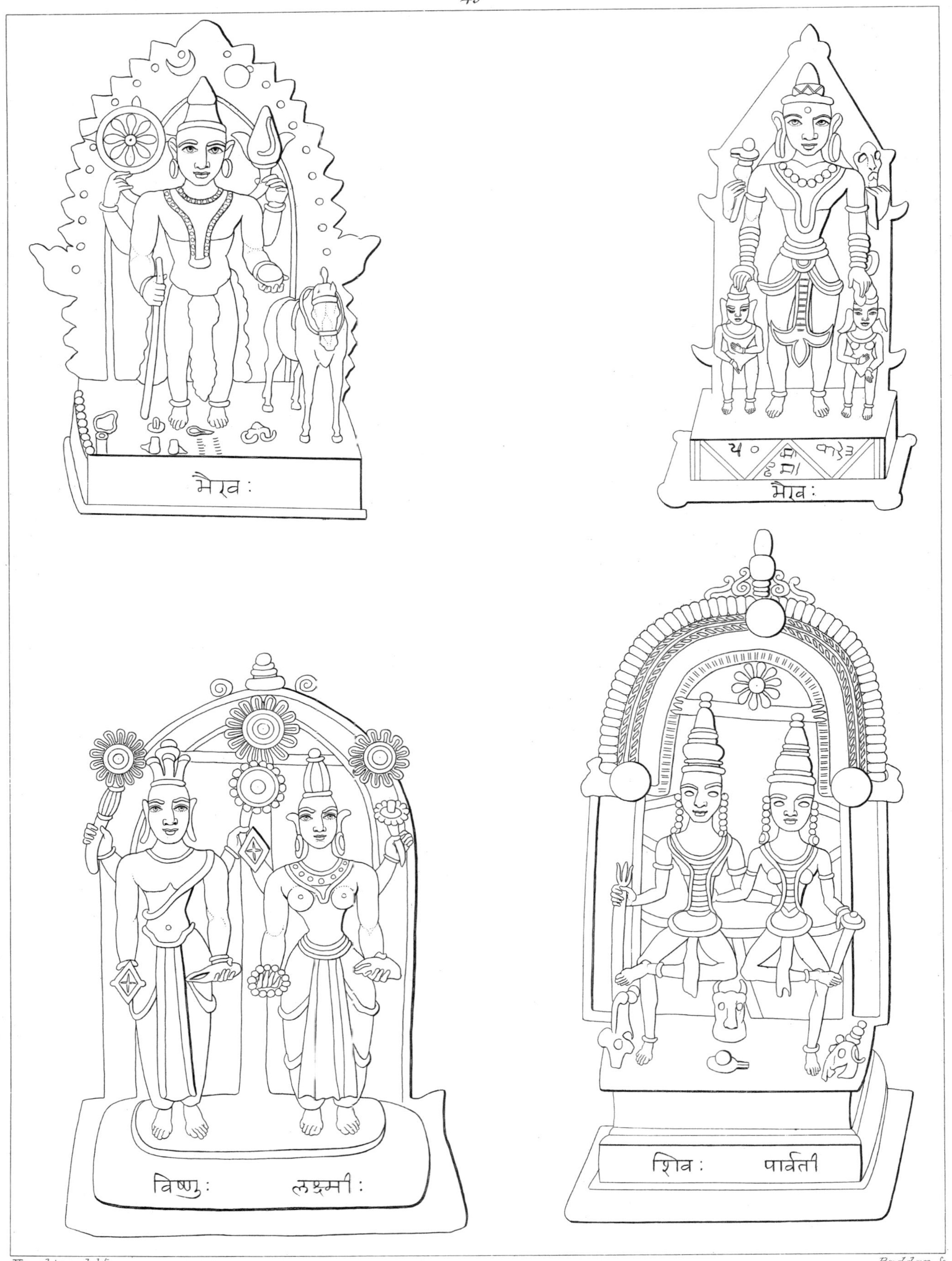

DĒVĪ and others.

From casts in Brass &c.

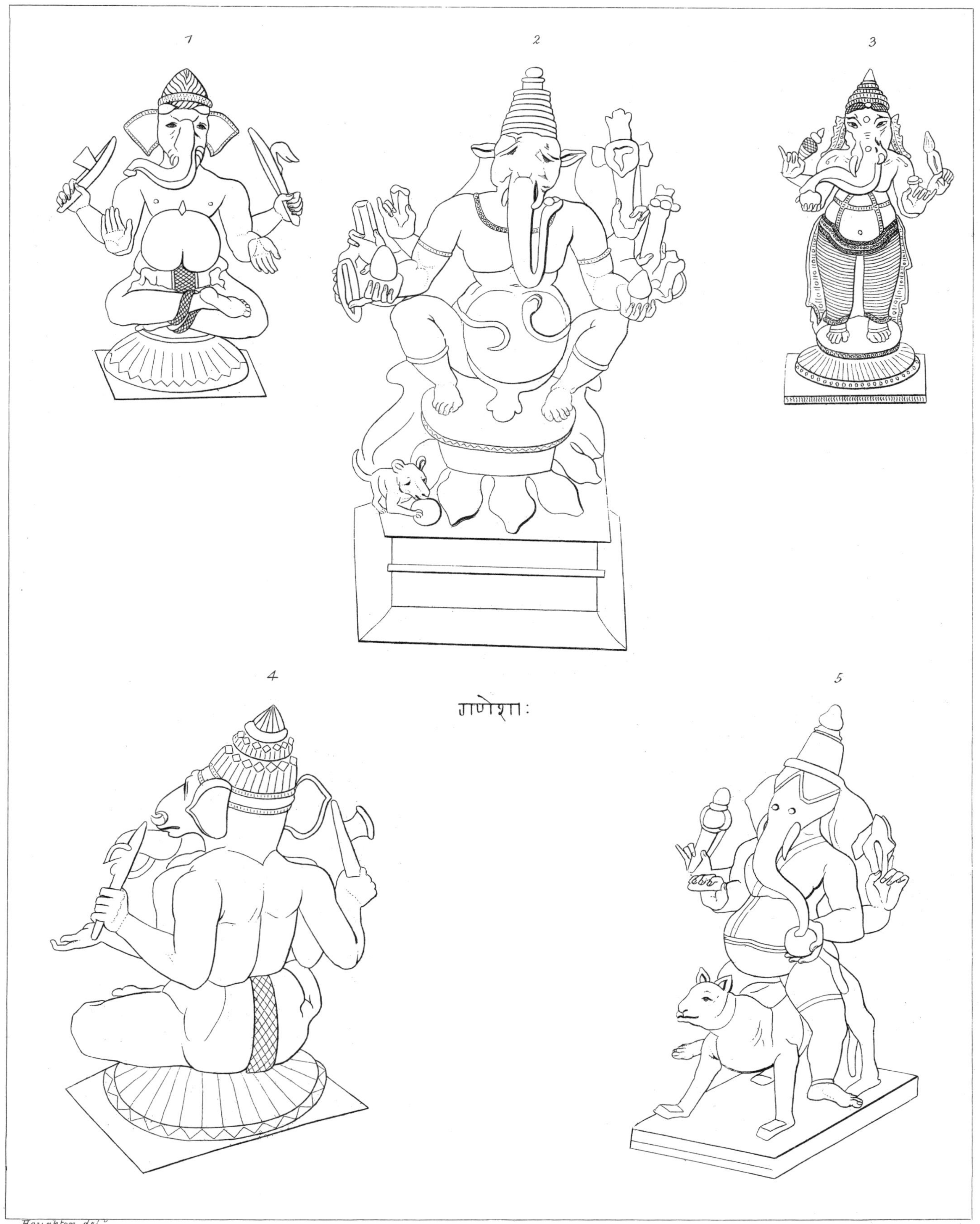

ग‍णेशाः

GANĒSA.

From Images in Brass and Bronze.

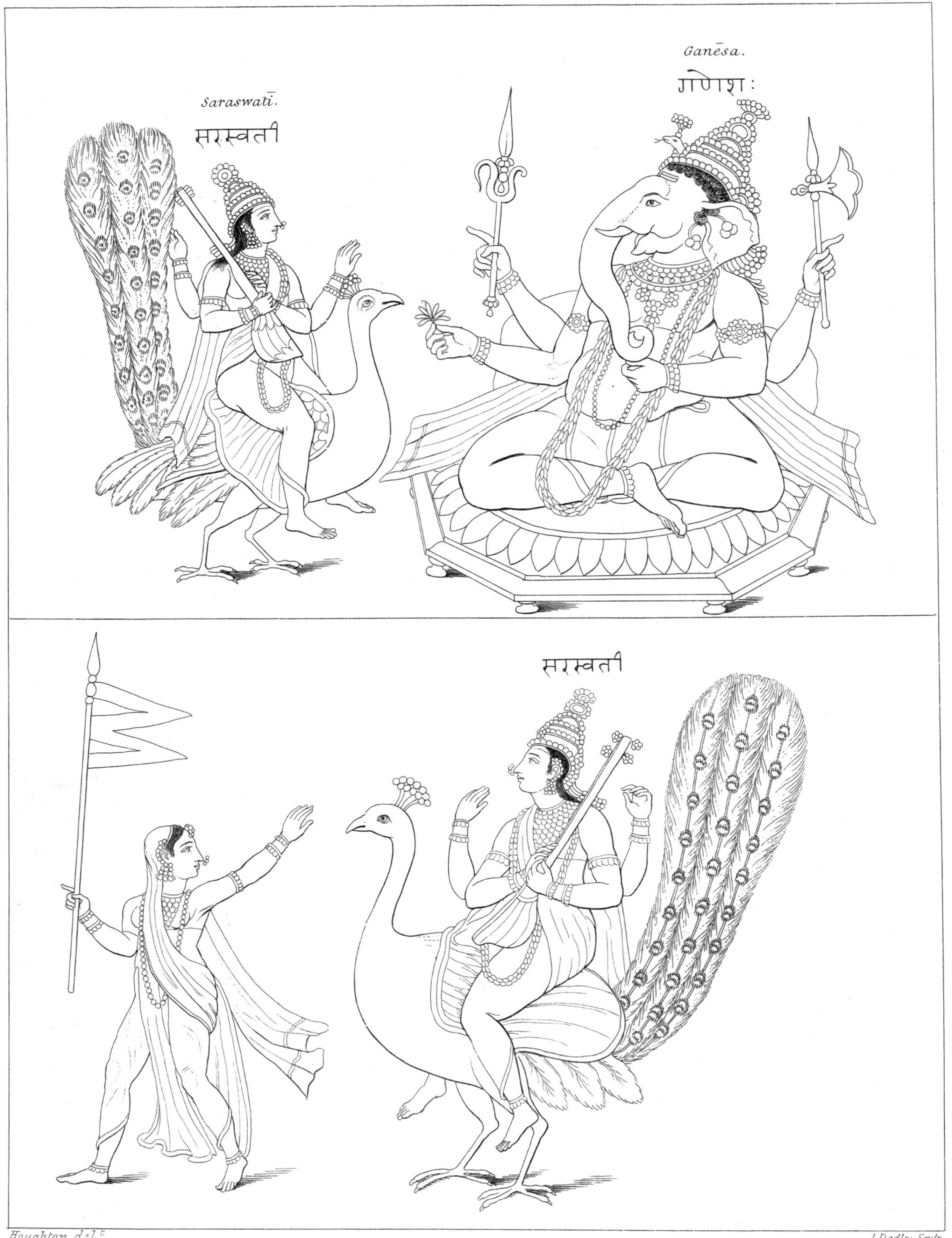

Houghton delt.

J. Dadley, Sculp.

GANĒSA and SARASWATĪ.

From Pictures.

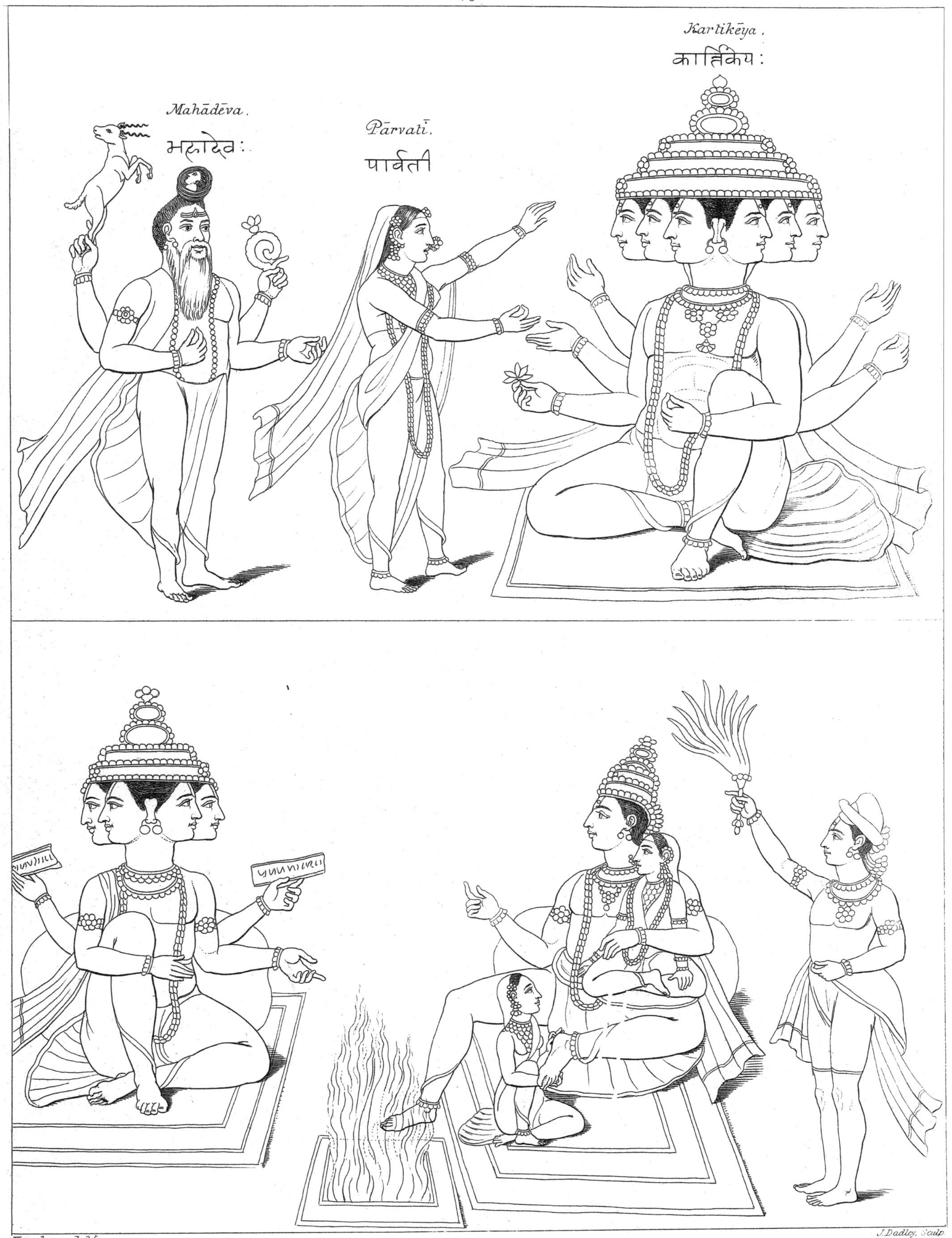

From Pictures.

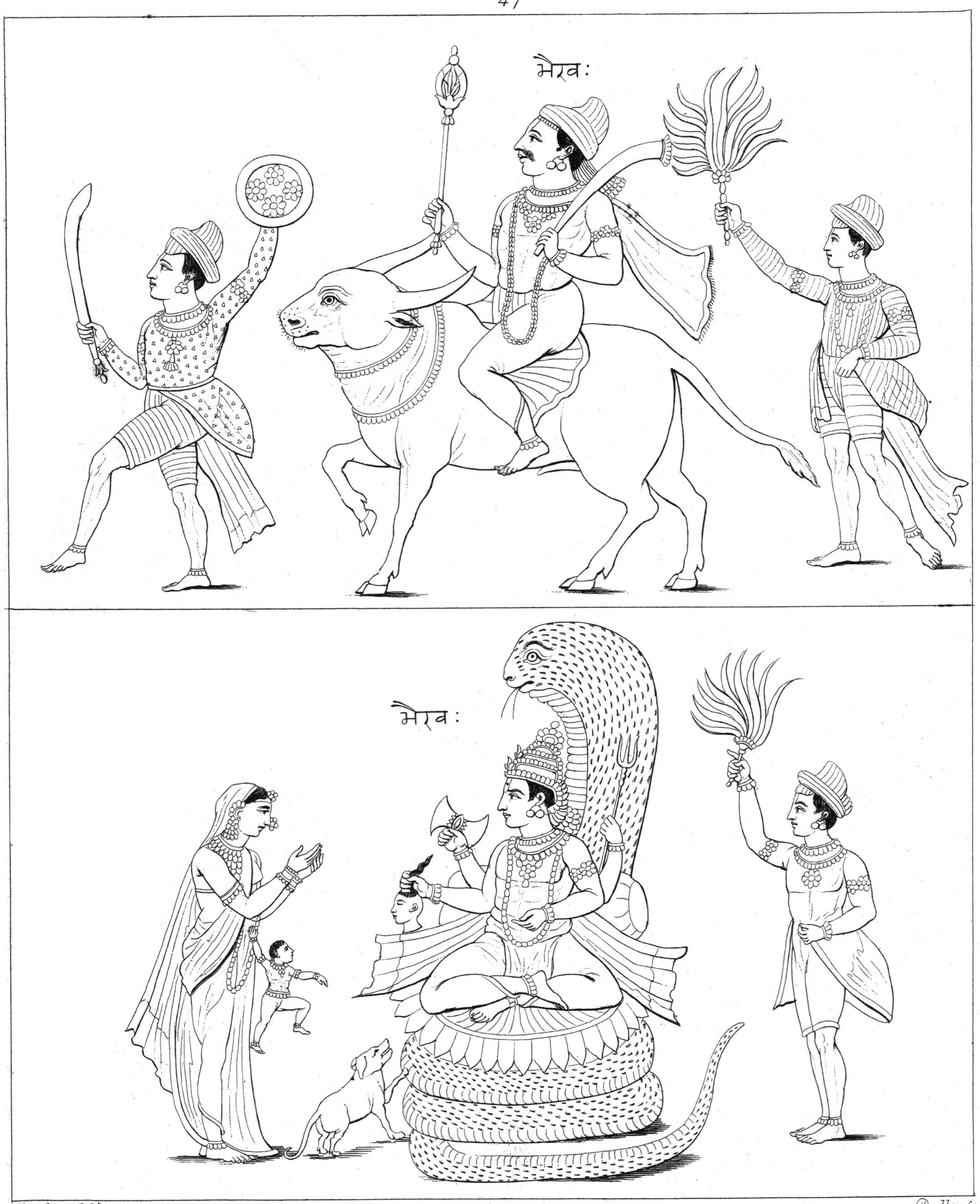

BHAIRAVA an AVATĀRA or son of SIVA.

From pictures.

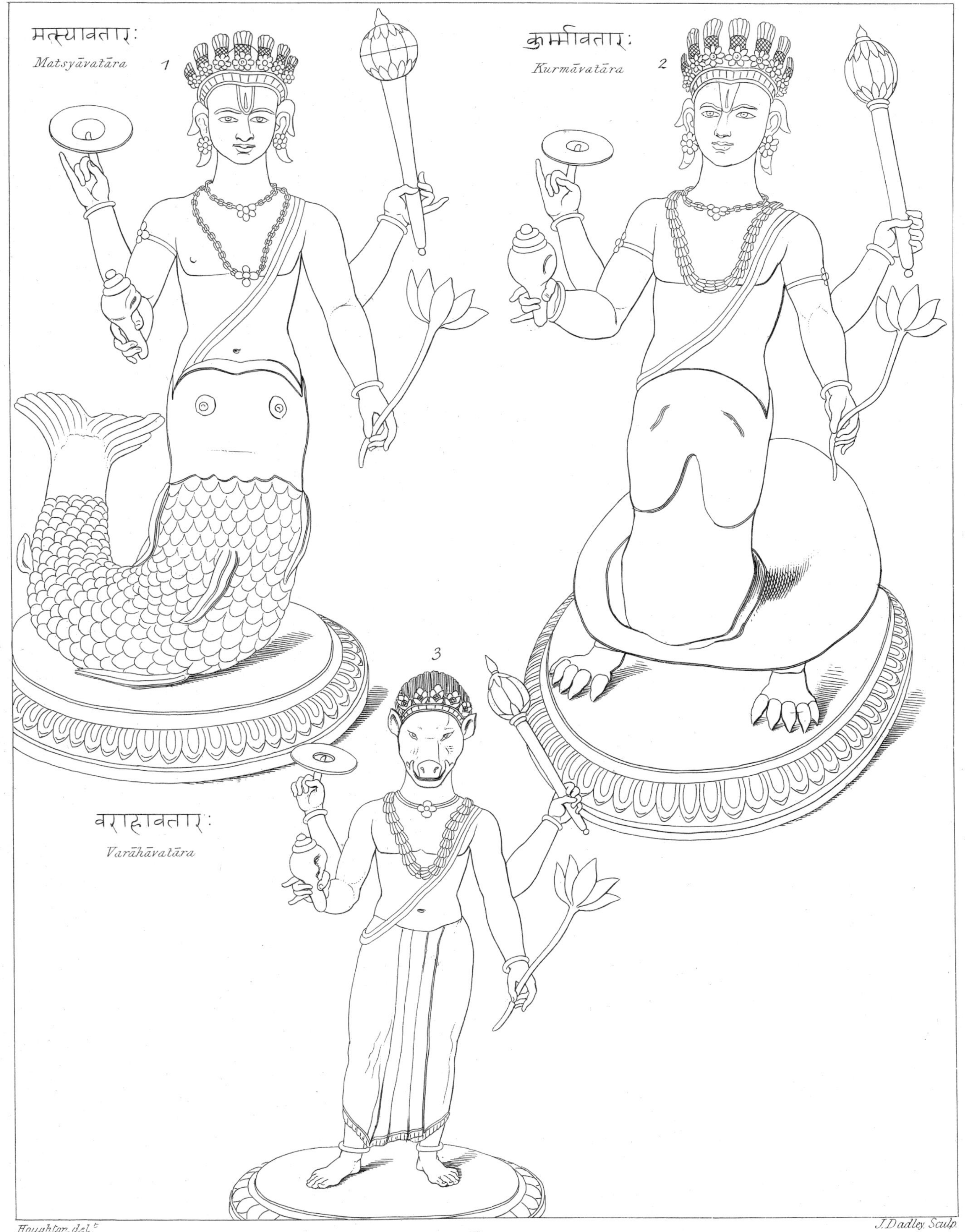

The three first AVATĀRAS *of* VISHNU,

in the forms of a FISH, *a* TORTOISE, *and a* BOAR.

From Zinc images in the museum at the India House.

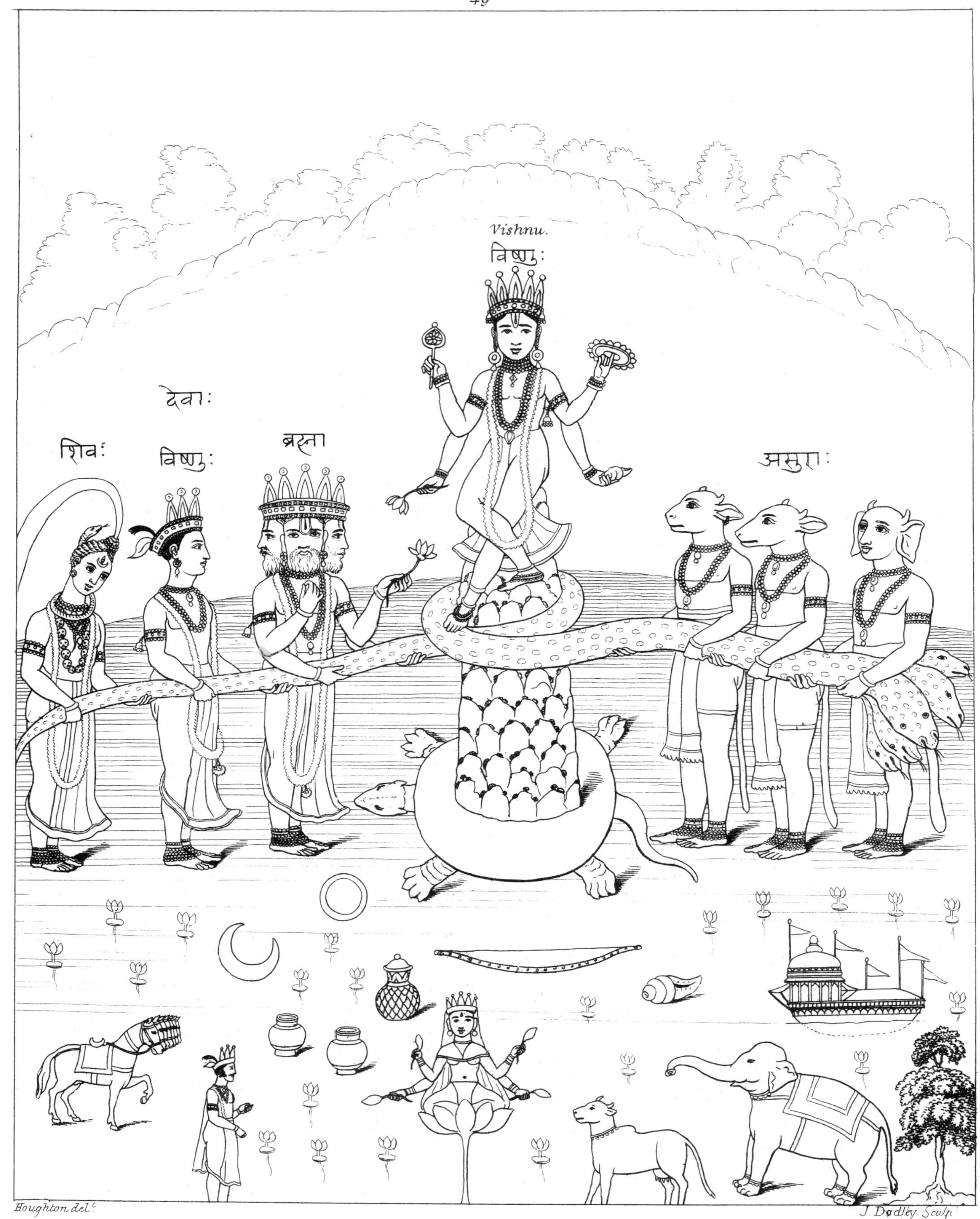

The 2nd or KURMĀVATĀRA of VISHNU.

Houghton delt.

J. Dudley Sculp.

From a picture.

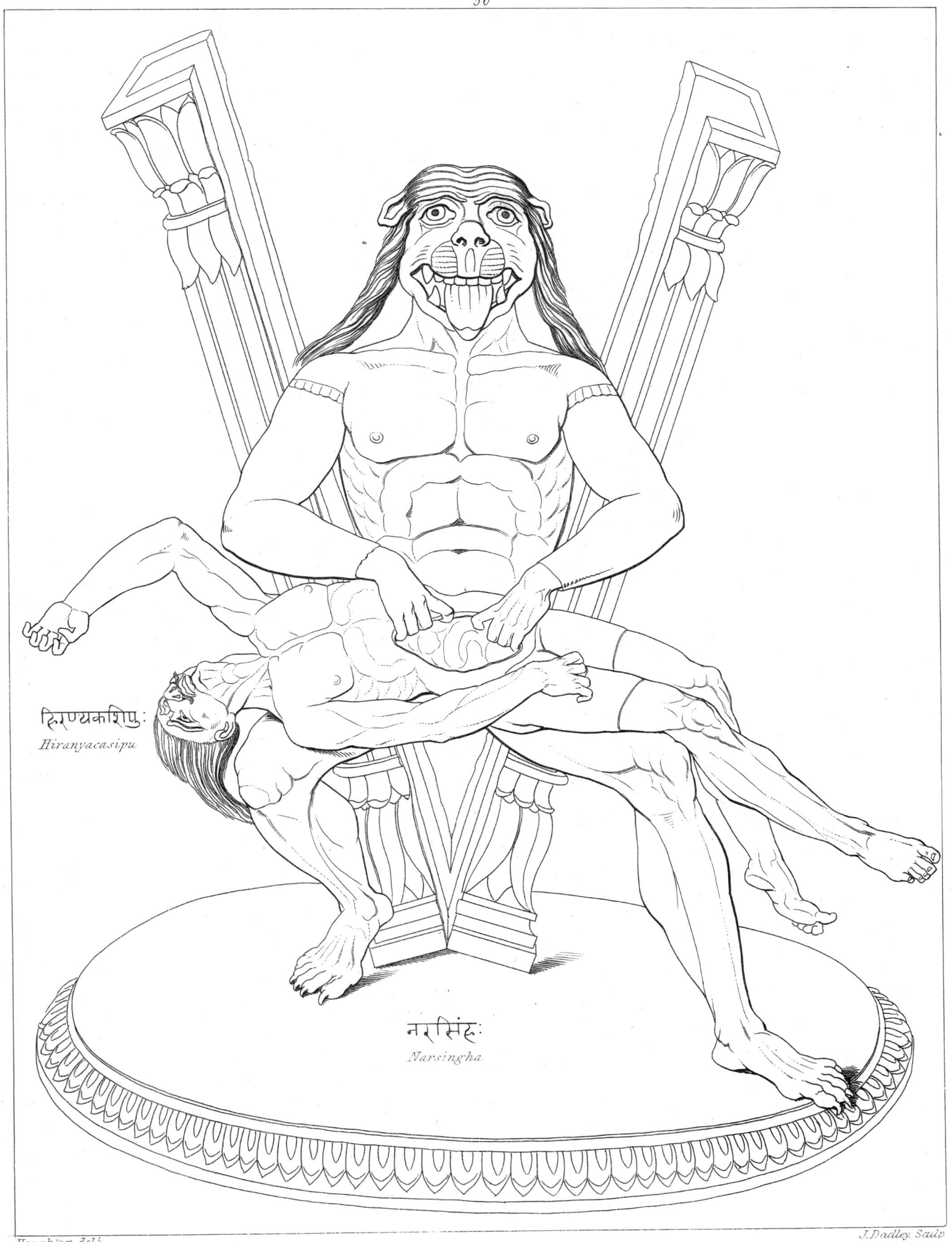

Houghton delt.   J. Dadley, Sculp.

The fourth *AVATĀRA* of VISHNU as NARSINHA.

From a Zinc cast in the museum at the India House.

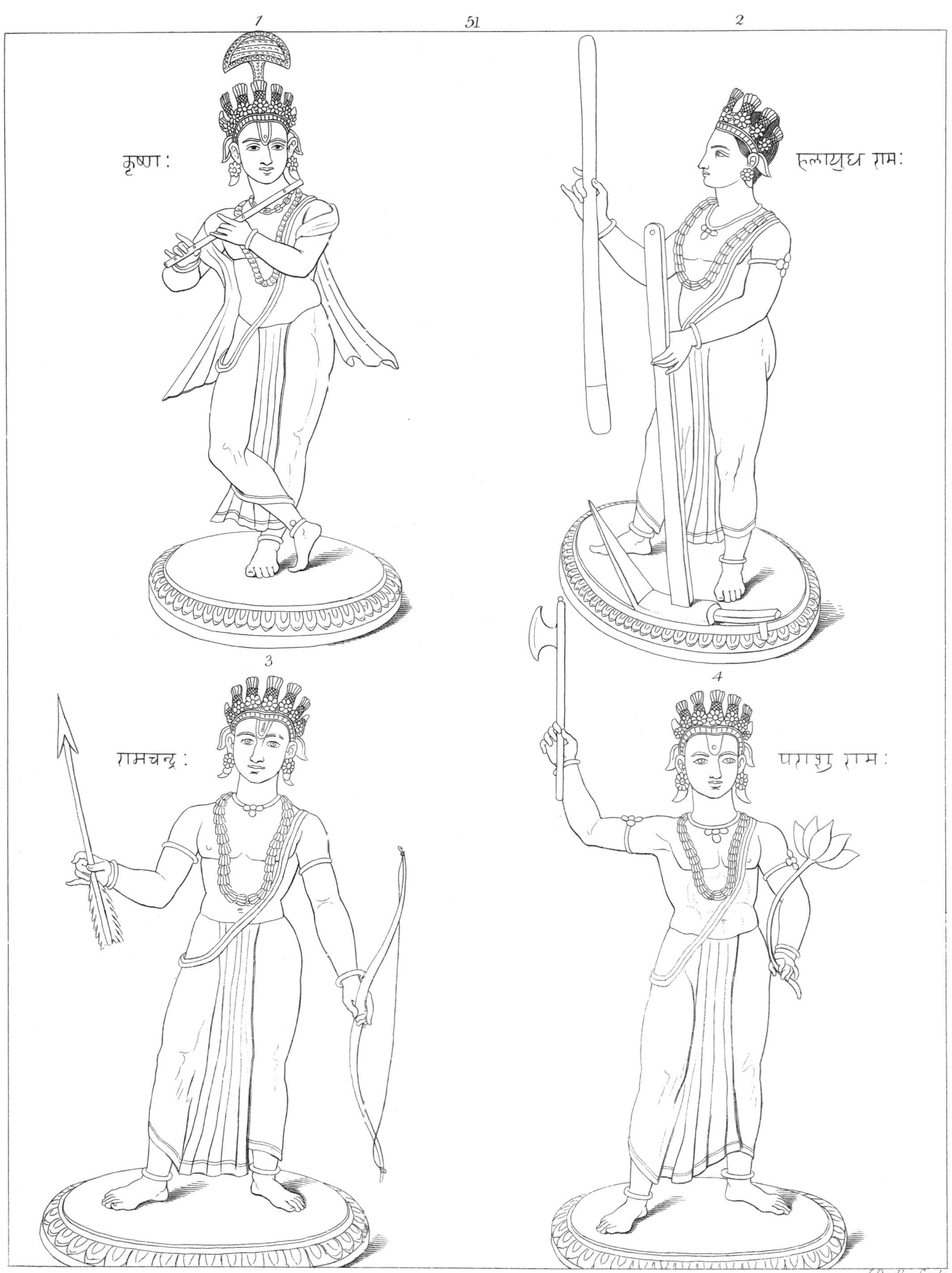

The AVATĀRAS of VISHNU in the persons of KRISHNA and the three RĀMAS.

From Images in the Museum at the East India House

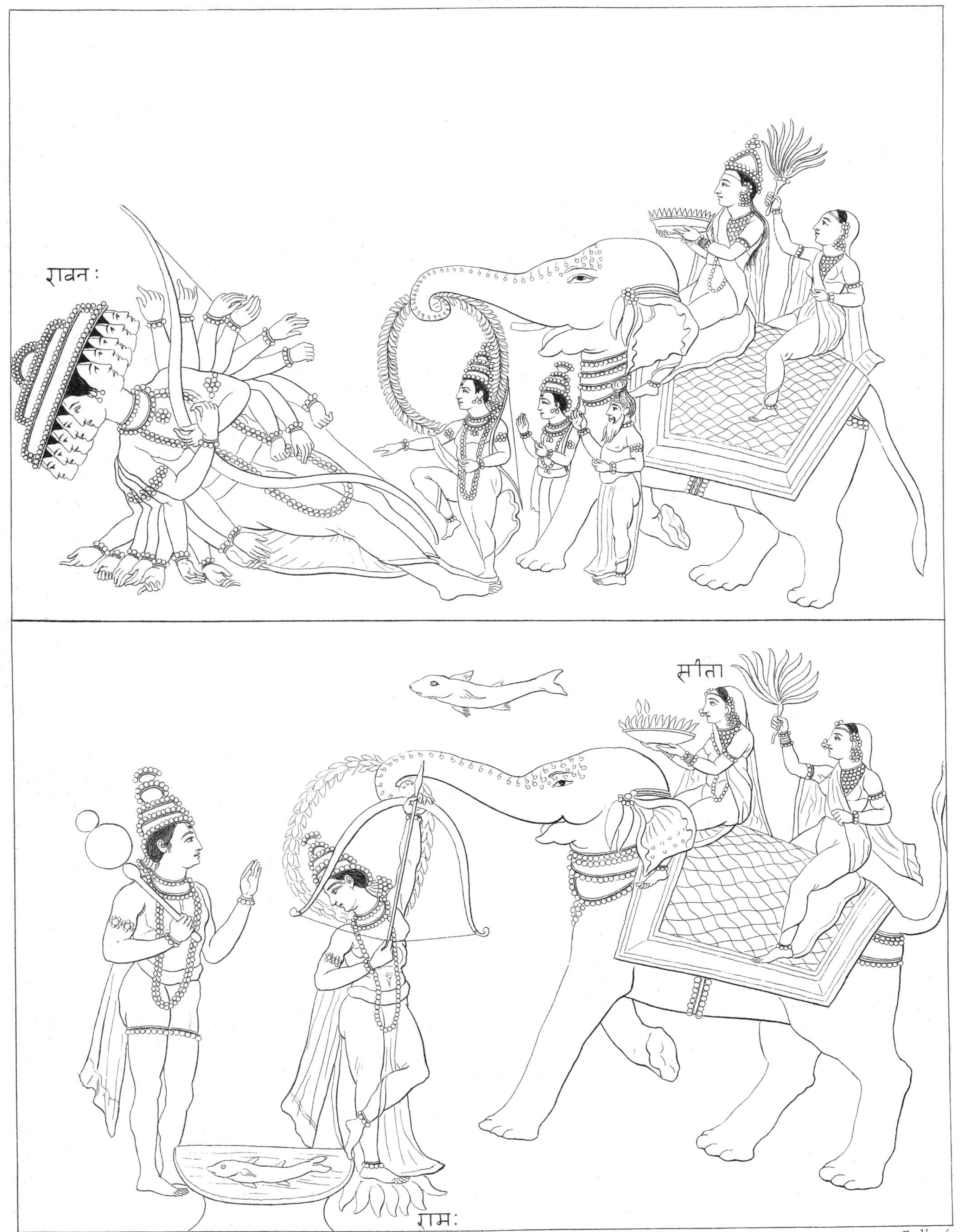

RĀMA *winning* SĪTĀ, *after the discomfiture of his competitor* RĀVANA.

From drawings taken from the Ramayana.

HANUMĀN assisted by SUGRĪVA and his associates, building RĀMA'S bridge from the CONTINENT to CEYLON to attack RĀVANA.

From the Ramayana.

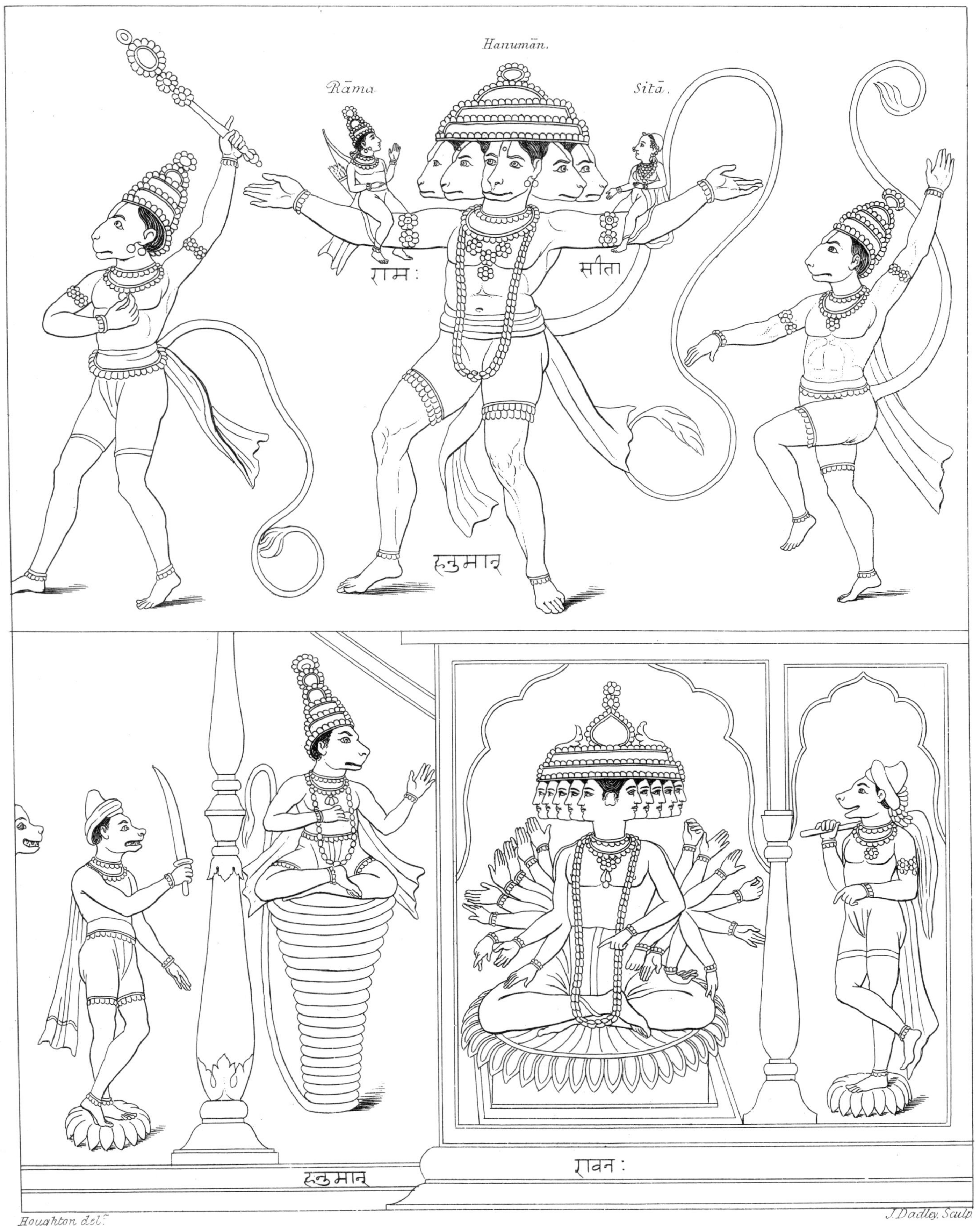

HANUMĀN and RĀVANA.

From Legends in the Ramayana.

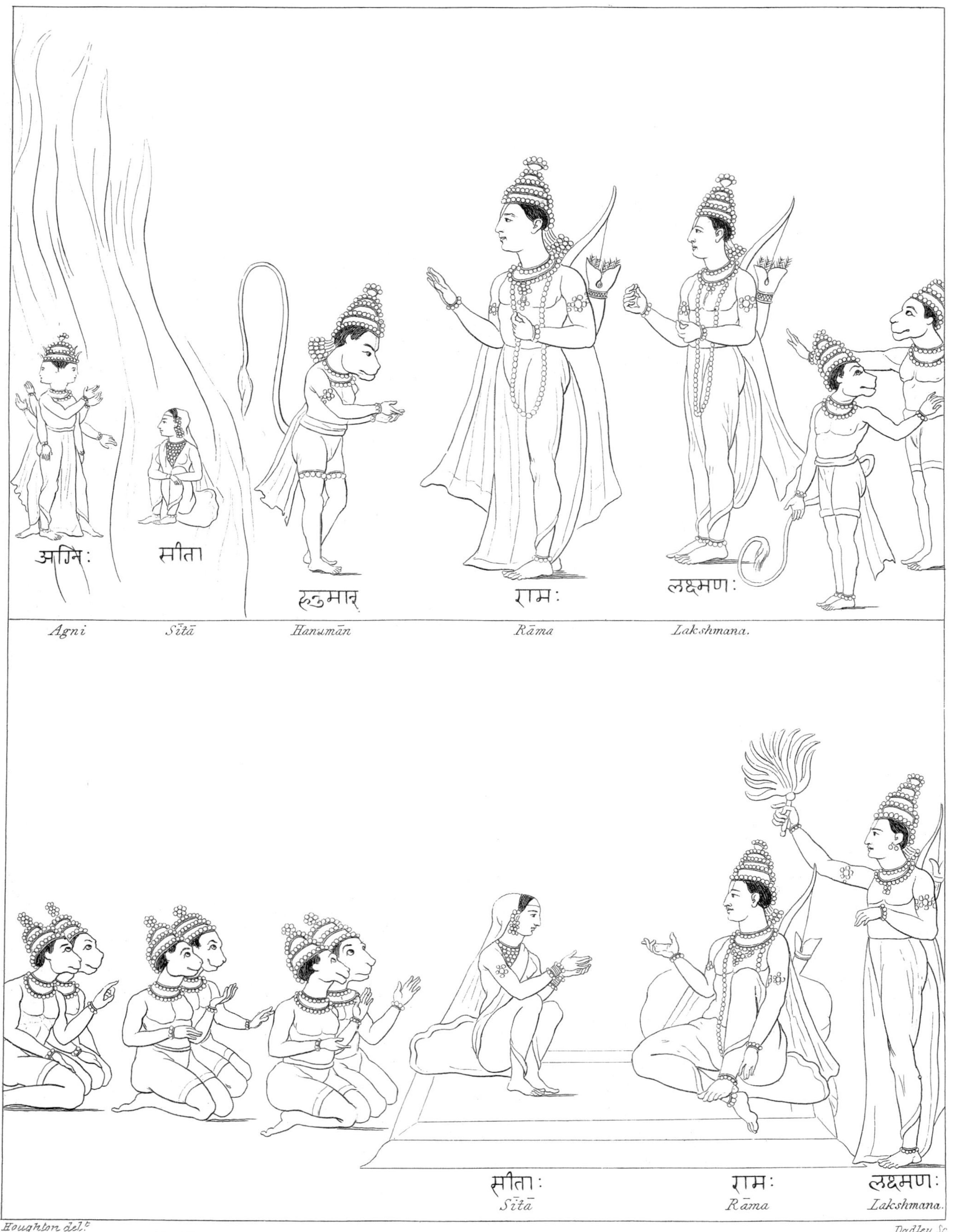

SĪTĀ *learning from* RĀMA *the necessity of her purification by* FIRE,

in which she is (above) supported and comforted by AGNI *it's Regent.*

From the Ramayan.

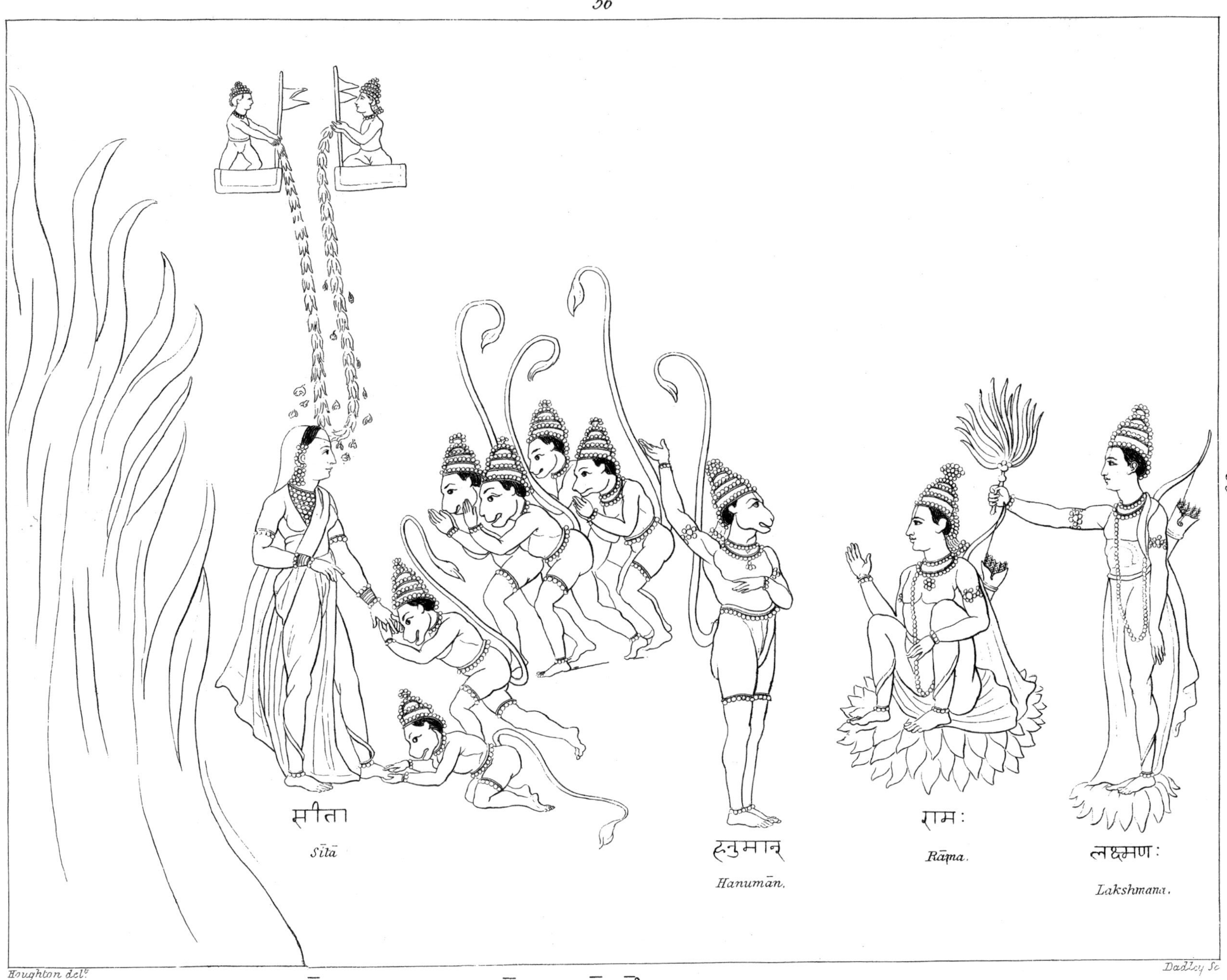

HANUMĀN anounceing to RĀMA SĪTĀ'S honorable acquital by the Fiery Ordeal.

From the Rāmāyana.

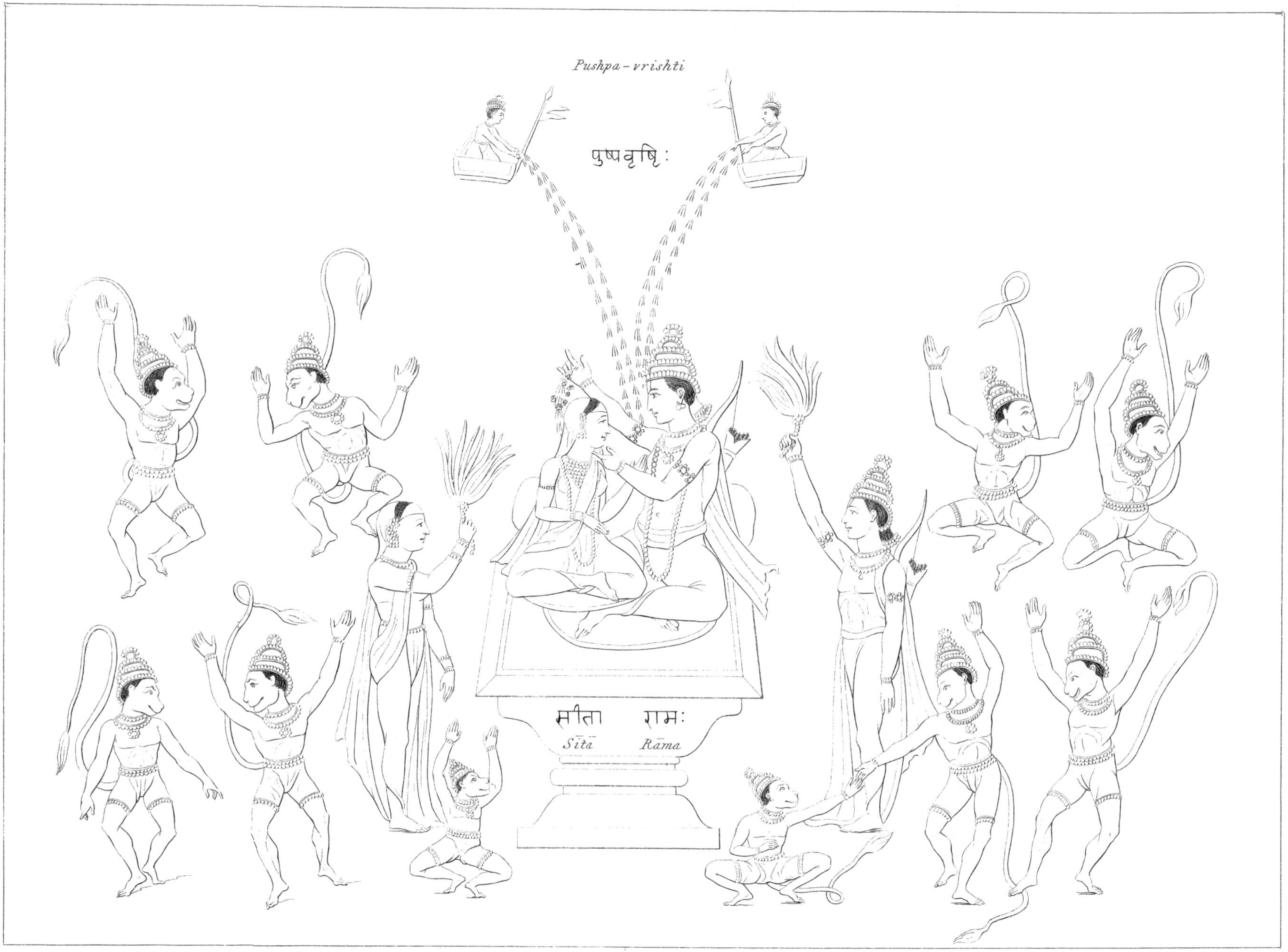

Pushpa-vrishti

पुष्पवृष्टि:

सीता   राम:
Sītā   Rāma

Houghton, del.t

Dudley Sc.

RĀMA and **SĪTĀ'S** Reunion, after her honorable acquital by the Fiery Ordeal.

From the Rāmāyana.

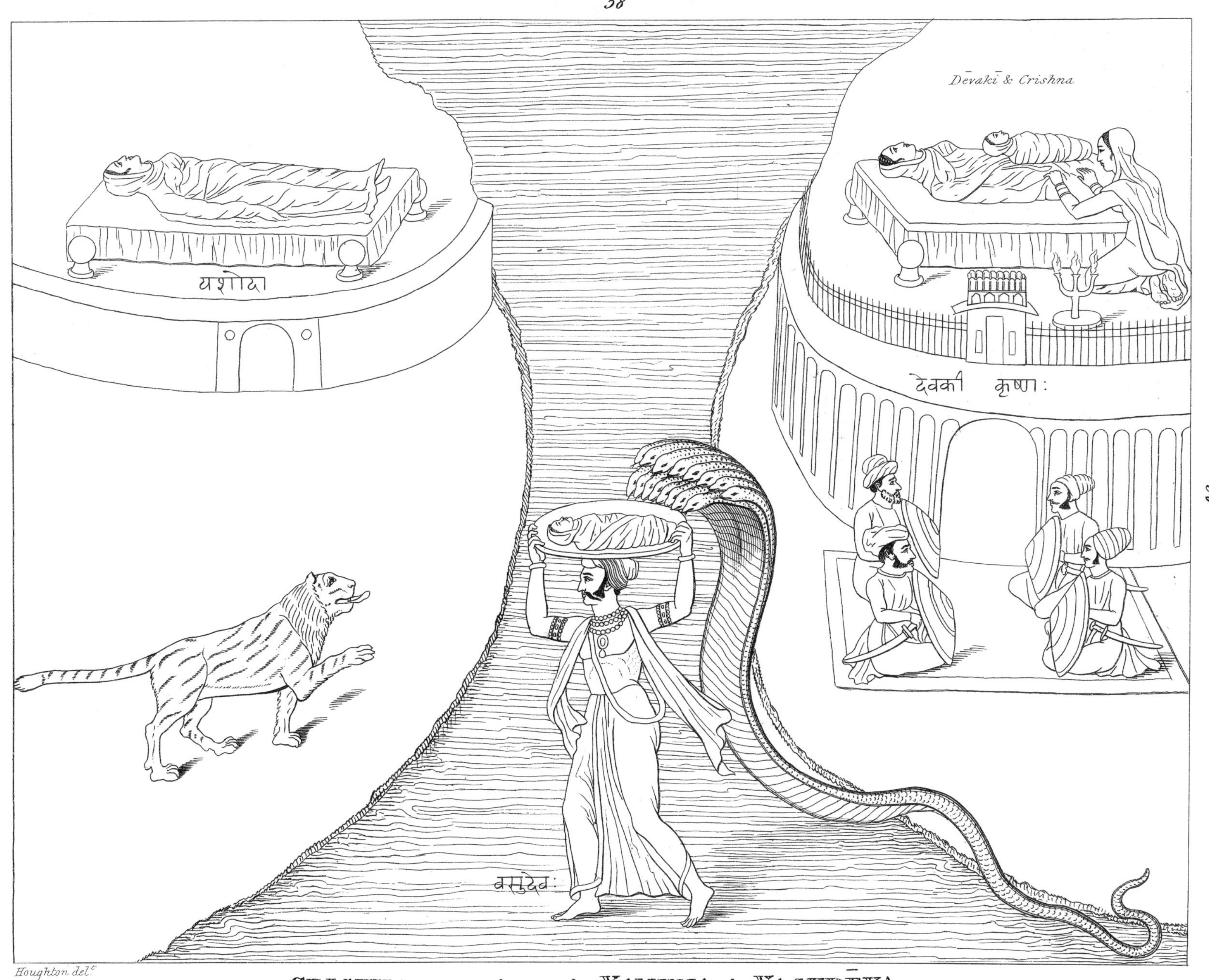

CRISHNA conveyed over the YAMUNA by VASUDĒVA,

Miraculously escapes from his uncle CANSA, the HEROD of HINDU Scripture History.

From the Srī Bhāgvata.

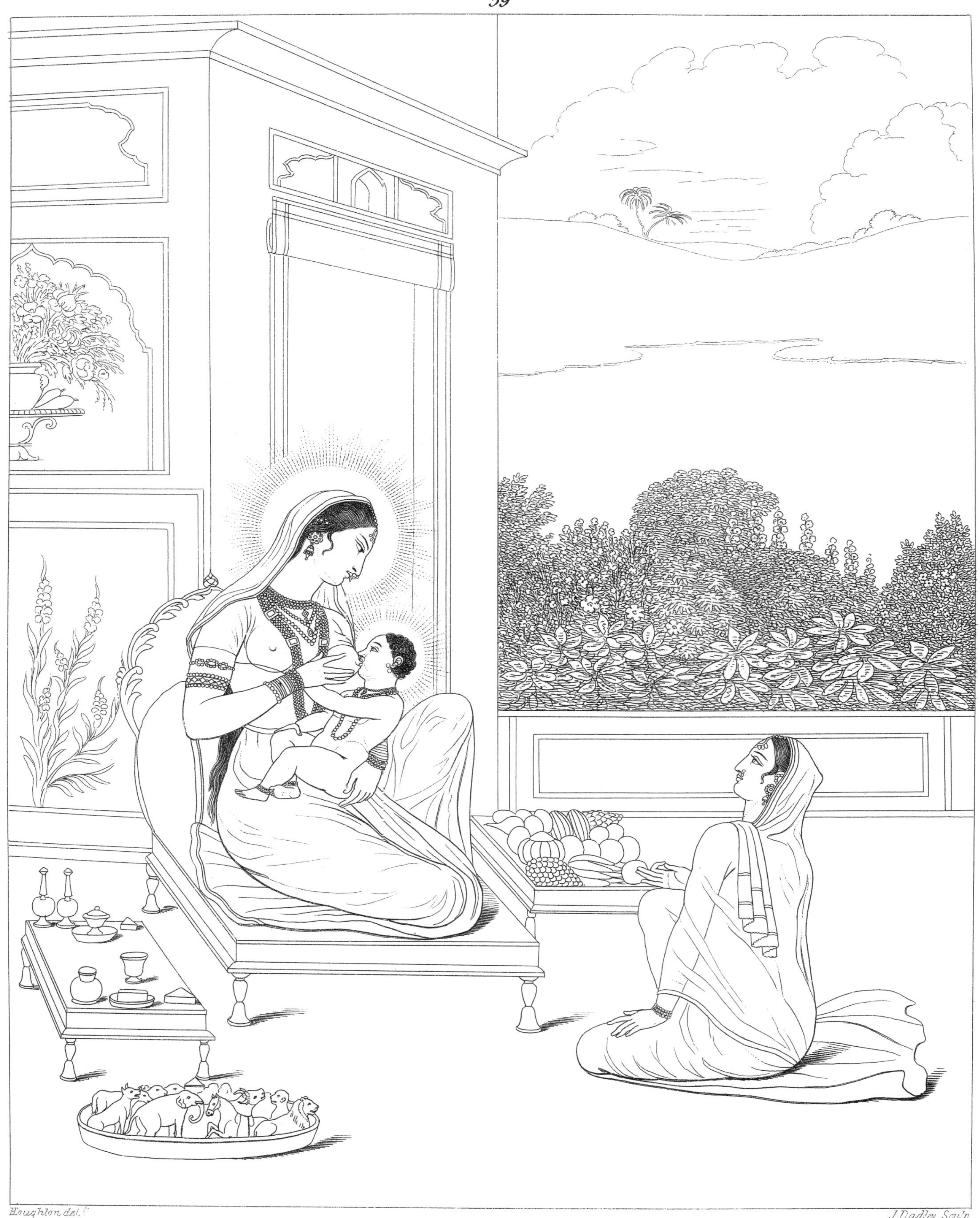

CRISHNA *nursed by* DĒVAKĪ.

From a highly finished picture.

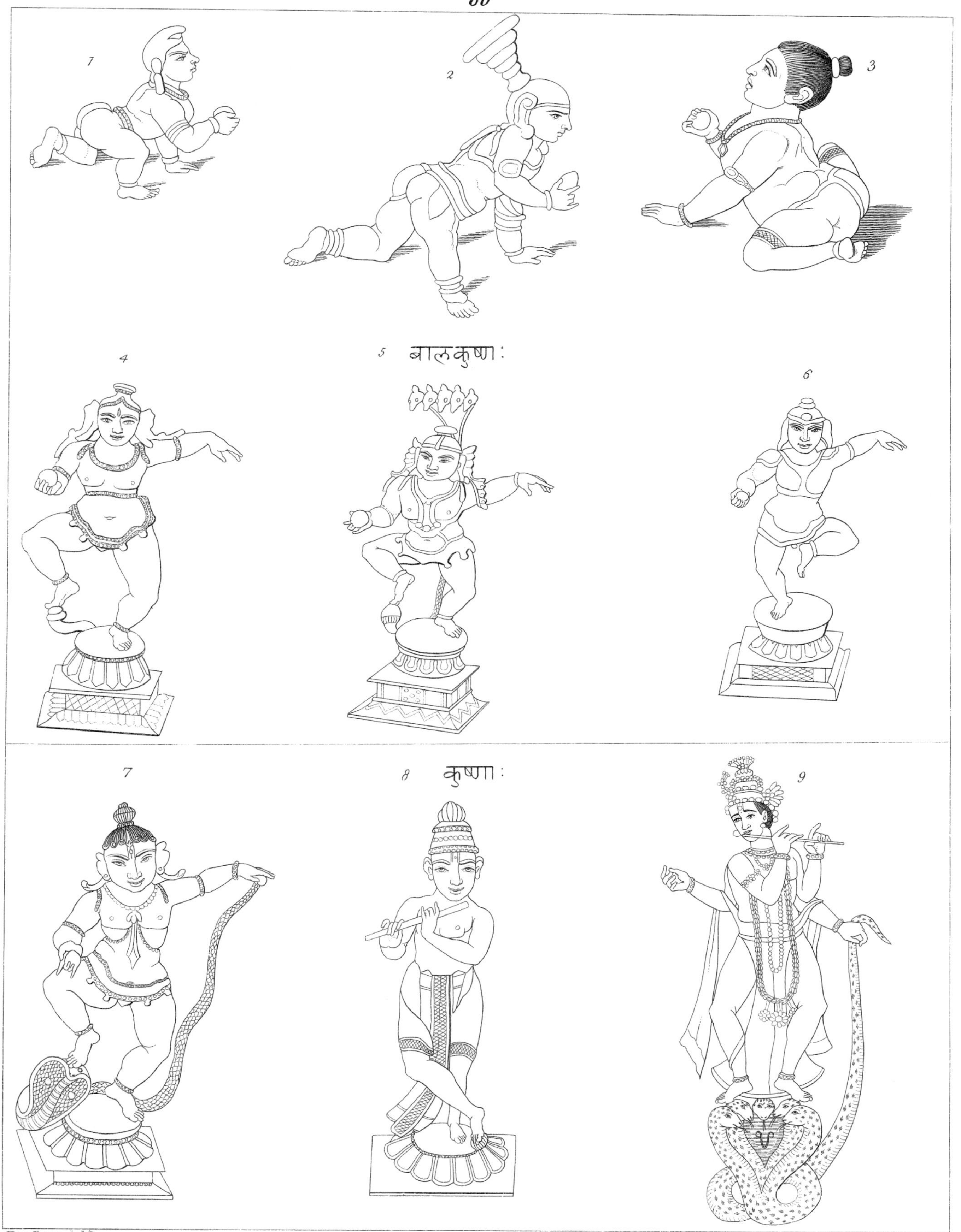

BĀLA KRISHNA.

From brafs and other images of the Infant Krishna.

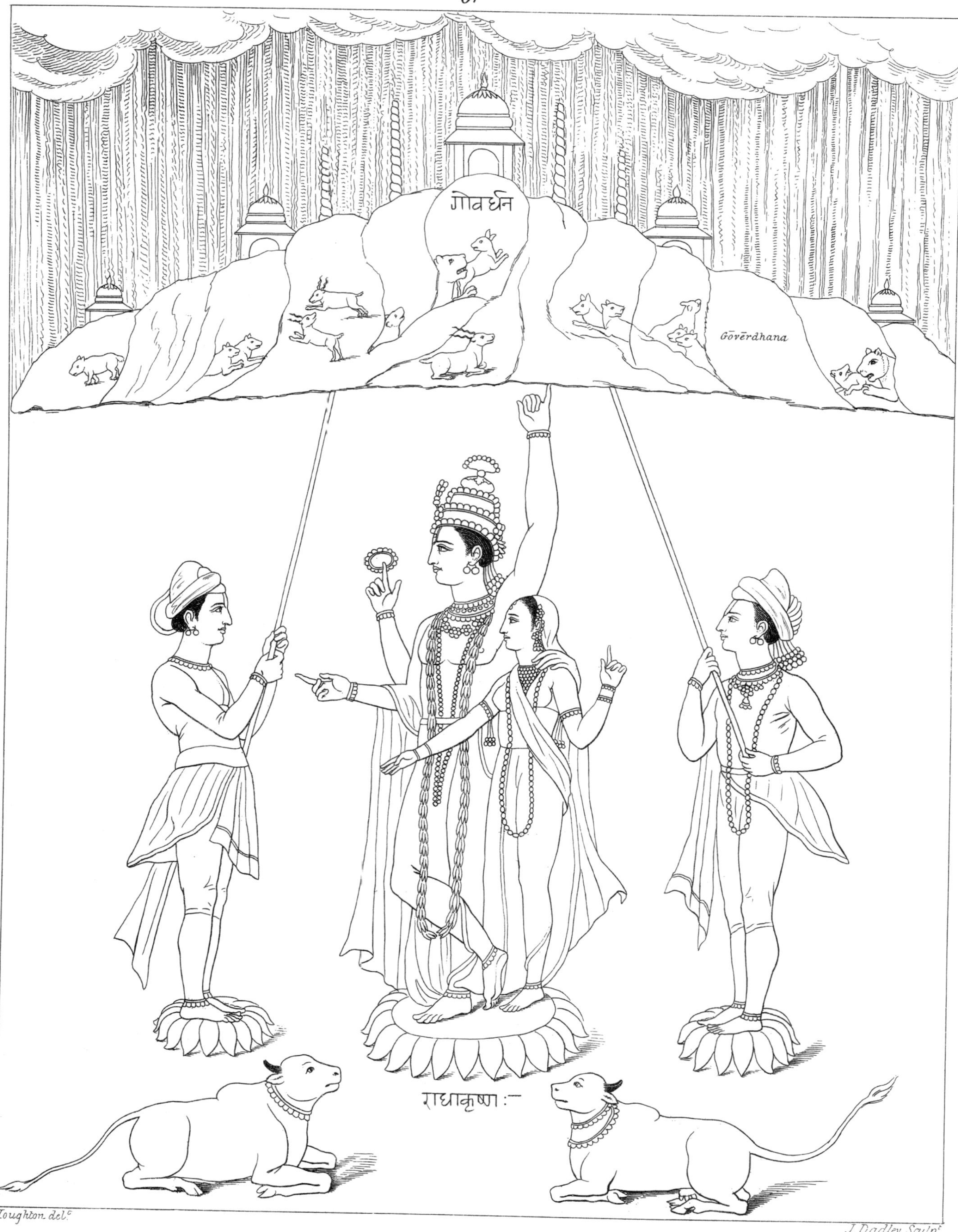

KRISHNA *uplifts the mountain* GŌVERDHANA *to Shelter his worshippers from the wrath of* INDRA.

From a picture.

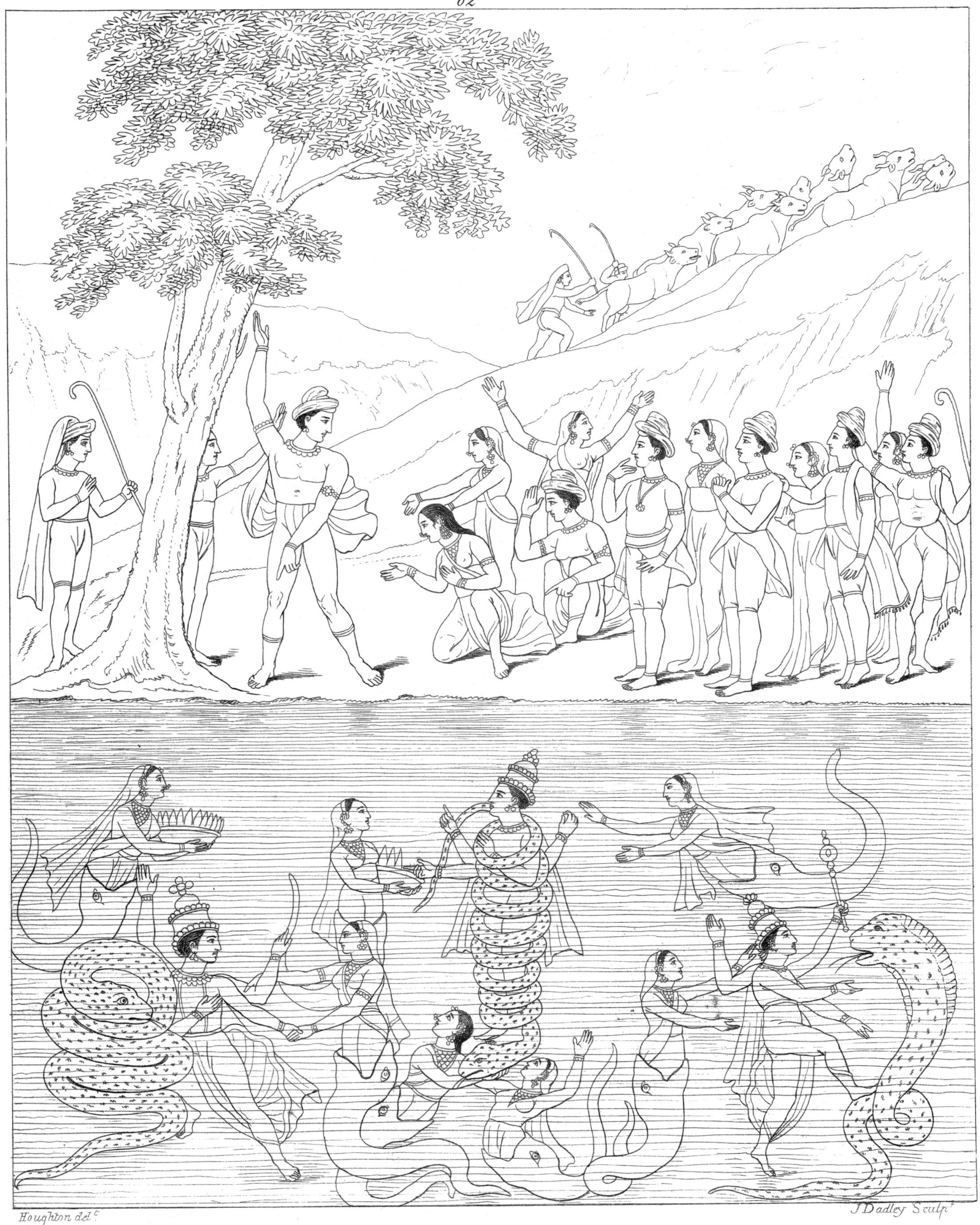

KRISHNA *about to destroy the Serpent* KALIYA, *the* NEREIDS, *his wives, interceding.*

From a Sketch.

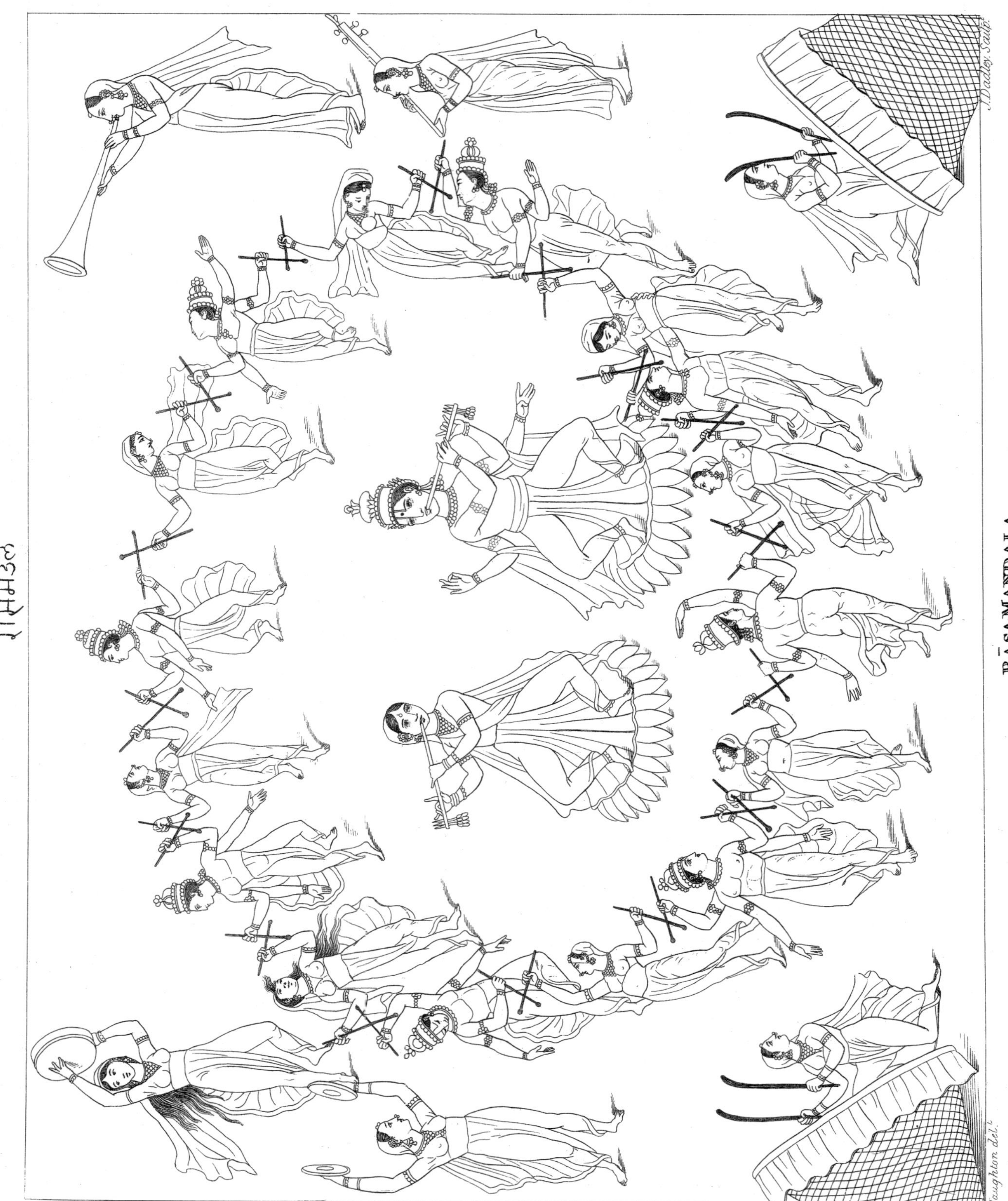

RĀSA-MANDALA,

KRISHNA (the SUN) and the celestial bodies in harmonious movements round him.

From a Sketch.

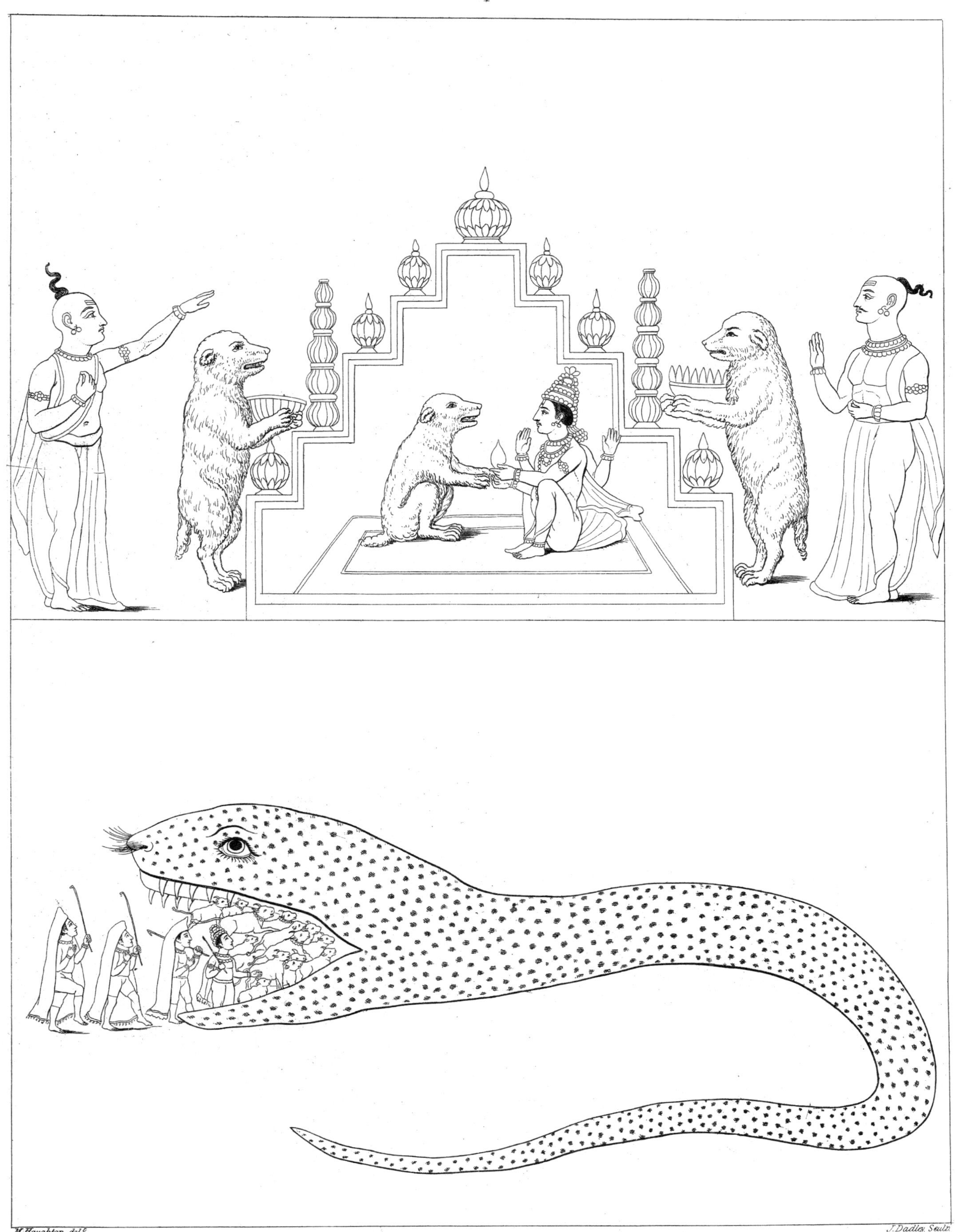

from Pictures in the SRÍ BHAGAVATA, or life of KRISHNA.

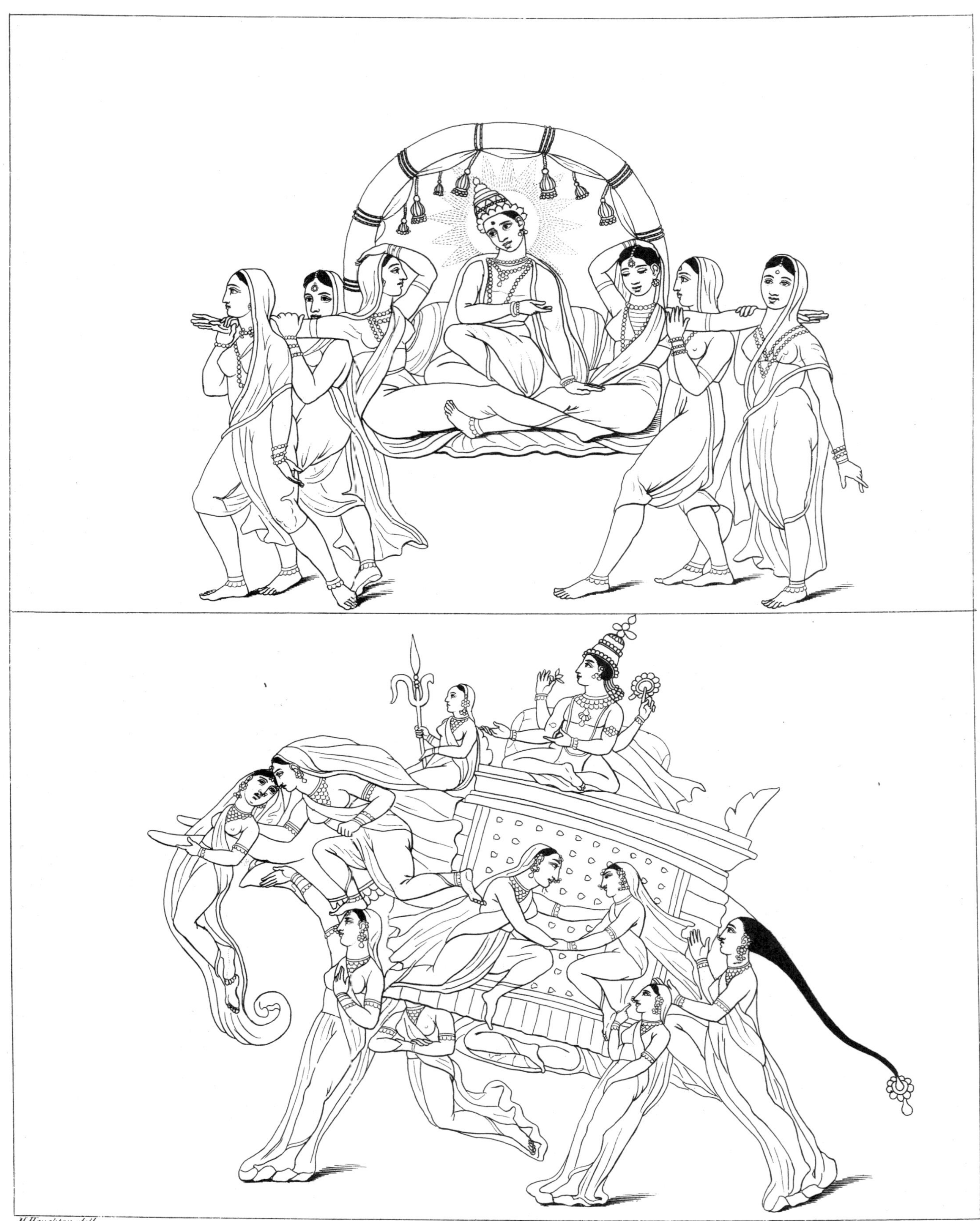

KRISHNA *and the* GŌPIA.

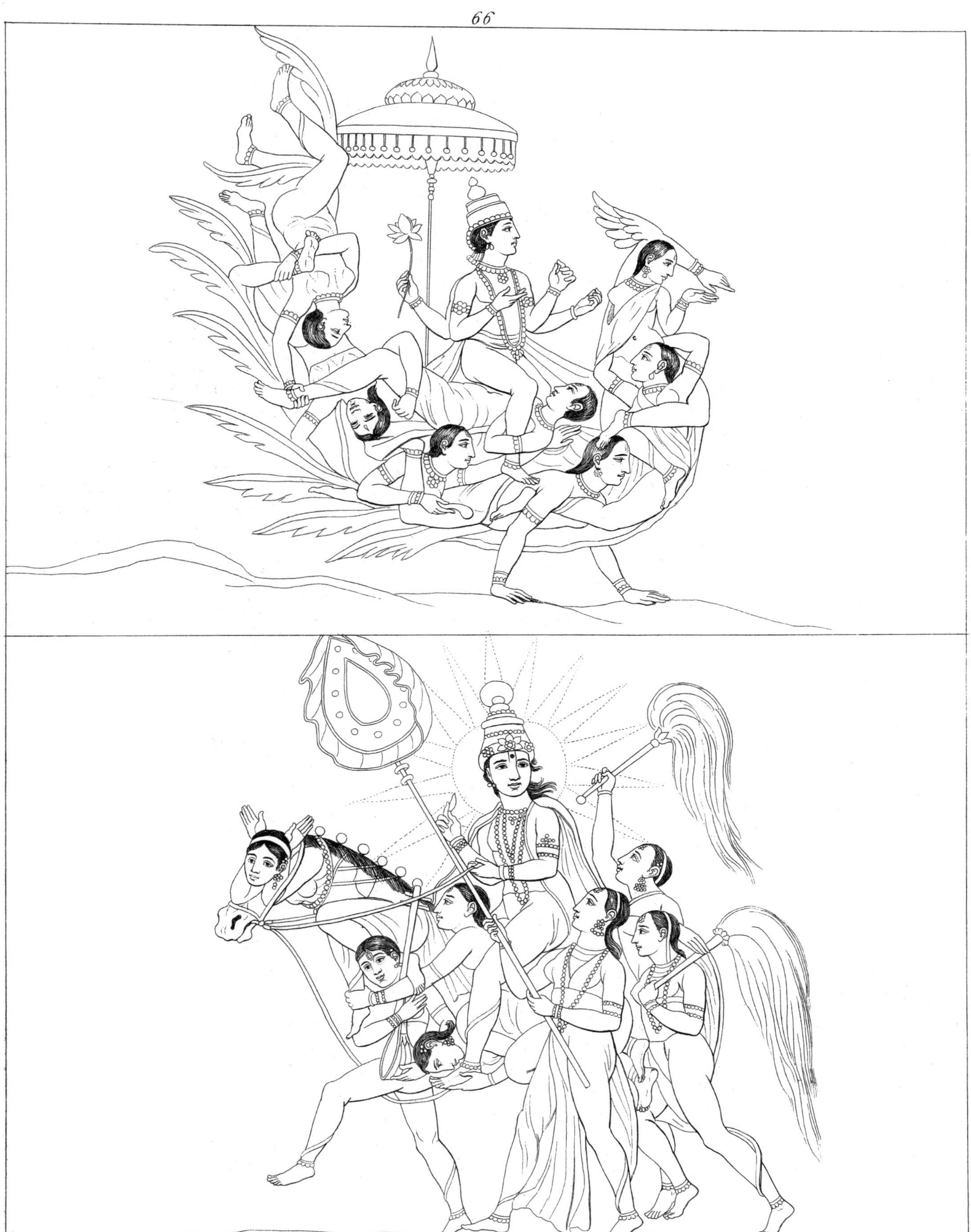

KRISHNA *and the* GOPIA.

in whimsical combinations. from Pictures.

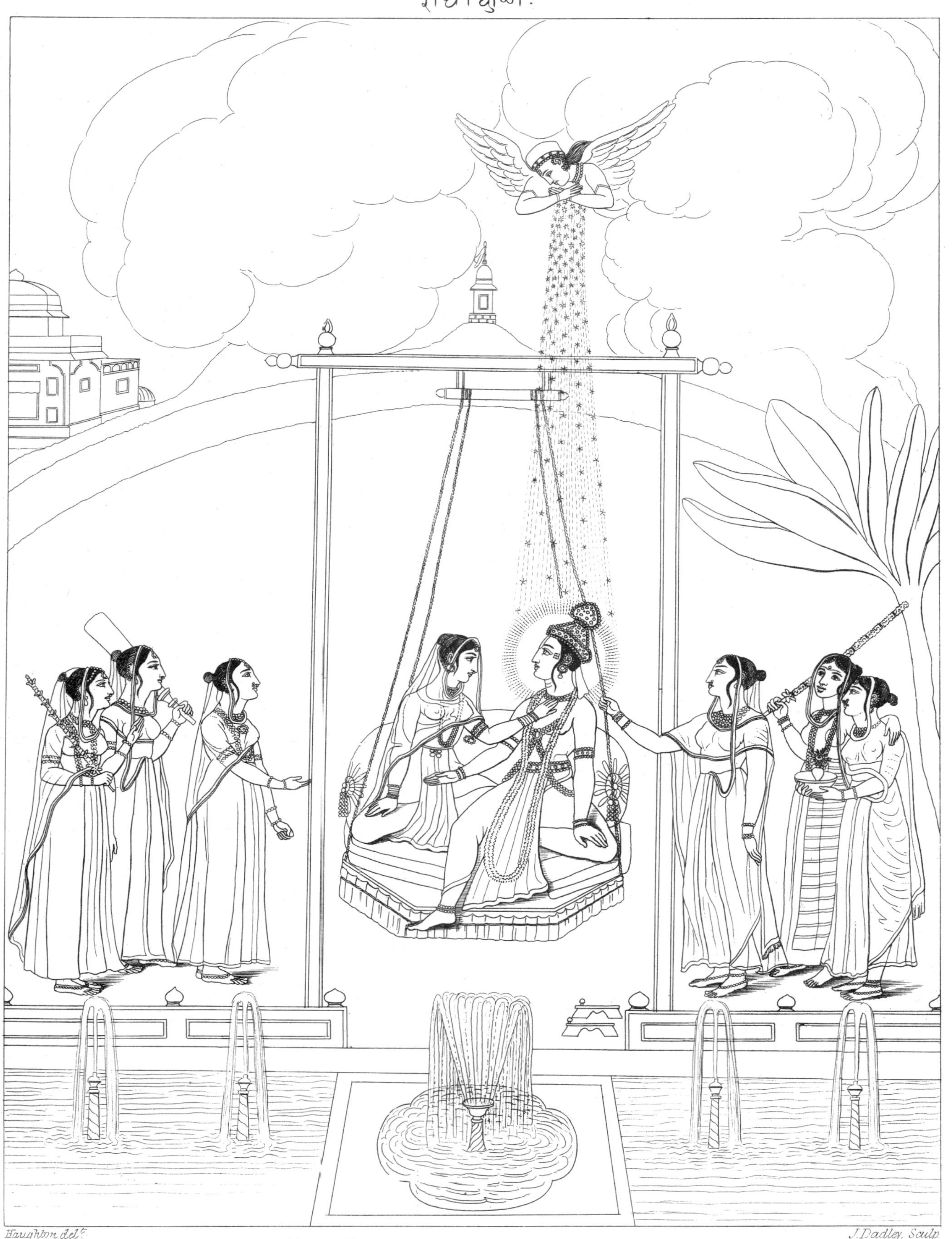

RĀDHĀ, KRISHNA, and attendant GOPIA.

From a Picture.

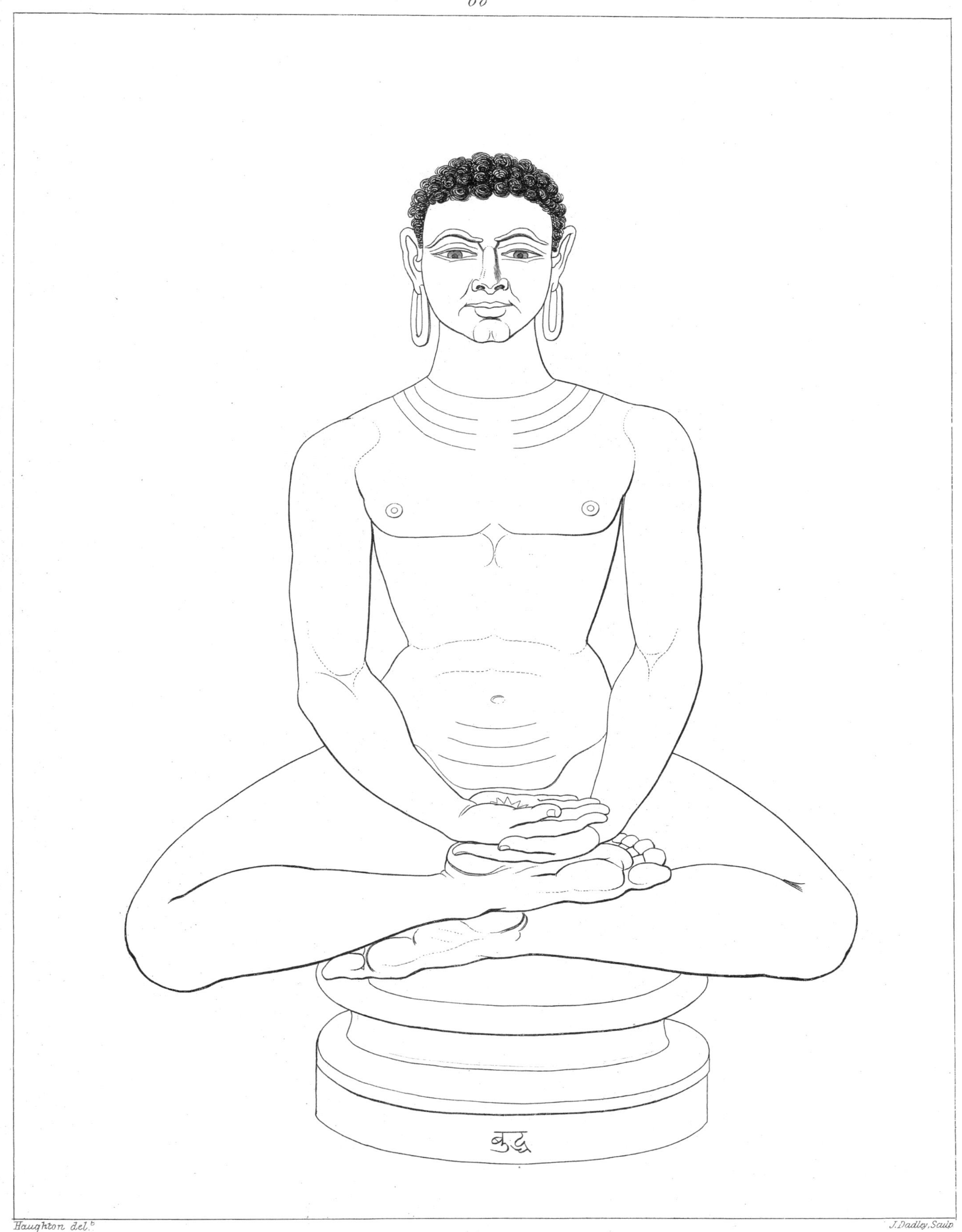

BUDDHA.

From a Statue in black marble in the Museum at the India House.

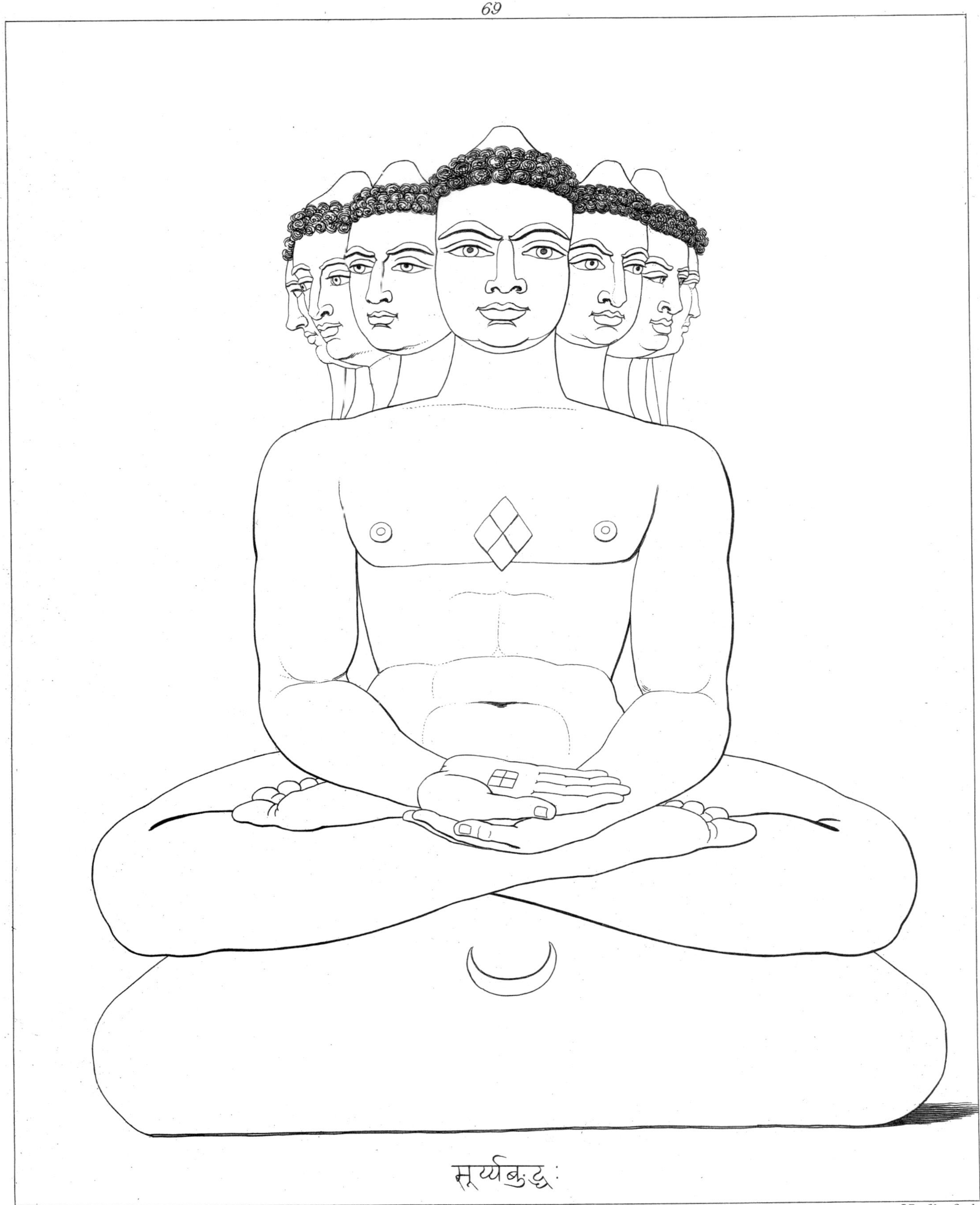

SŪRYA BUDDHA.

From a Statue in the Museum at the India House.

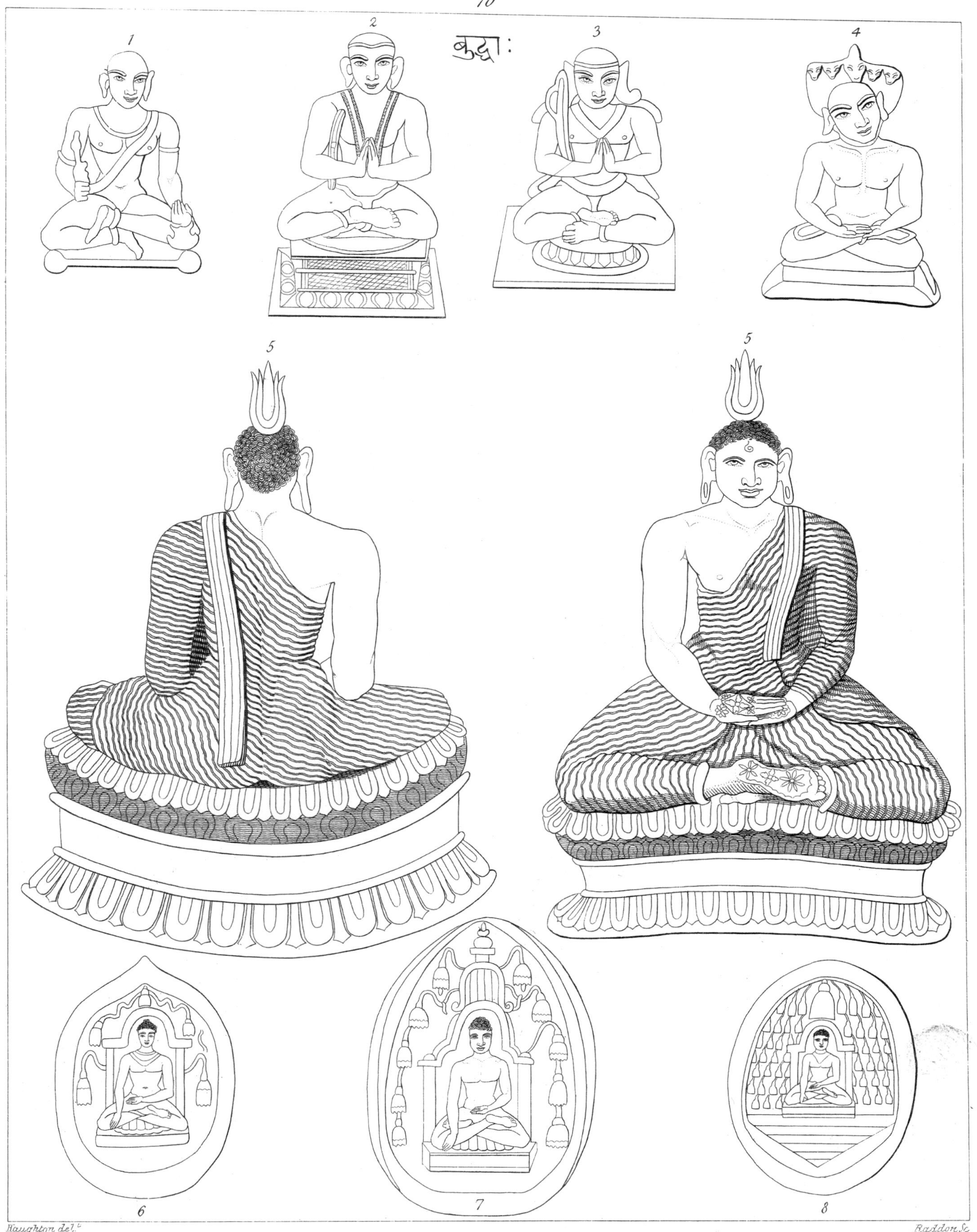

बुद्धाः

BUDDHĀ

Nos. 1.2.3.4. *JAIN* images in brass of the *DECCAN*. 5. in gilt brass from *CEYLON*. 6.7.8. of *LAK* dug up at *GAYA*.

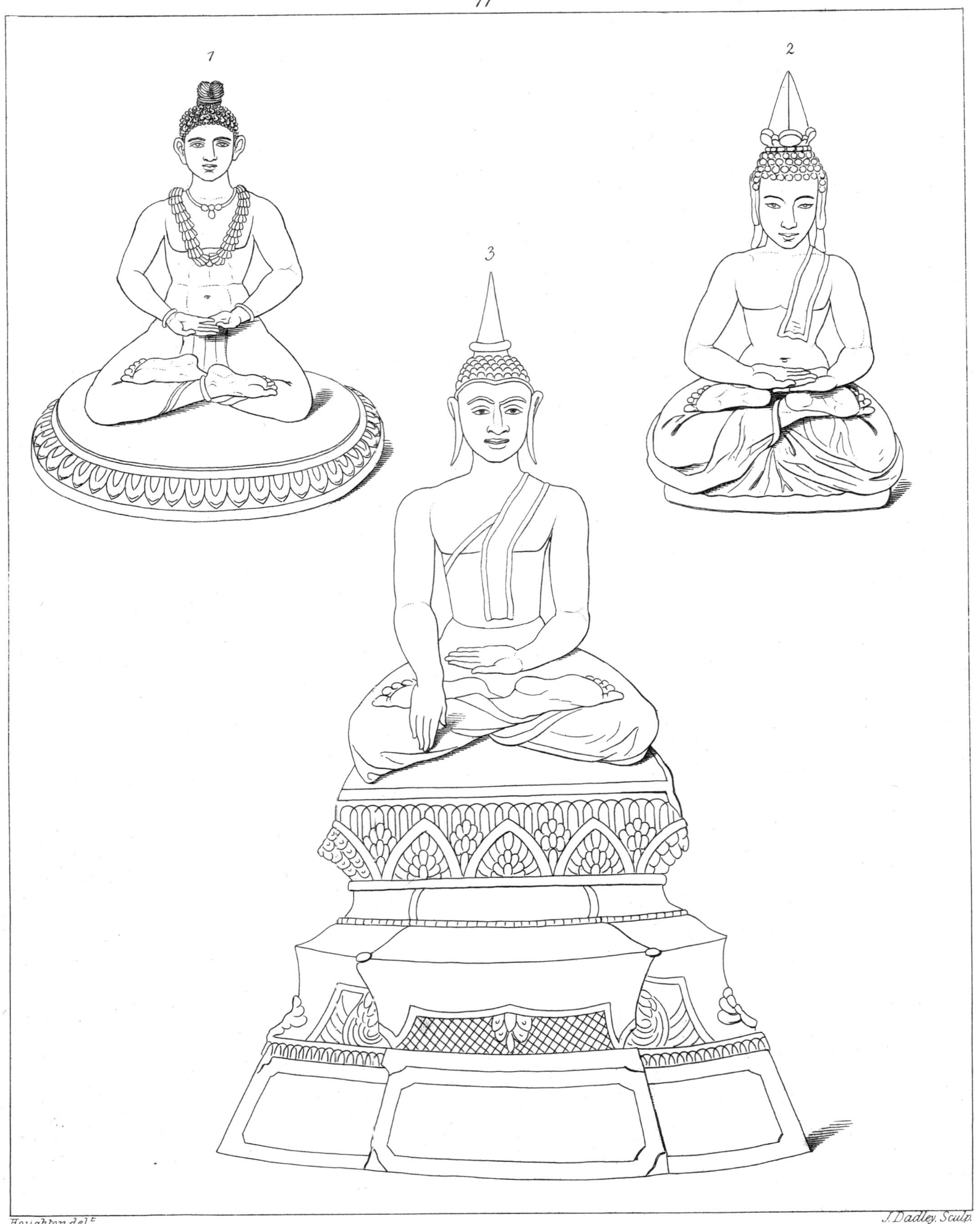

BUDDHĀ.

Nᵒ.1. of zinc cast at BENARES. 2. of marble from CHINA. 3. in Silver from AVA.

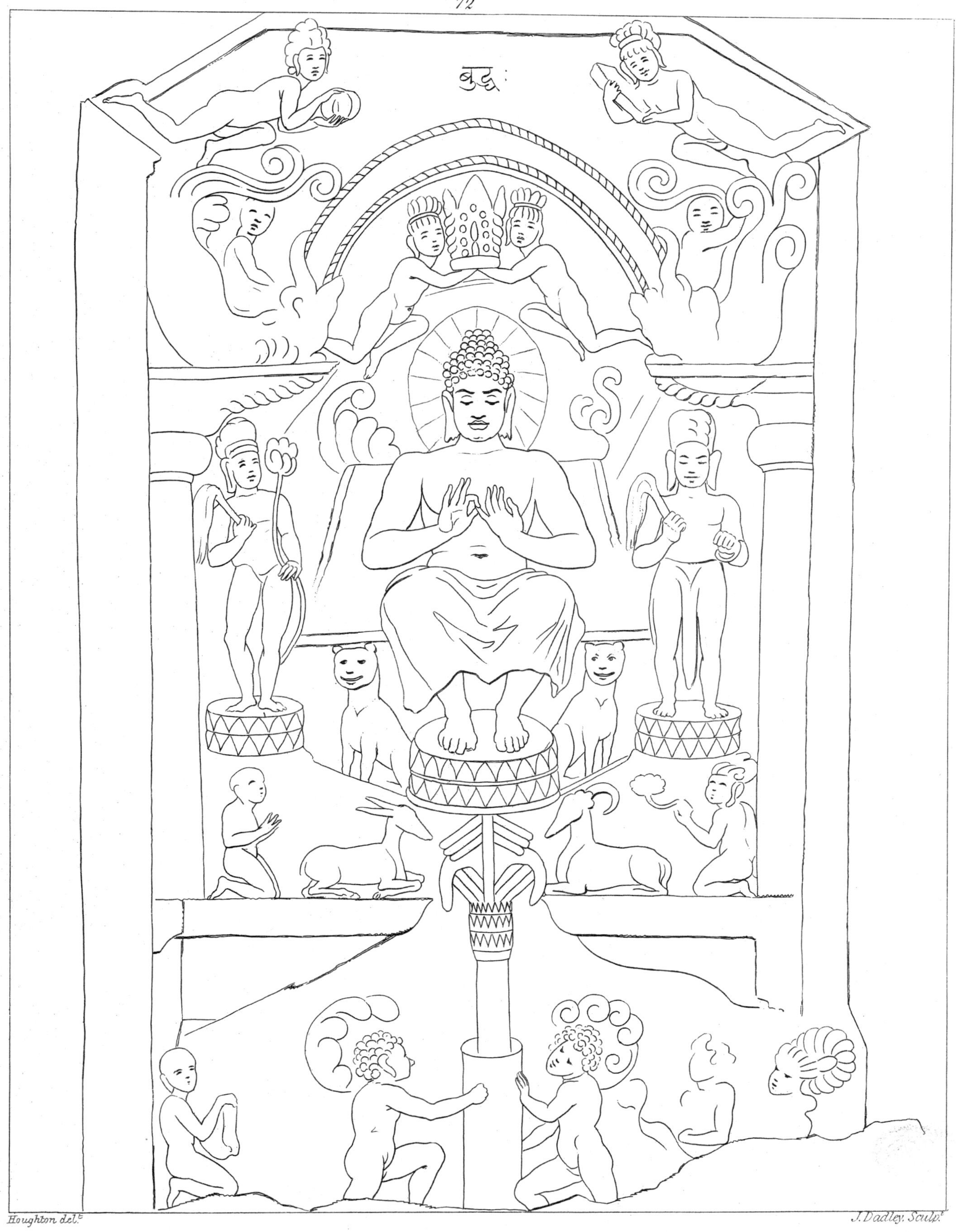

BUDDHA *from a* SCULPTURE *in* KARLY CAVE, *between* POONA & BOMBAY.

Copied from a SKETCH *in the collection of the* RIGHT HON. VISCOUNT VALENTIA.

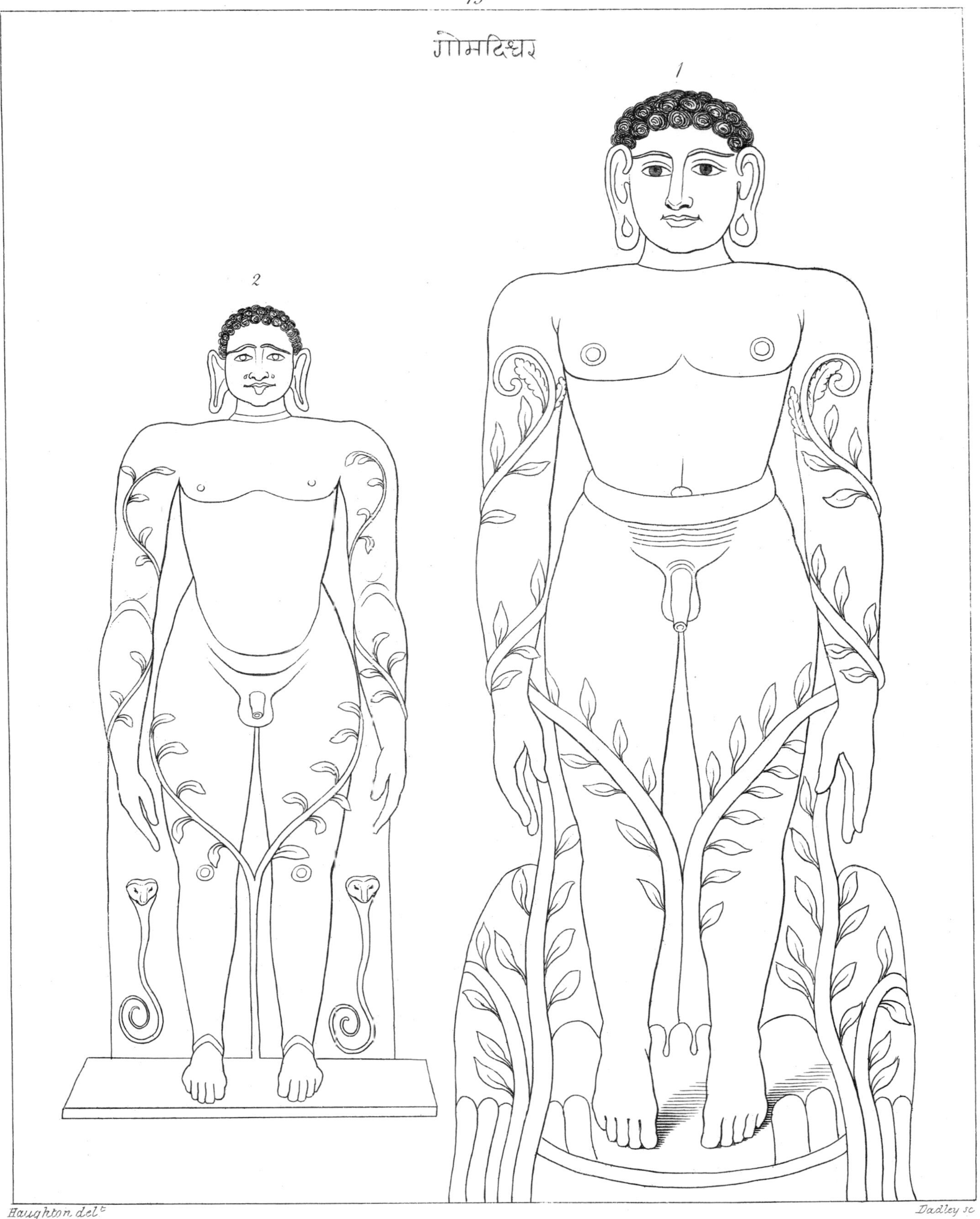

गोमटिश्वर

STATUE of GŌMAD ISWARA at SRAVANA BELGULA in KANARA 70 feet in height.

From a picture in the collection of the Right Honorable Sir ARTHUR WELLESLEY.

2. Of the same at EINURU or YENNOOR in KANARA 35 feet high.

गोमटिश्वर:

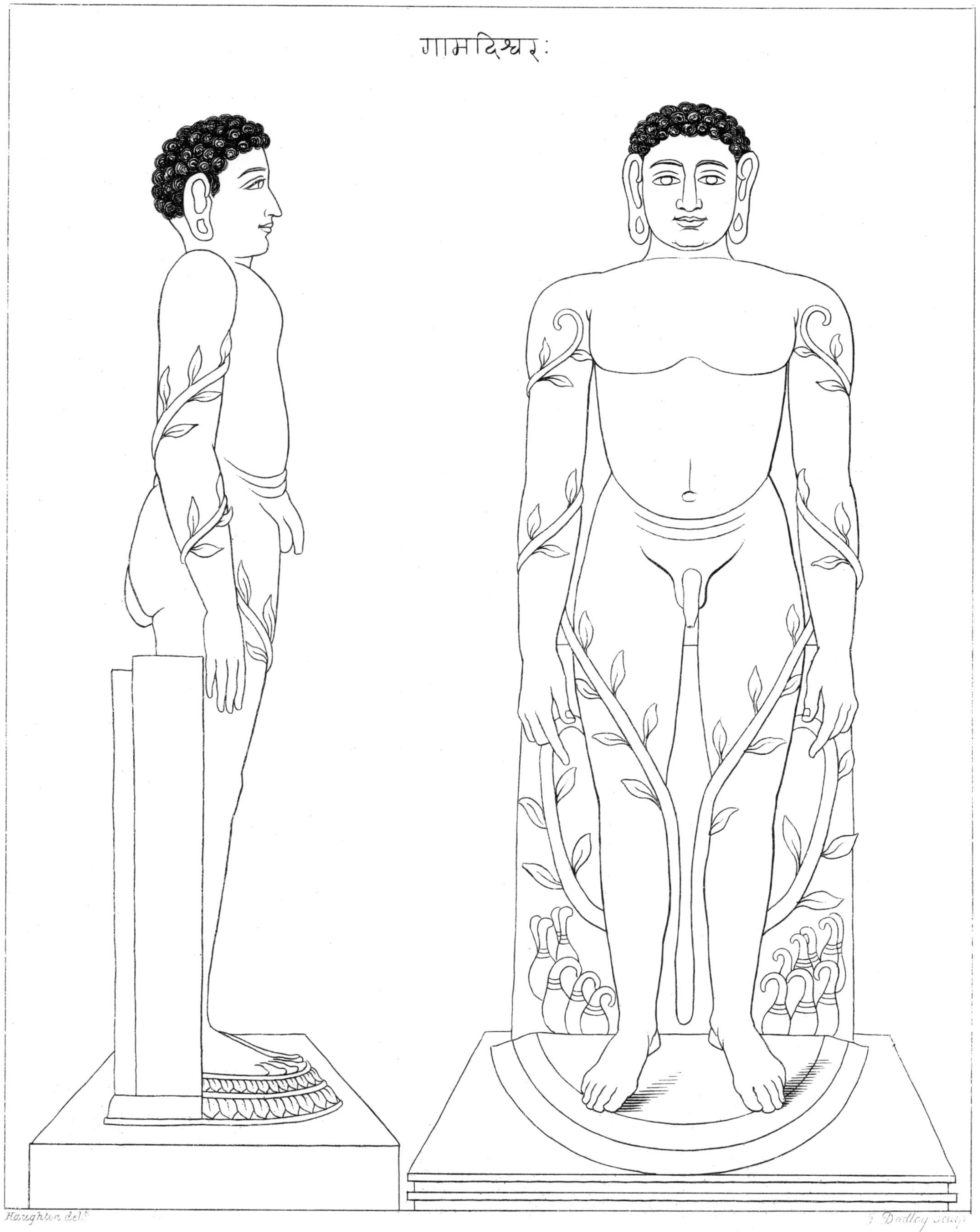

Statue of *GOMAD ISWARA* or *GOMUTA RAYA* at *KARKULLY* in *KANARA*.

36 feet 6 Inches in height.

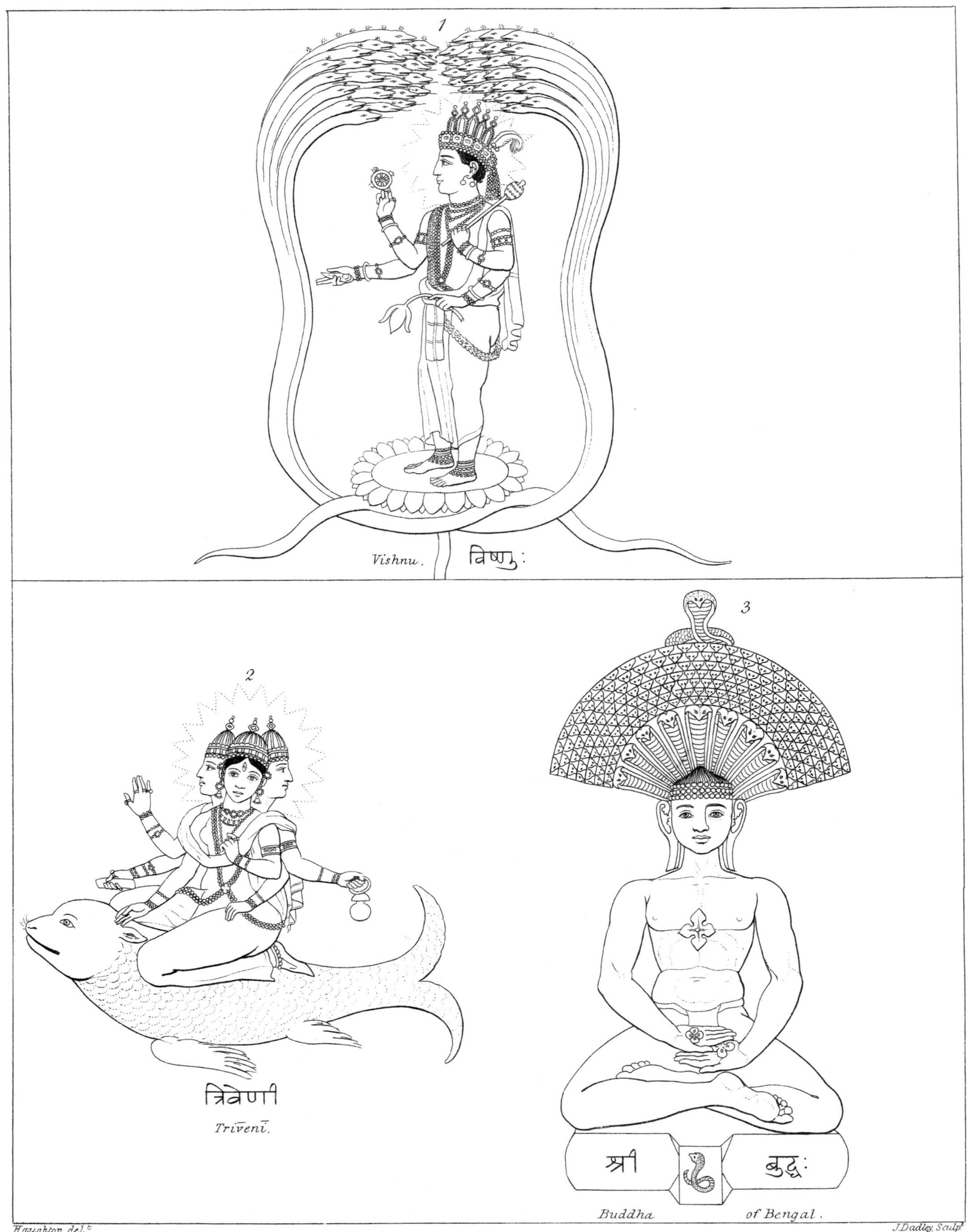

Buddha   of Bengal.

Haughton del.ᵗ

J. Dadley, Sculpᵗ

From PICTURES in the collection of COLONEL STUART.

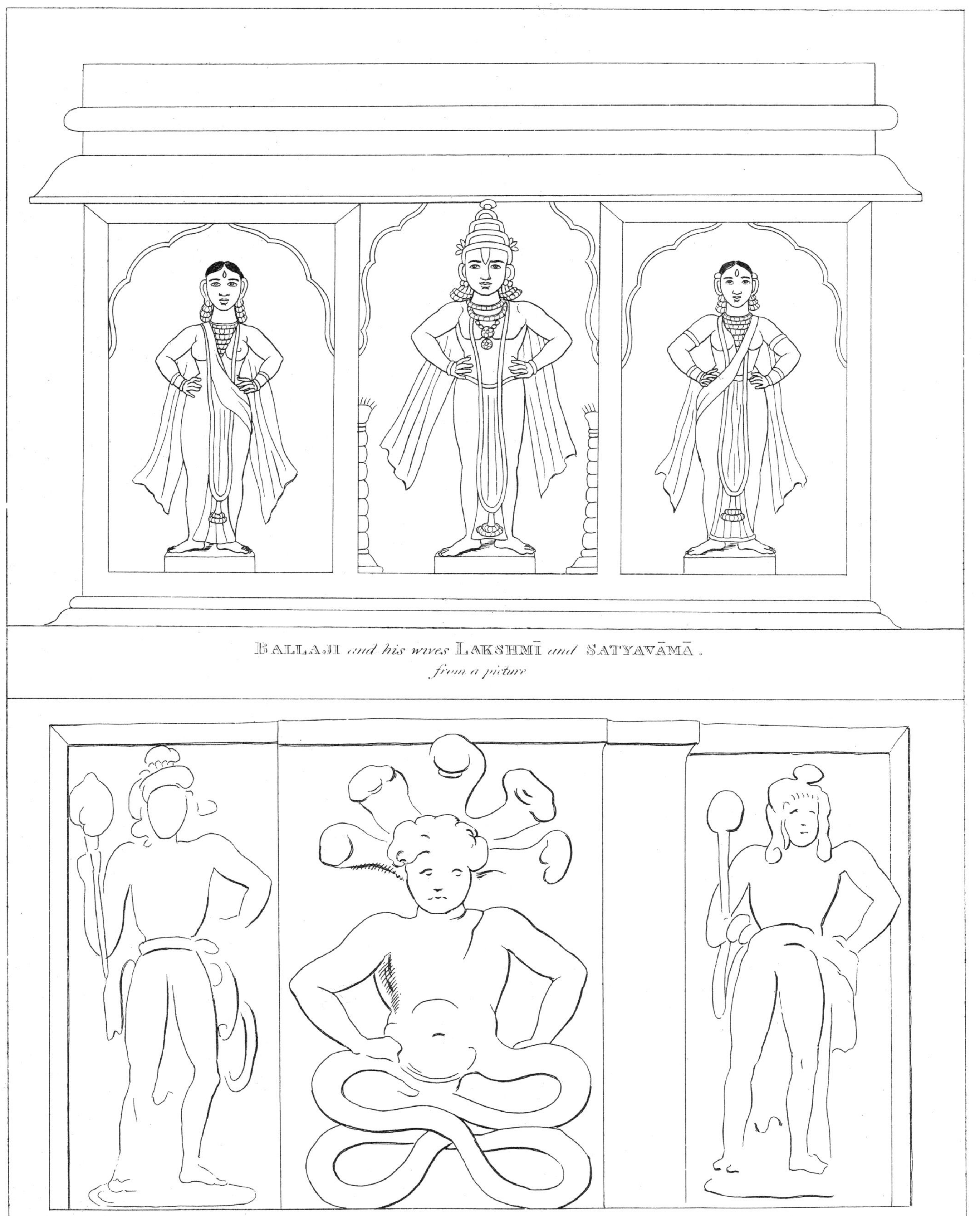

BALLAJI *and his wives* LAKSHMĪ *and* SATYAVĀMĀ.

from a picture

BUDDHA.

From a ruined temple at SIVA SAMUDRA, *on an Island in the* CAVERI.

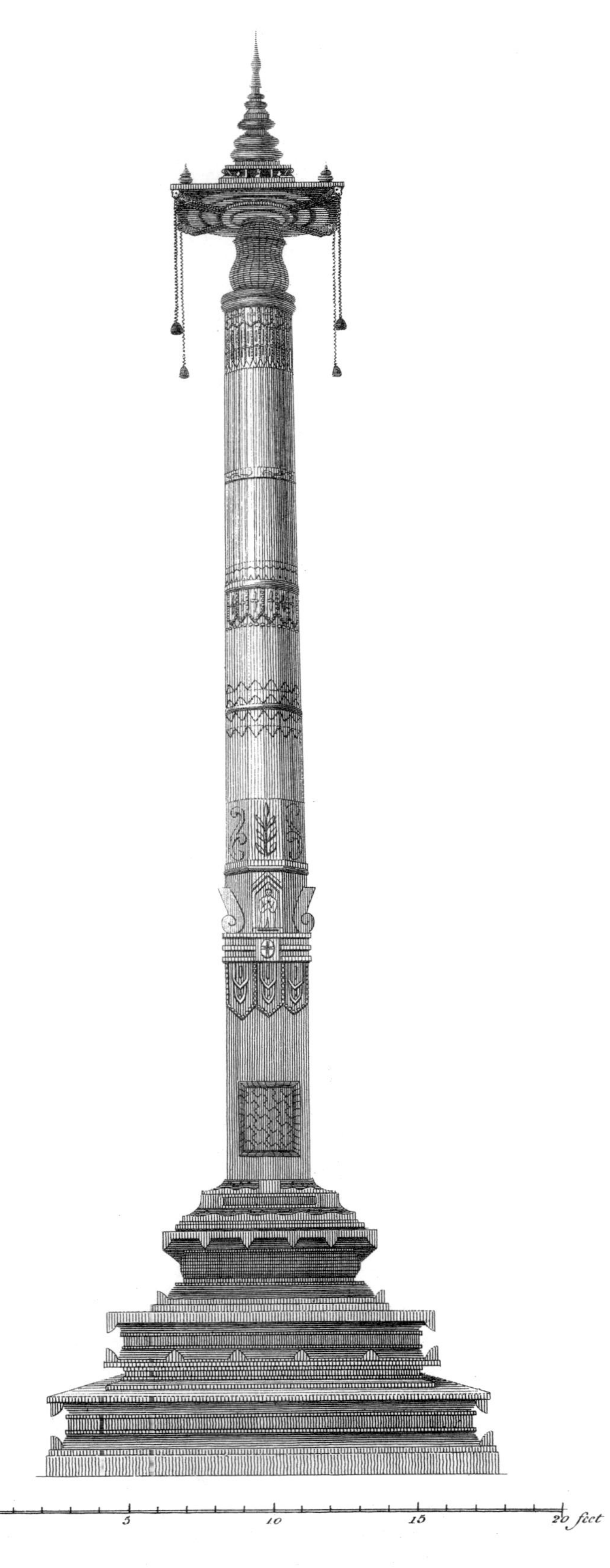

Elevation and View of an OBELISK of granite 52½ feet in height, facing a JAIN Temple at MUDUBIDERY, or MORBIDRY, near MANGALORE in KANARA.

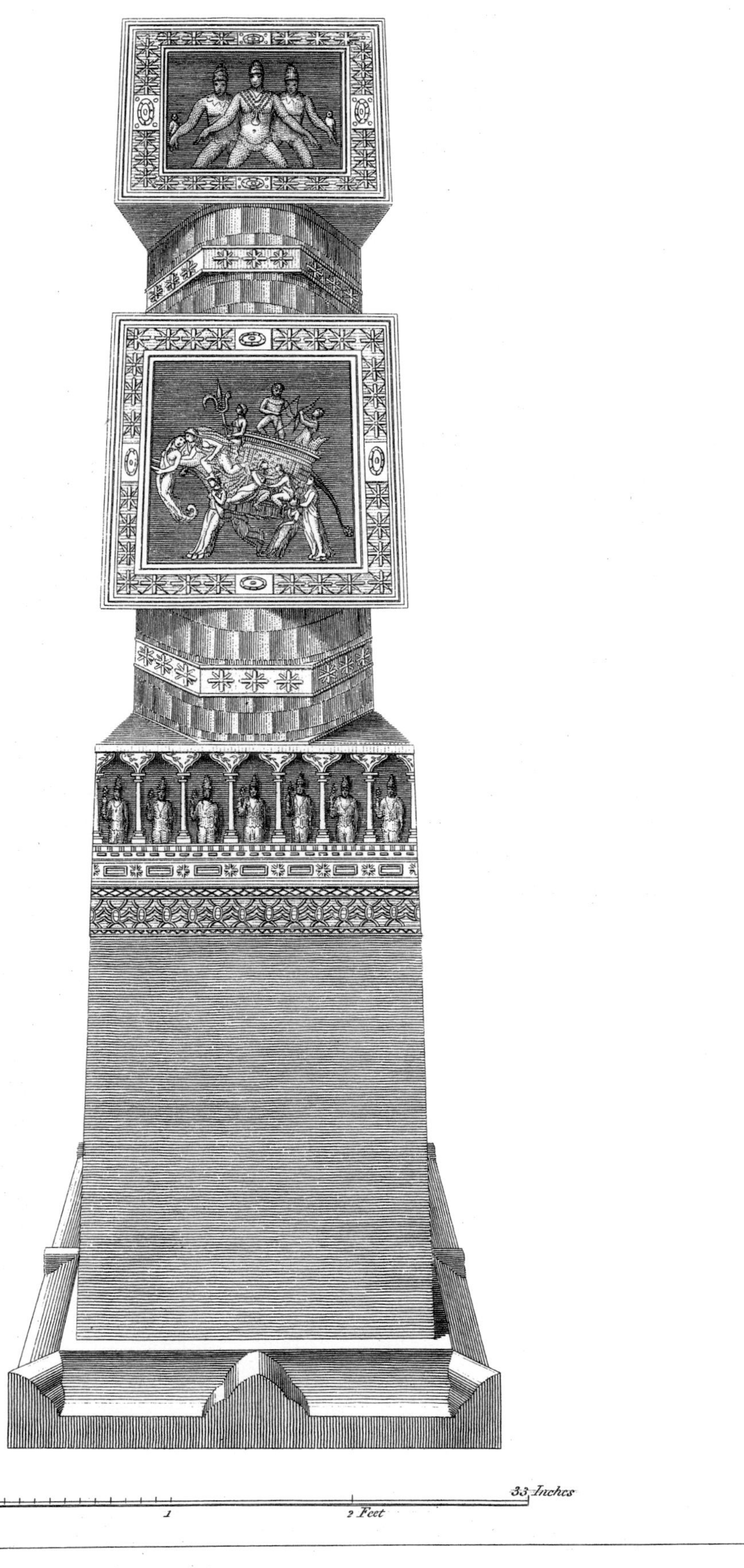

A WOODEN PILLAR in the PALACE at MUDU BIDERY, or MOORBIDRY near MANGALORE in KANARA.

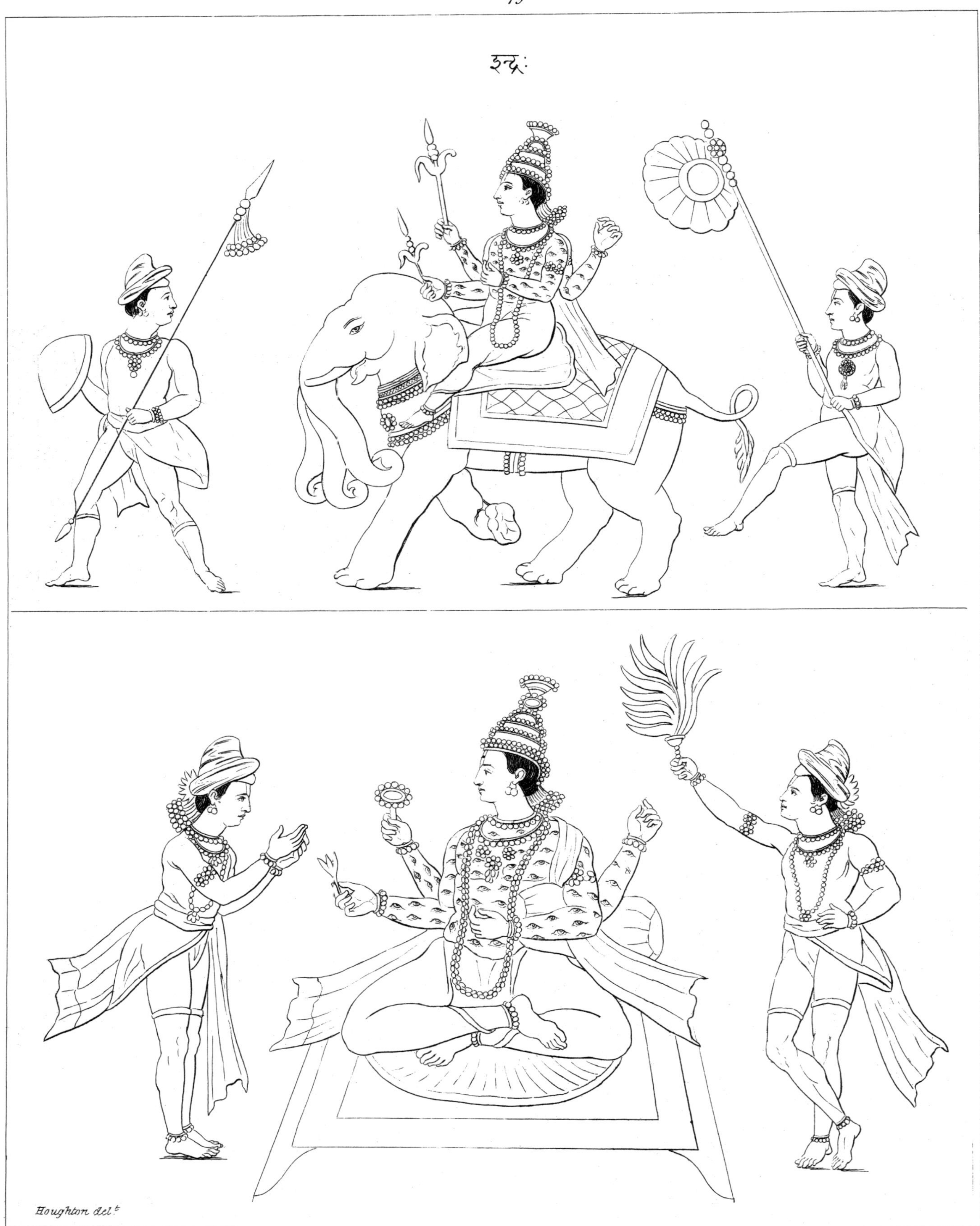

INDRA, *GOD of the* FIRMAMENT.

From pictures.

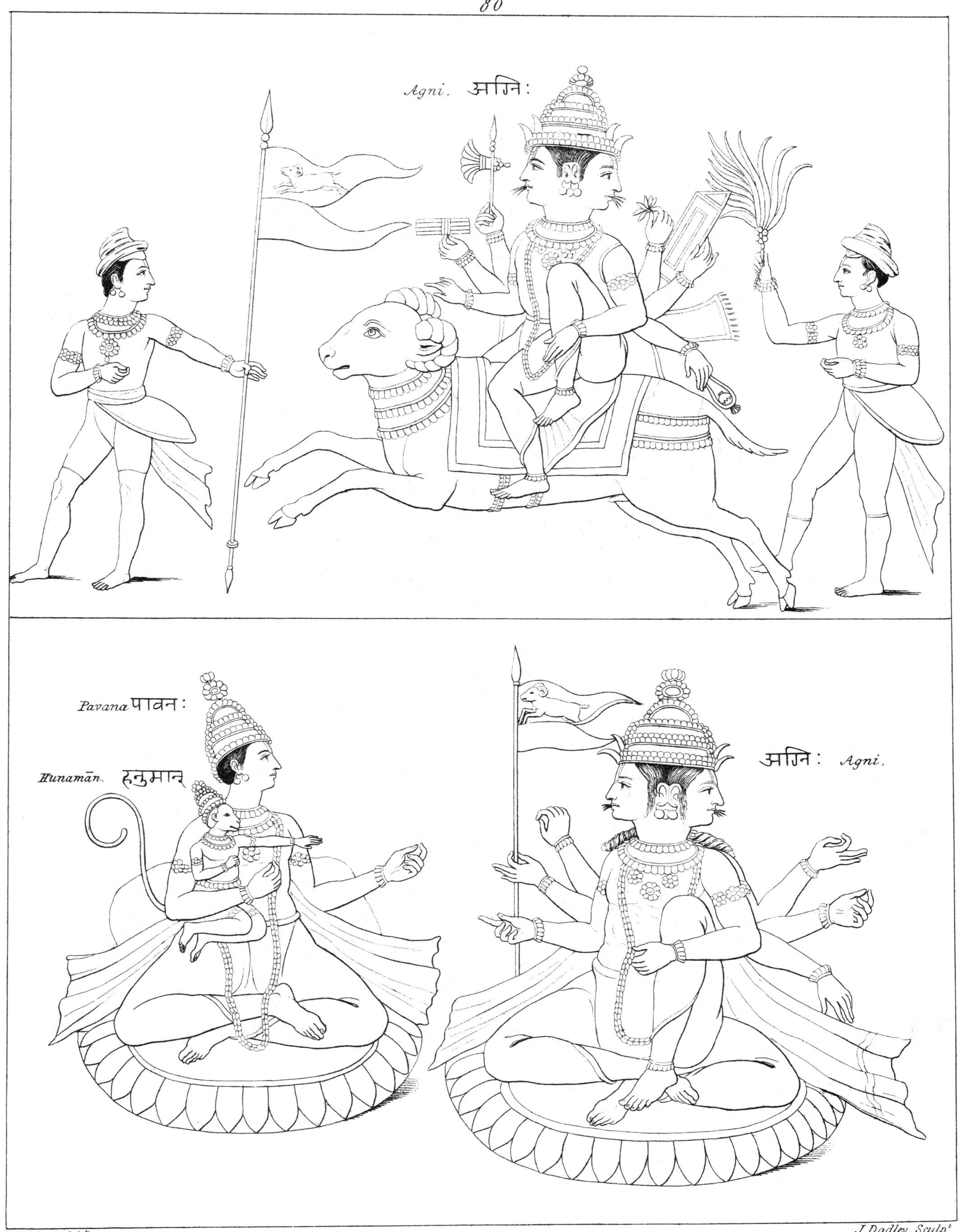

AGNI, GOD of FIRE. PĀVANA, REGENT of WINDS.

From Pictures.

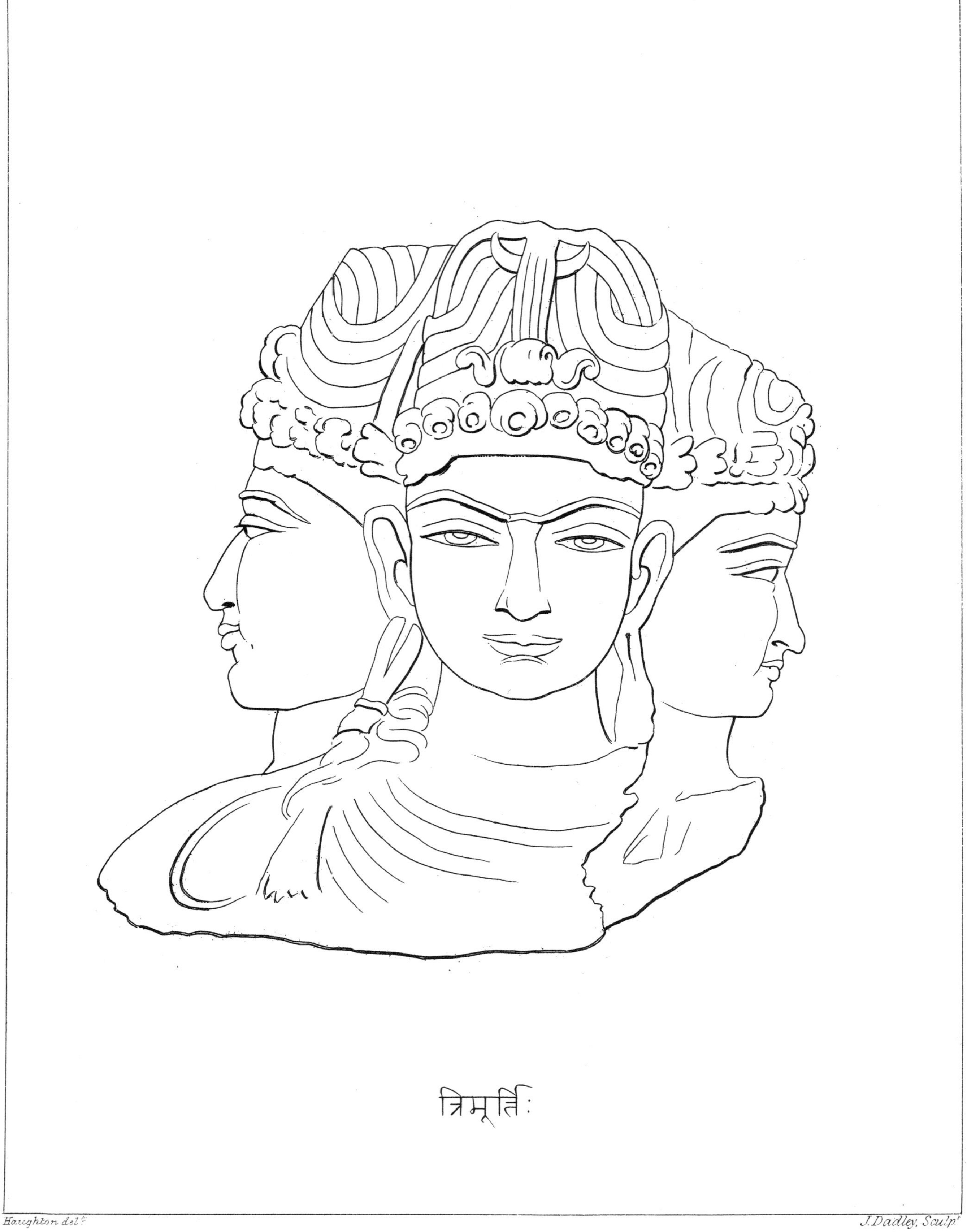

त्रिमूर्तिः

TRIMŪRTI the HINDU TRIAD.

From a very ancient Granite in the Museum at the India House.

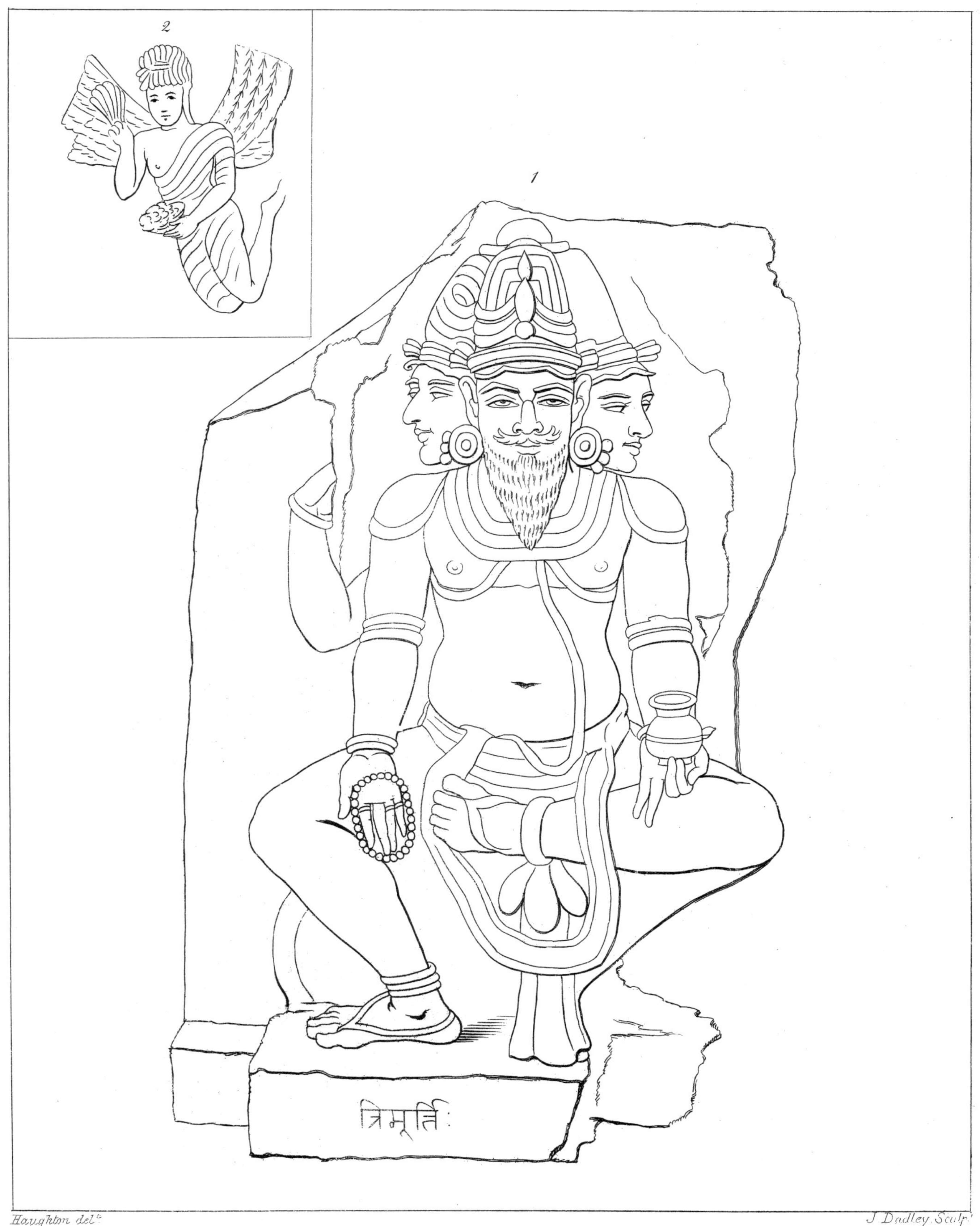

Haughton del.ᵗ   J. Dadley Sculp.ᵗ

TRIMŪRTI *the* HINDU TRIAD.

From a very ancient Granite in the Museum at the India House.

2. From the grand temple at KENEREH *on* SALSETTE.

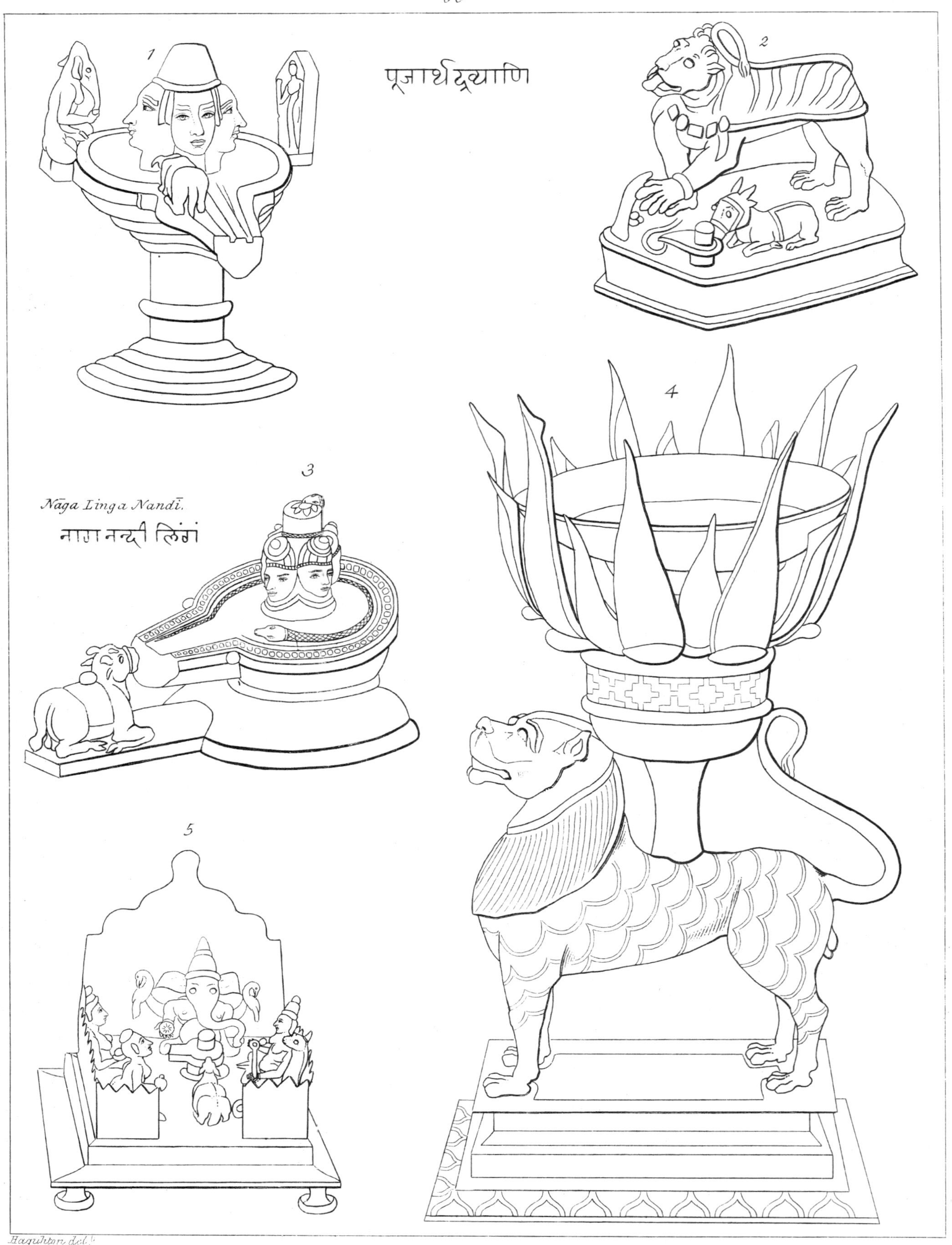

PŪJĀRTHA DRAVYĀNI., SACRIFICIAL IMPLEMENTS &c.

From subjects in brafs &c.

पूजार्थे द्रव्याणि

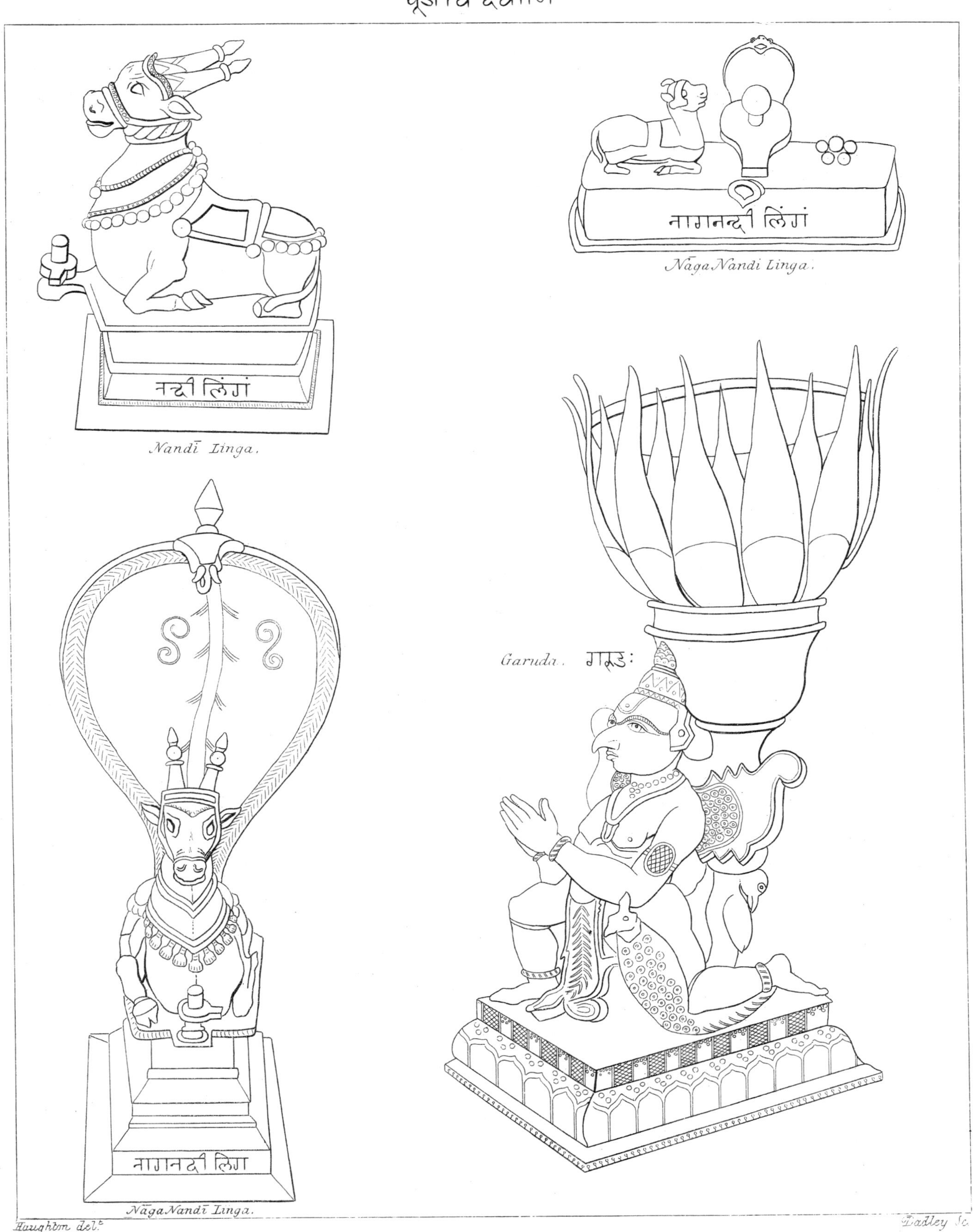

PŪJĀRTHA DRAVYĀNI.

From subjects in brass &c.

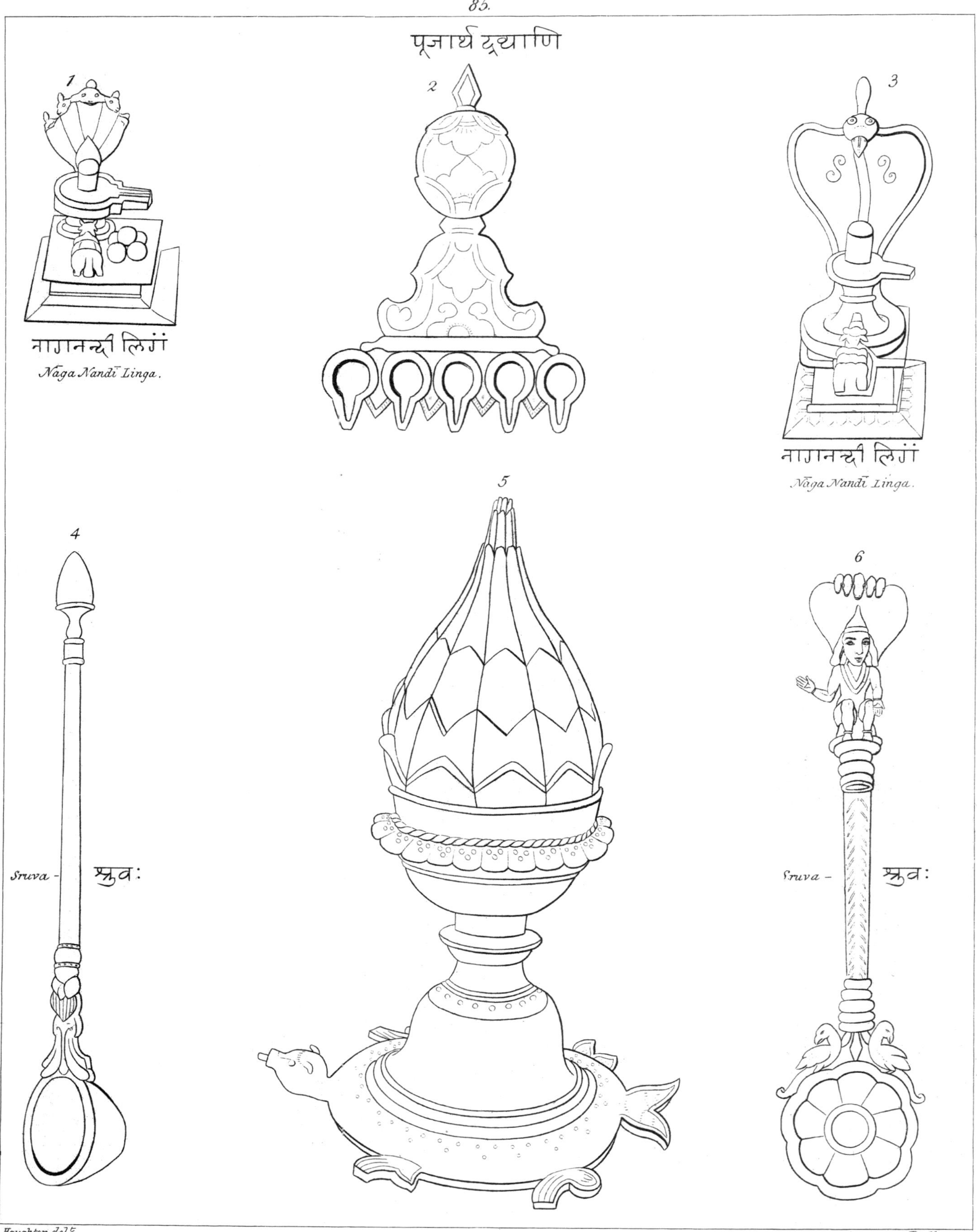

Haughton delt.

Dadley sc.

PŪJĀRTHA DRAVYĀNI, SACRIFICIAL UTENSILS.

From subjects in Copper, &c.

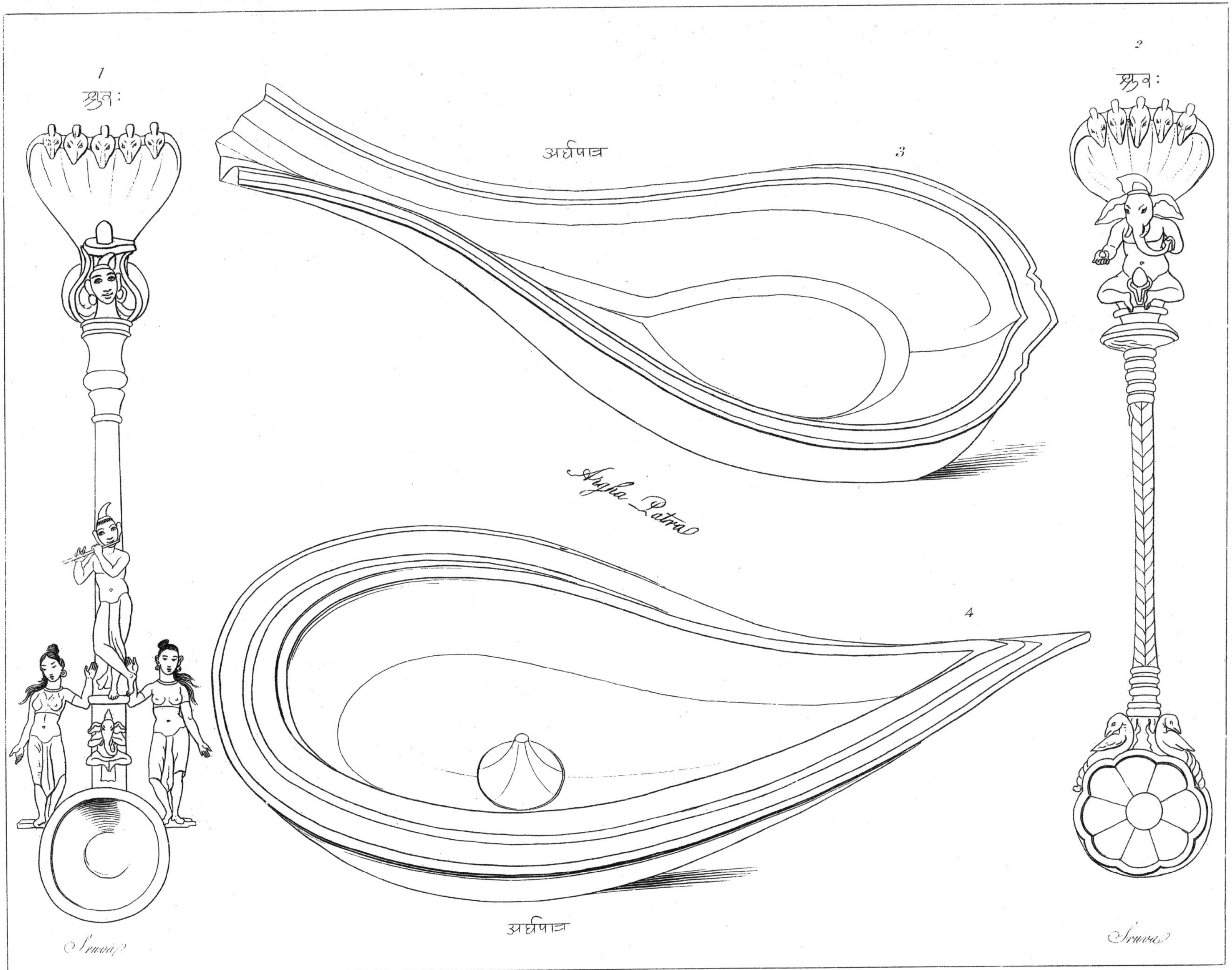

Argha Patra

IMPLEMENTS *used in* **PŪJĀ** *or* **WORSHIP**.

M. Houghton del.

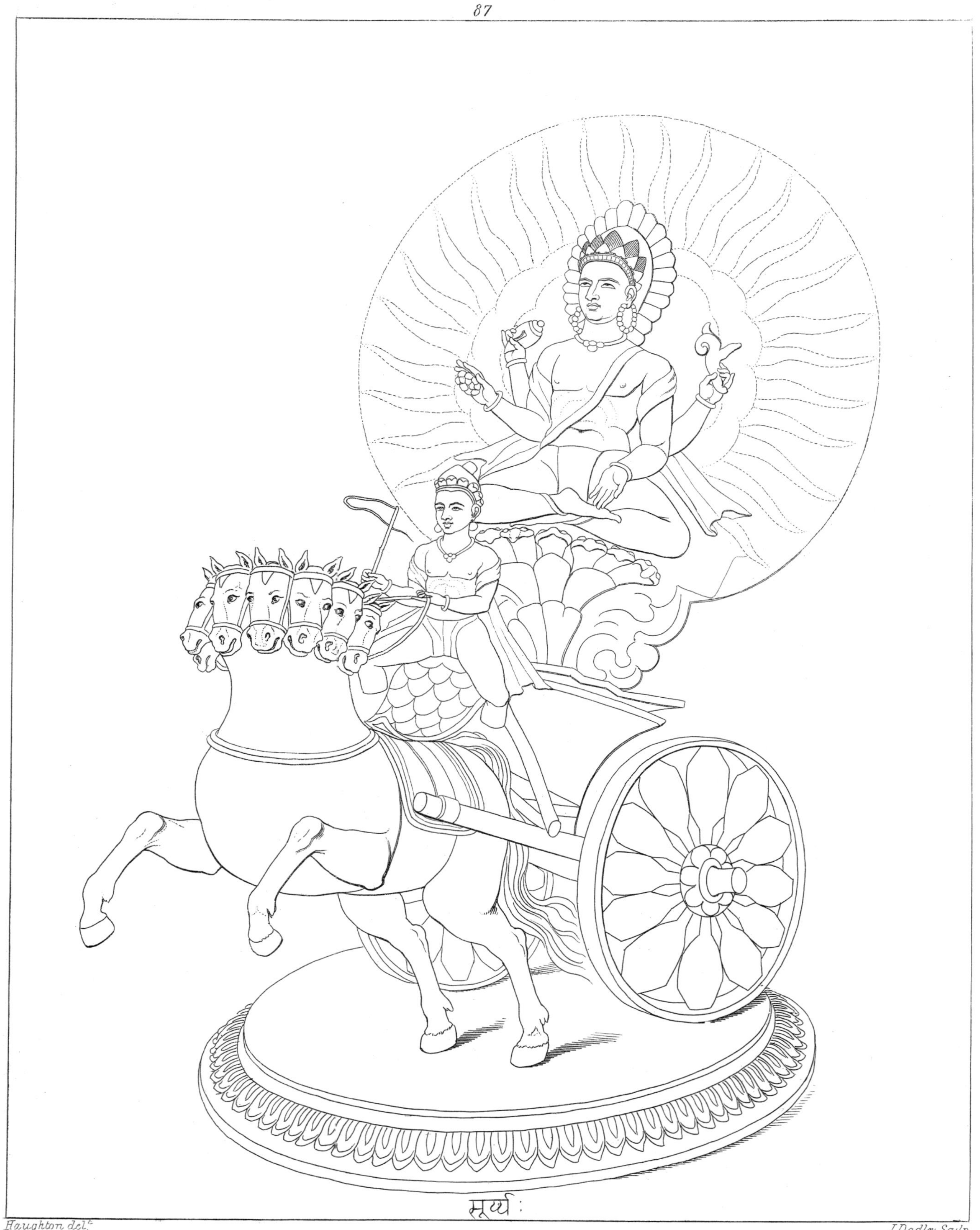

SŪRYA *the* SUN.

From a cast in the Museum at the India House.

Copied from a Sculpture in the temple of VISWESWARA *at* BENARES.

राशिचक्रं

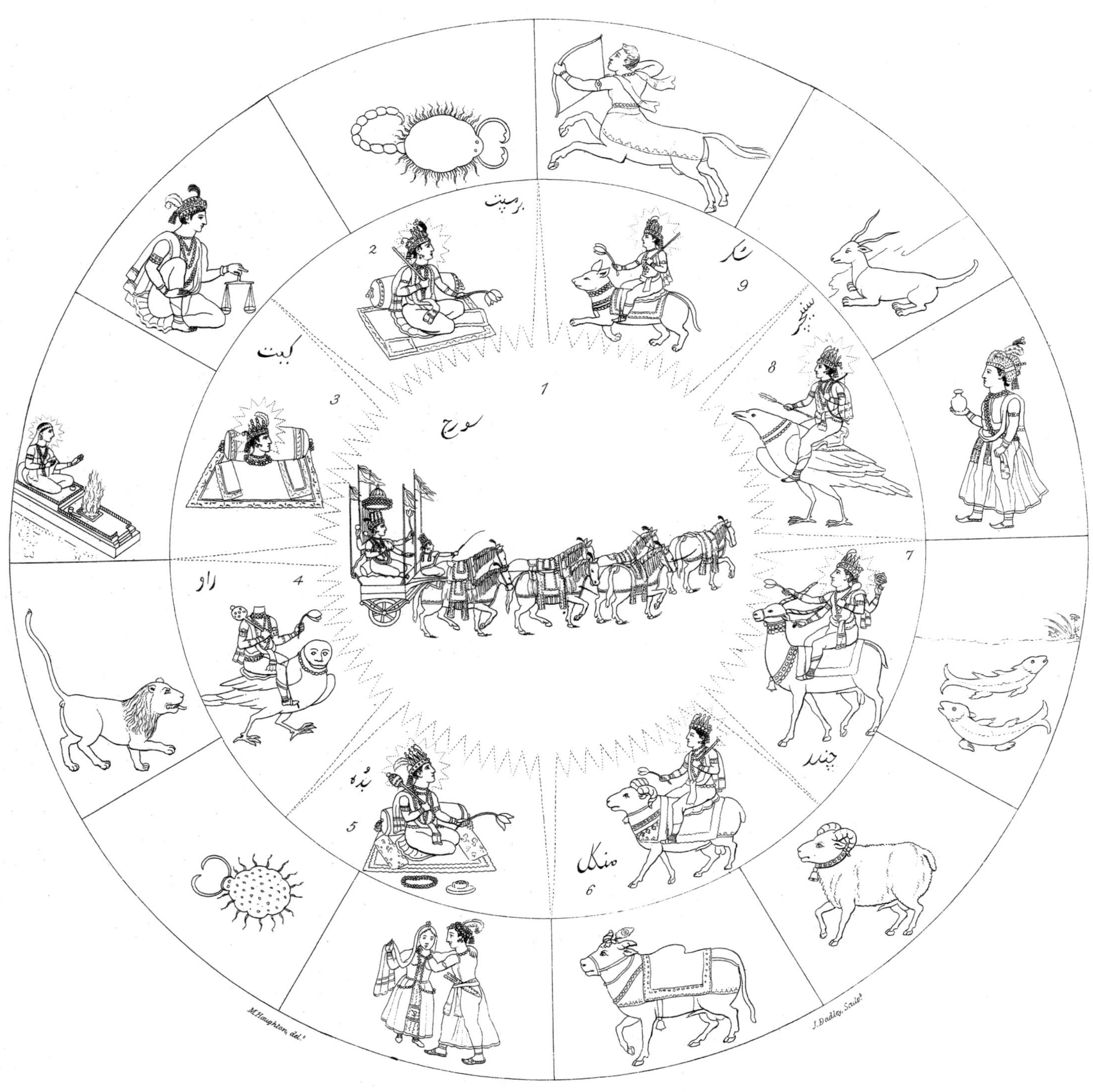

RĀSI CHAKRA.

The HINDU ZODIAC, and SOLAR SYSTEM

From a picture in the collection of Colonel Stuart.

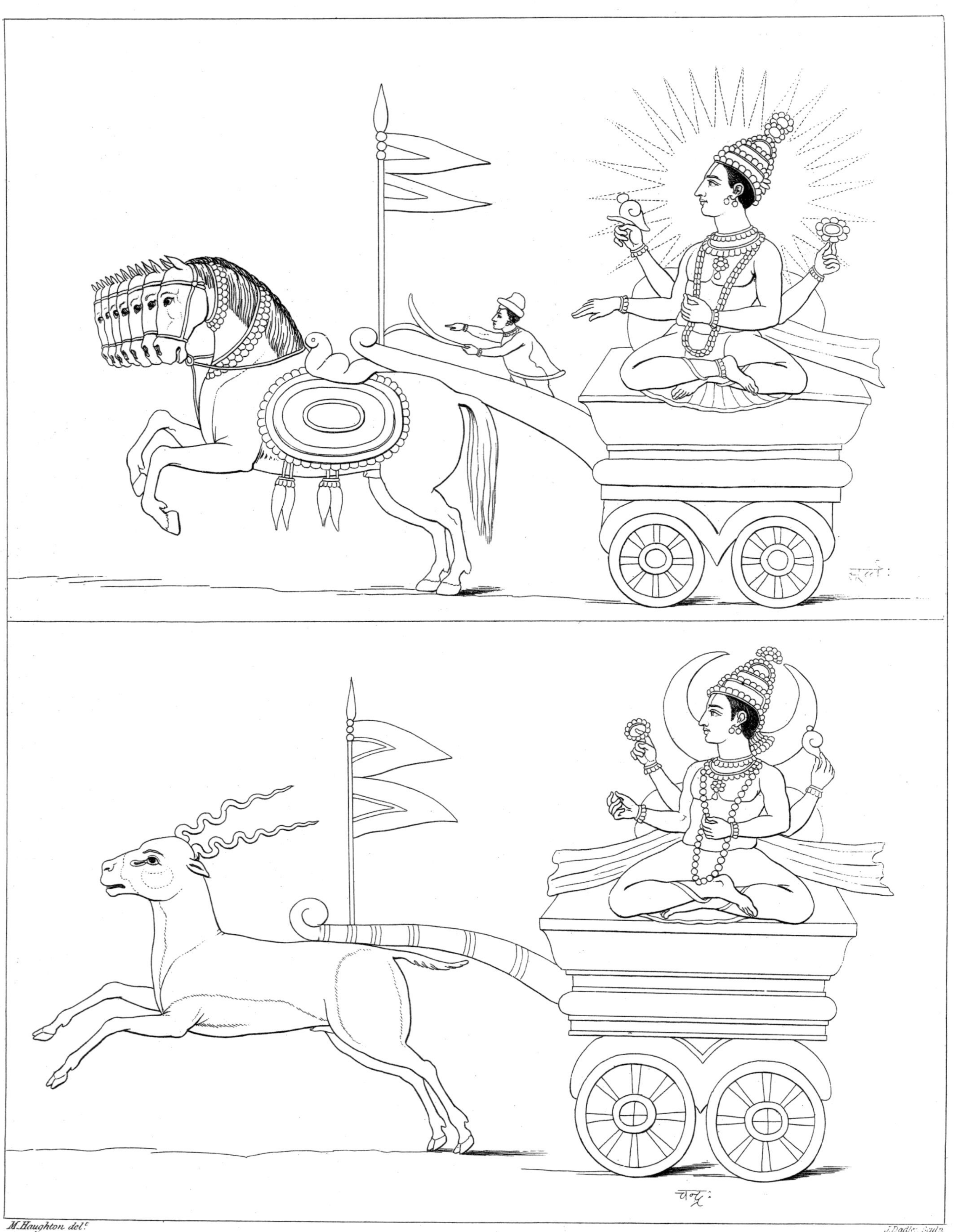

M.Haughton del.t

J.Dadle. Sculp.

SŪRYA and CHANDRA- The SUN and MOON.

from Pictures.

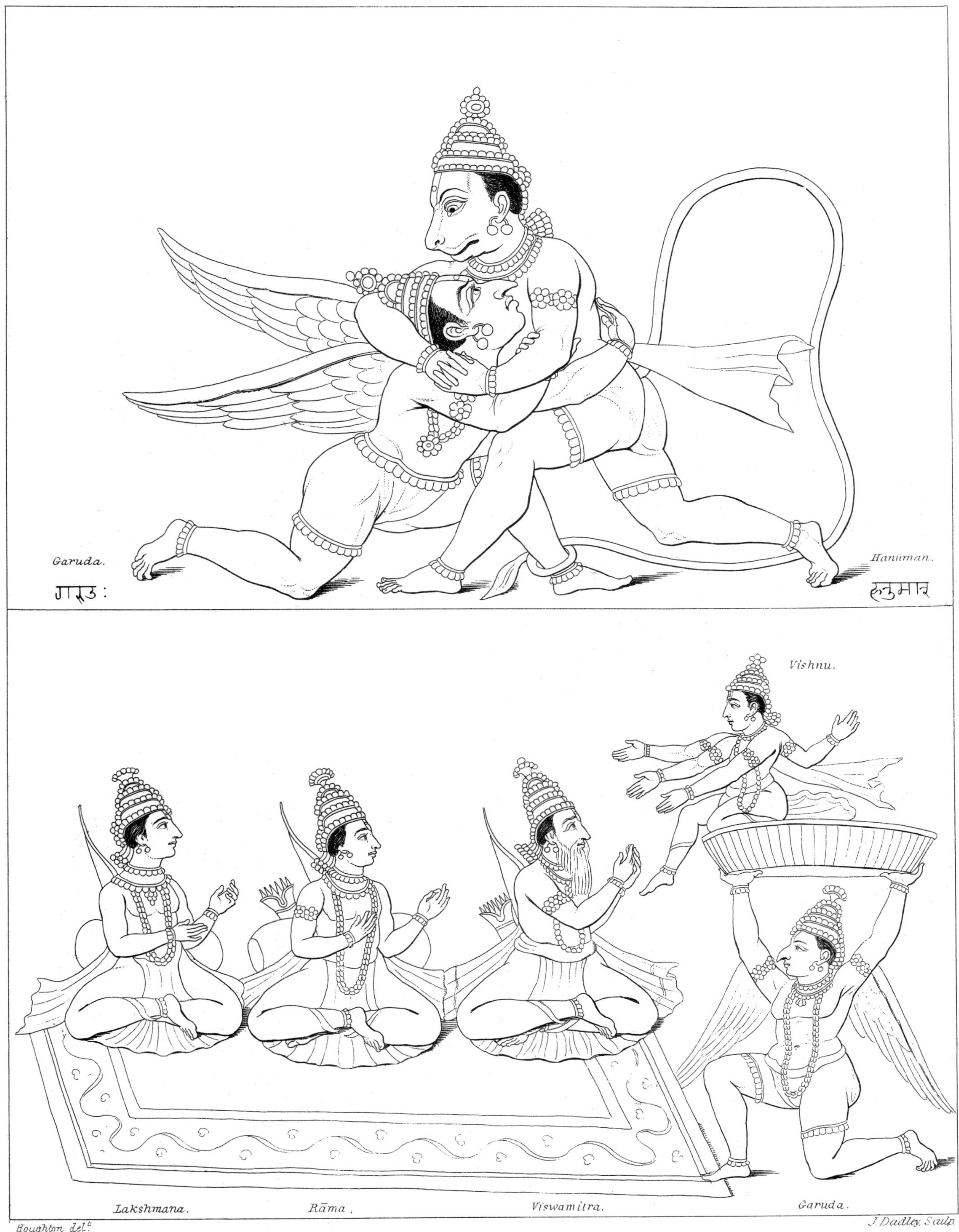

From pictures illustrating the RAMAYANA.

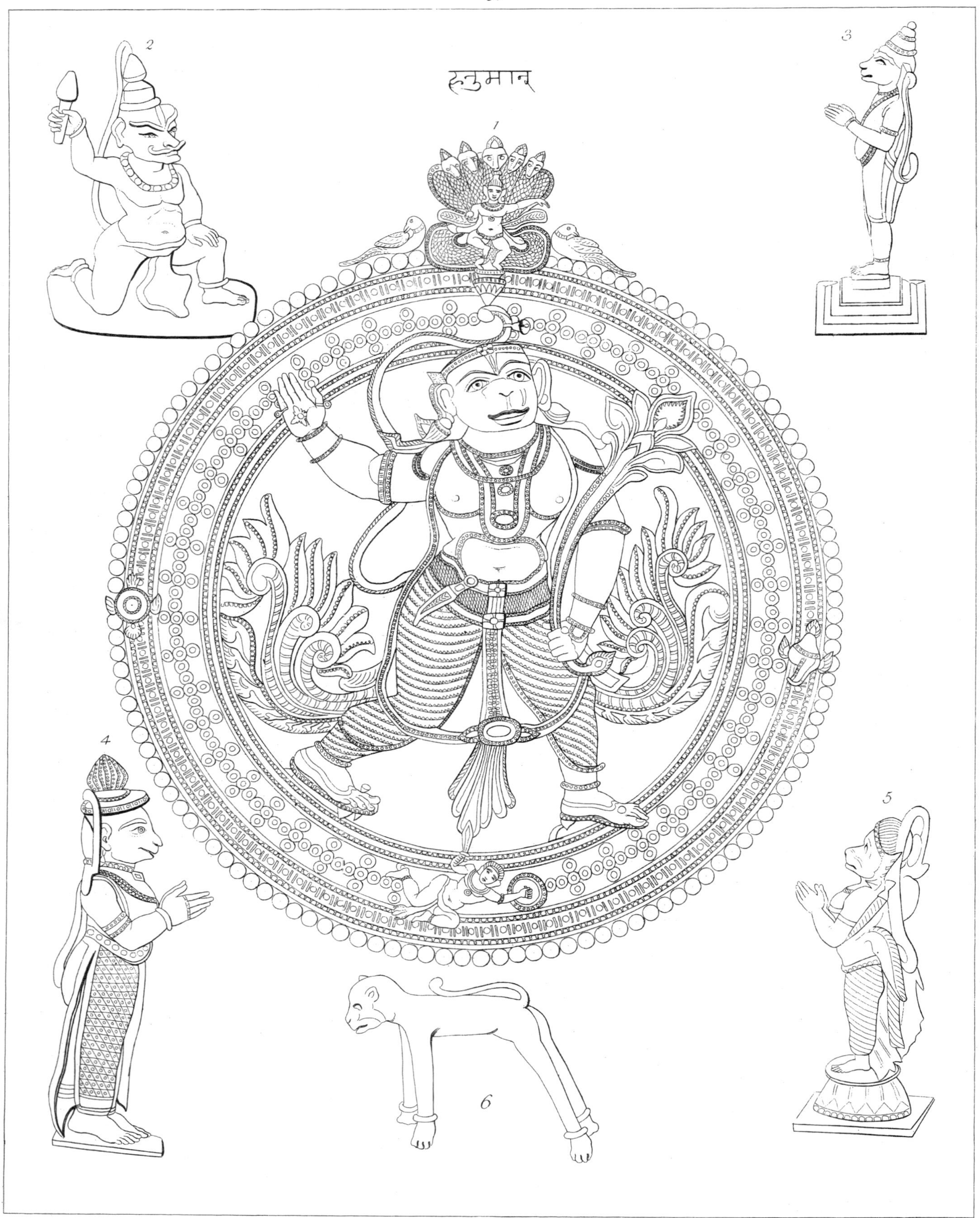

HANUMĀN.

From subjects in brass &c.

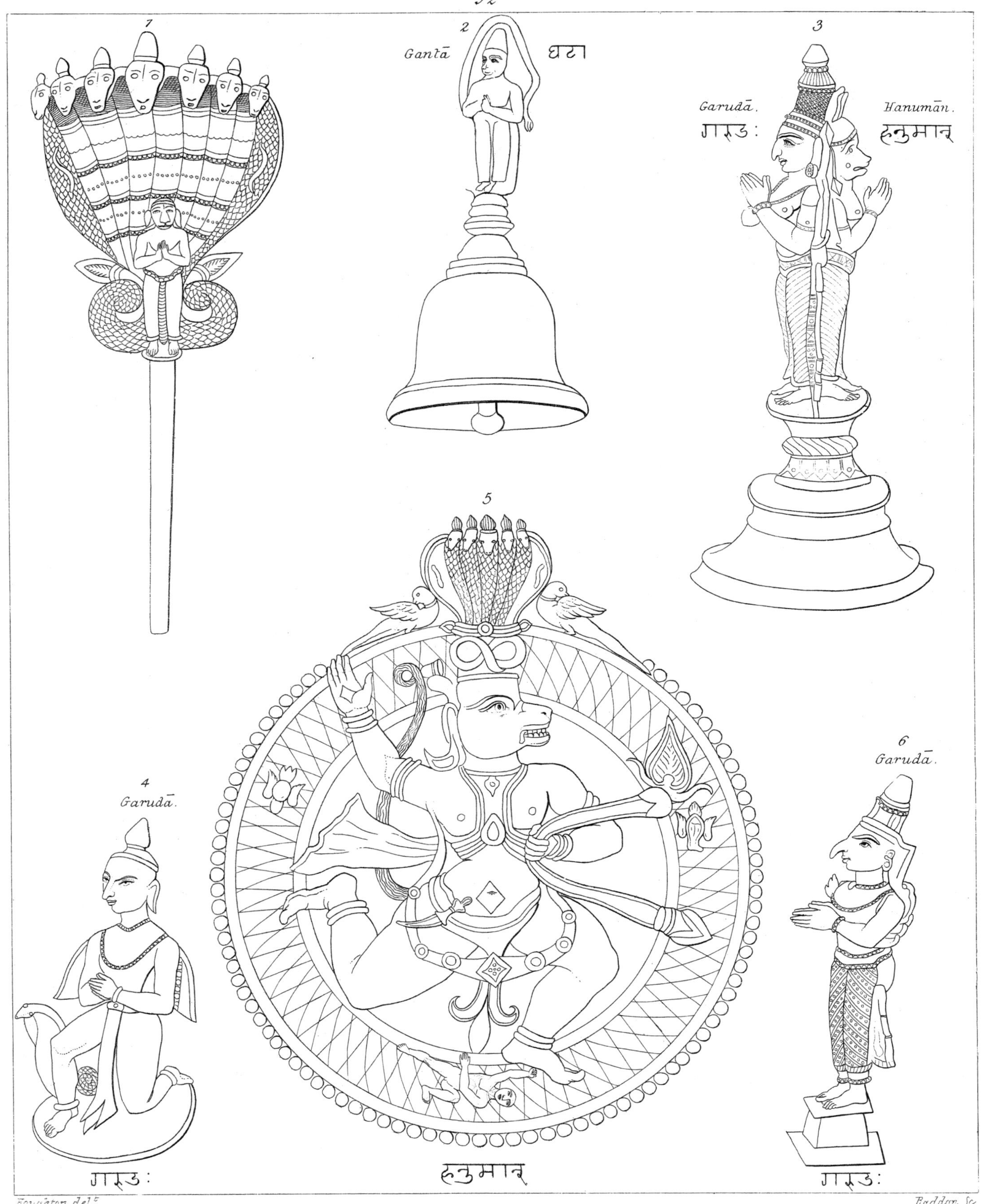

HANUMĀN. &c

From subjects in brass &c.

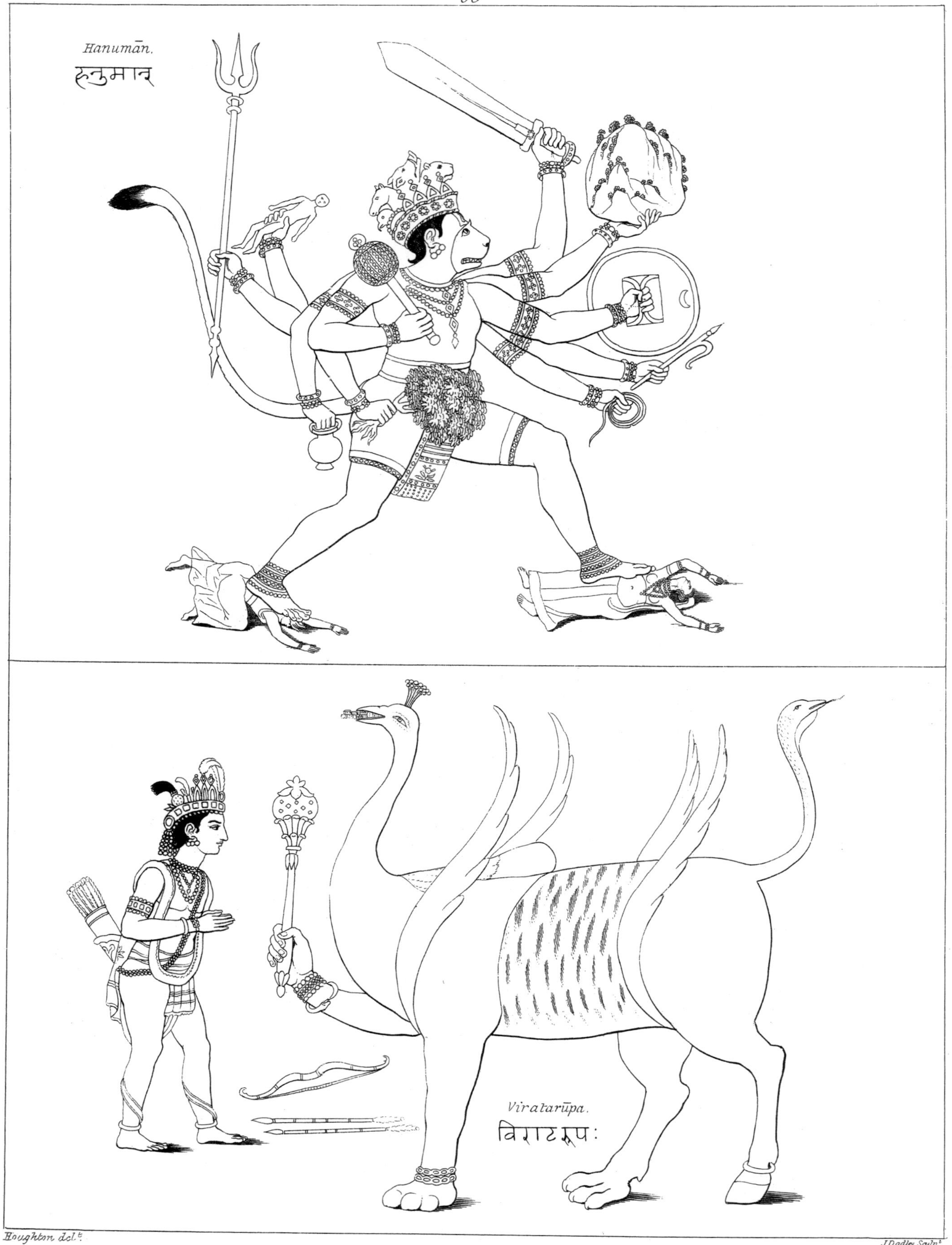

From pictures in the collection of Colonel Stuart.

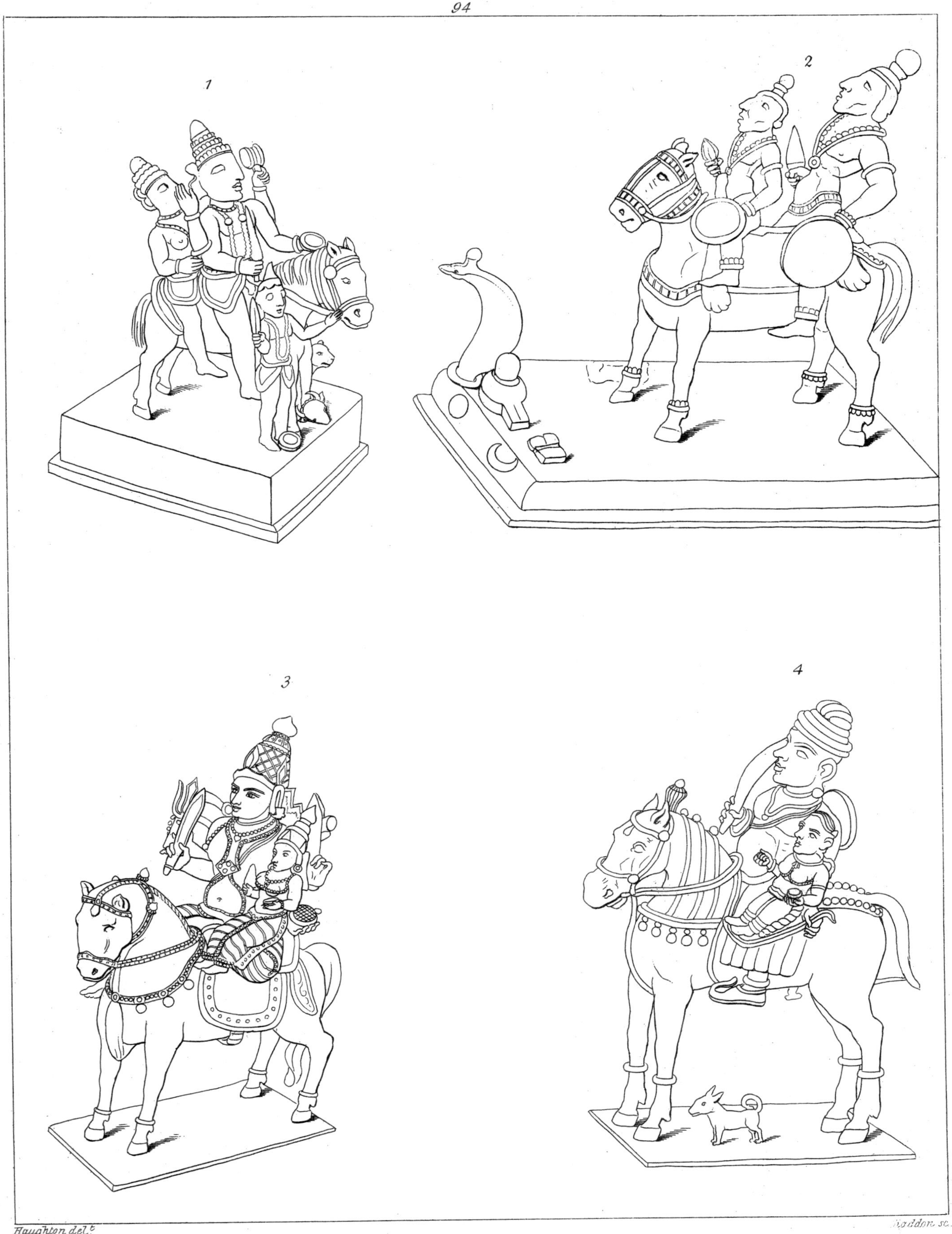

KANDARAO and MALSARA an *AVATĀRA* of MAHĀDĒVA and PĀRVATĪ.

From casts in brass &c.

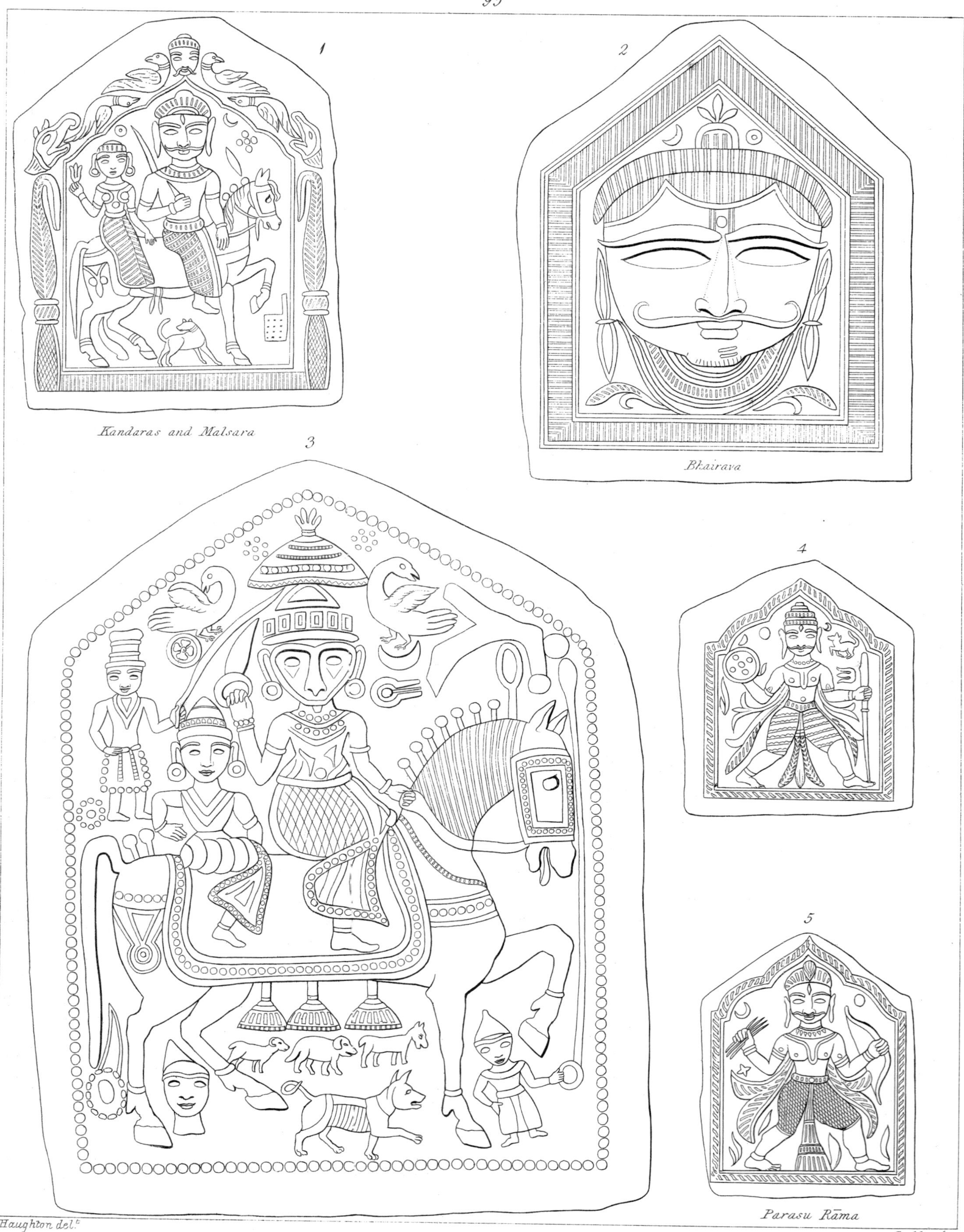

From thin plates of embossed copper.

From a Picture representing a Miracle performed near POONA by NANESHWER, an AVANTARA of VISHNU.

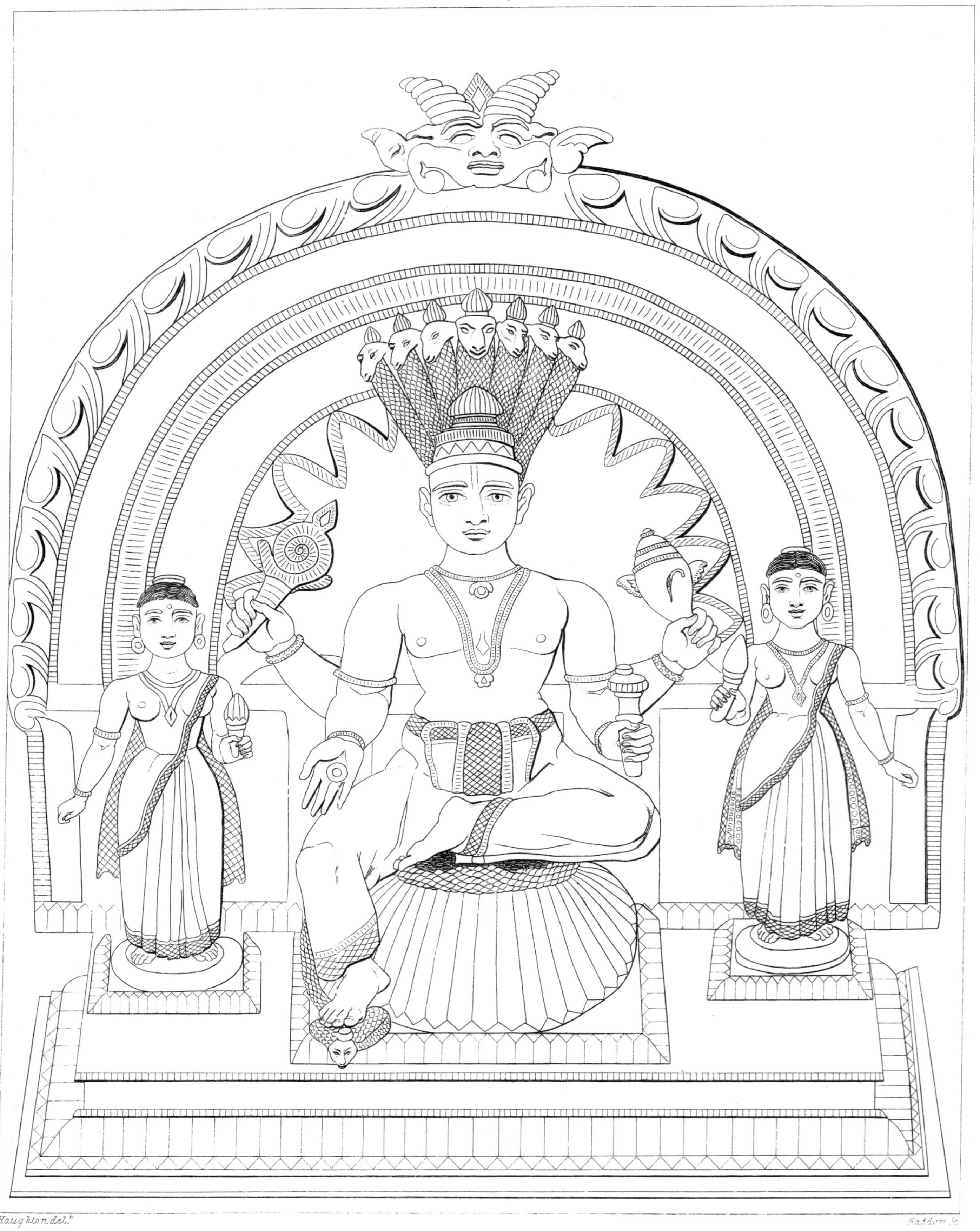

BALLAJI *an* AVATĀRA *of* VISHNU *and his wives* LAKSHMĪ *and* SATYA VĀMĀ.

From a subject in brass.

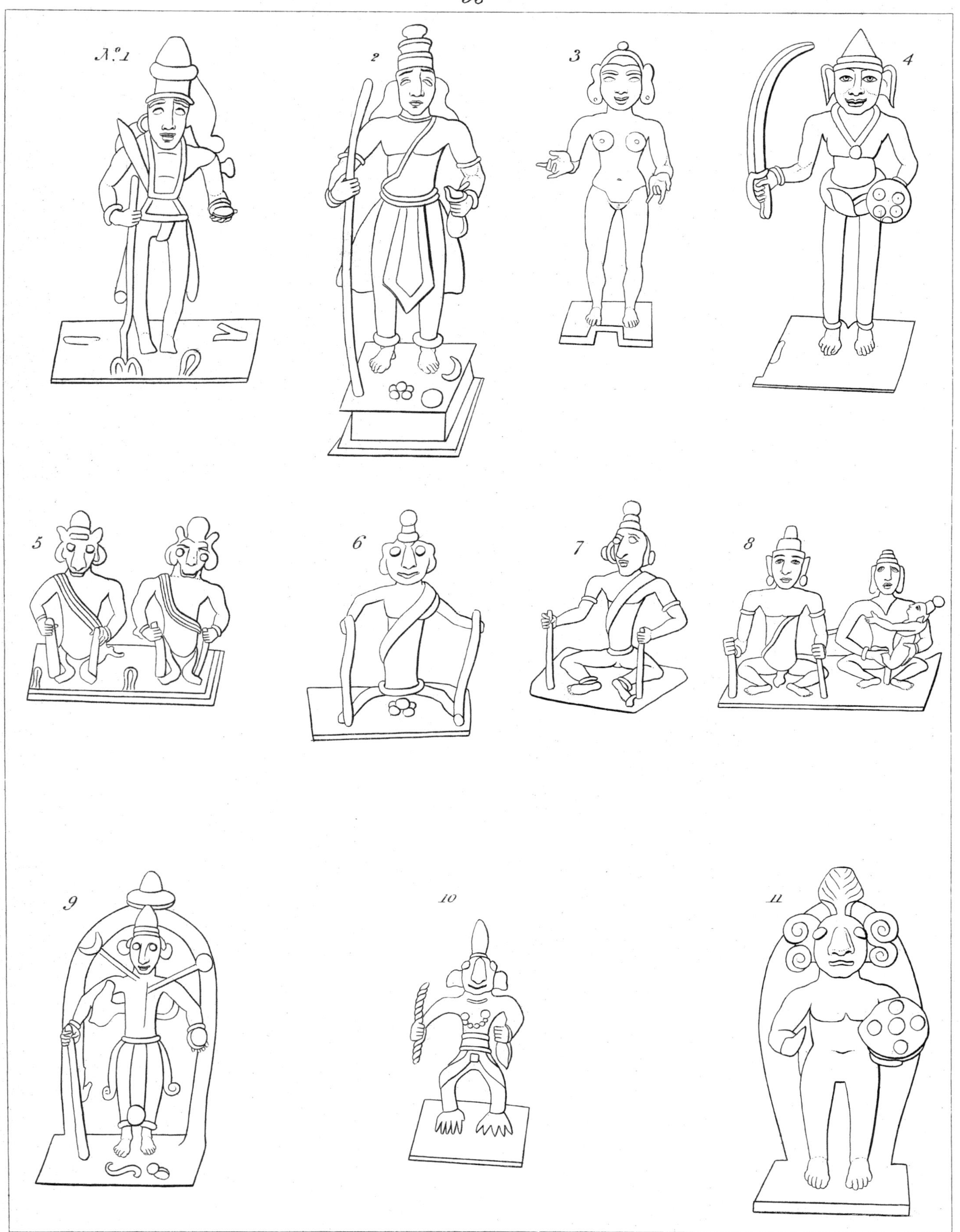

M. Haughton del.ᵗ

From very ancient and rude casts in brass &c.

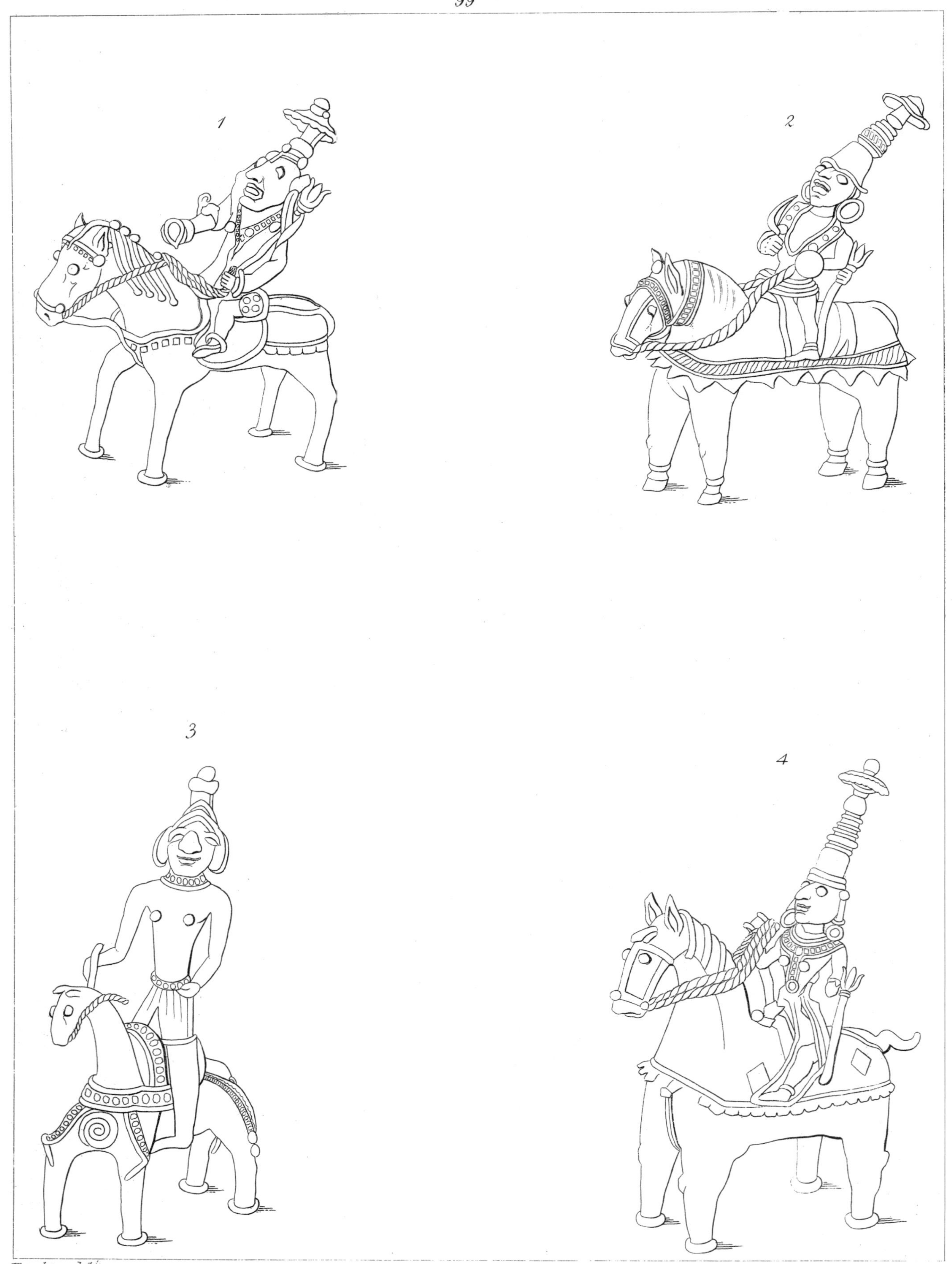

From very ancient casts in brafs &c.

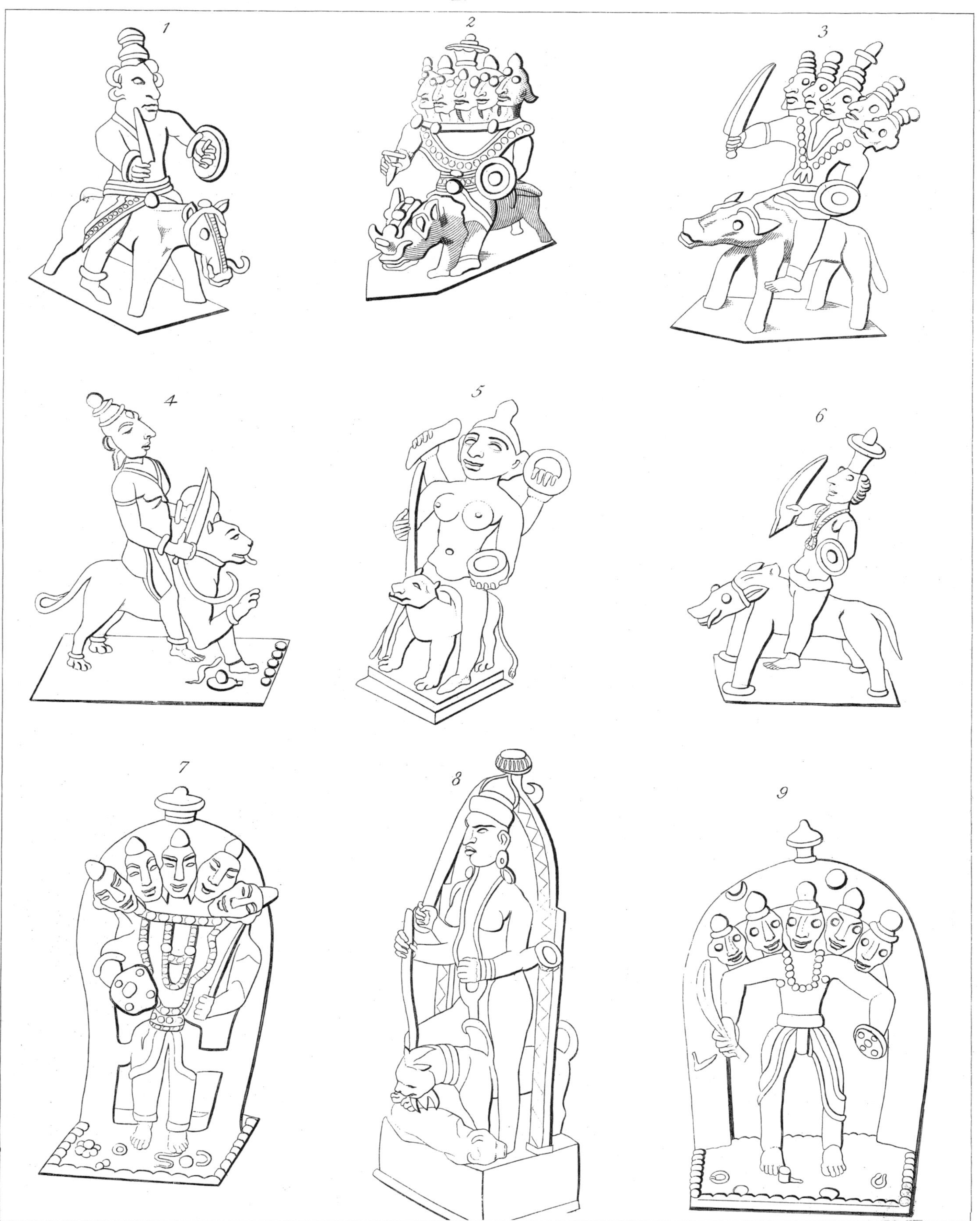

Swaine del et. Sc.

From very ancient casts in brass &c.

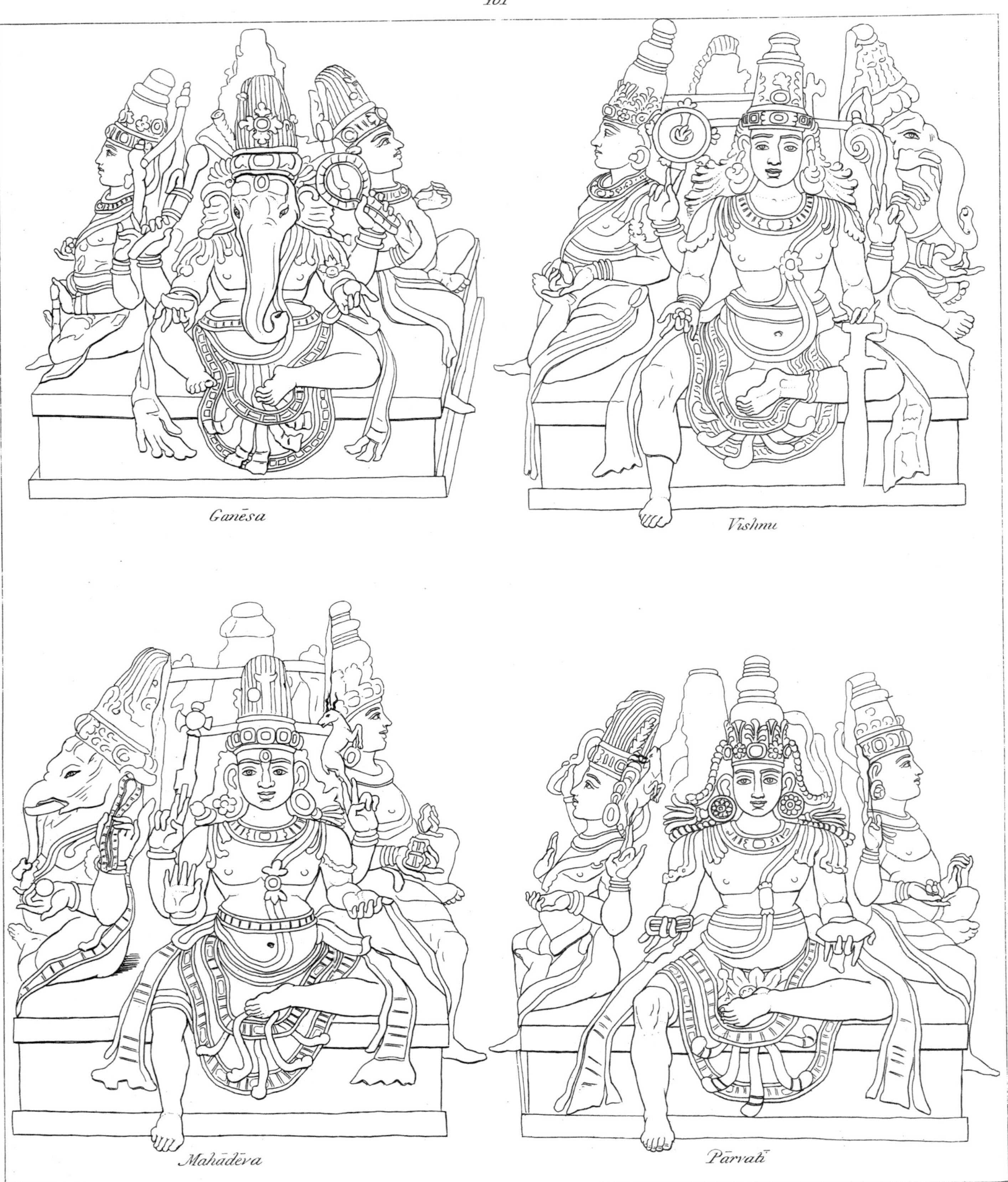

From a four sided cast in bronze

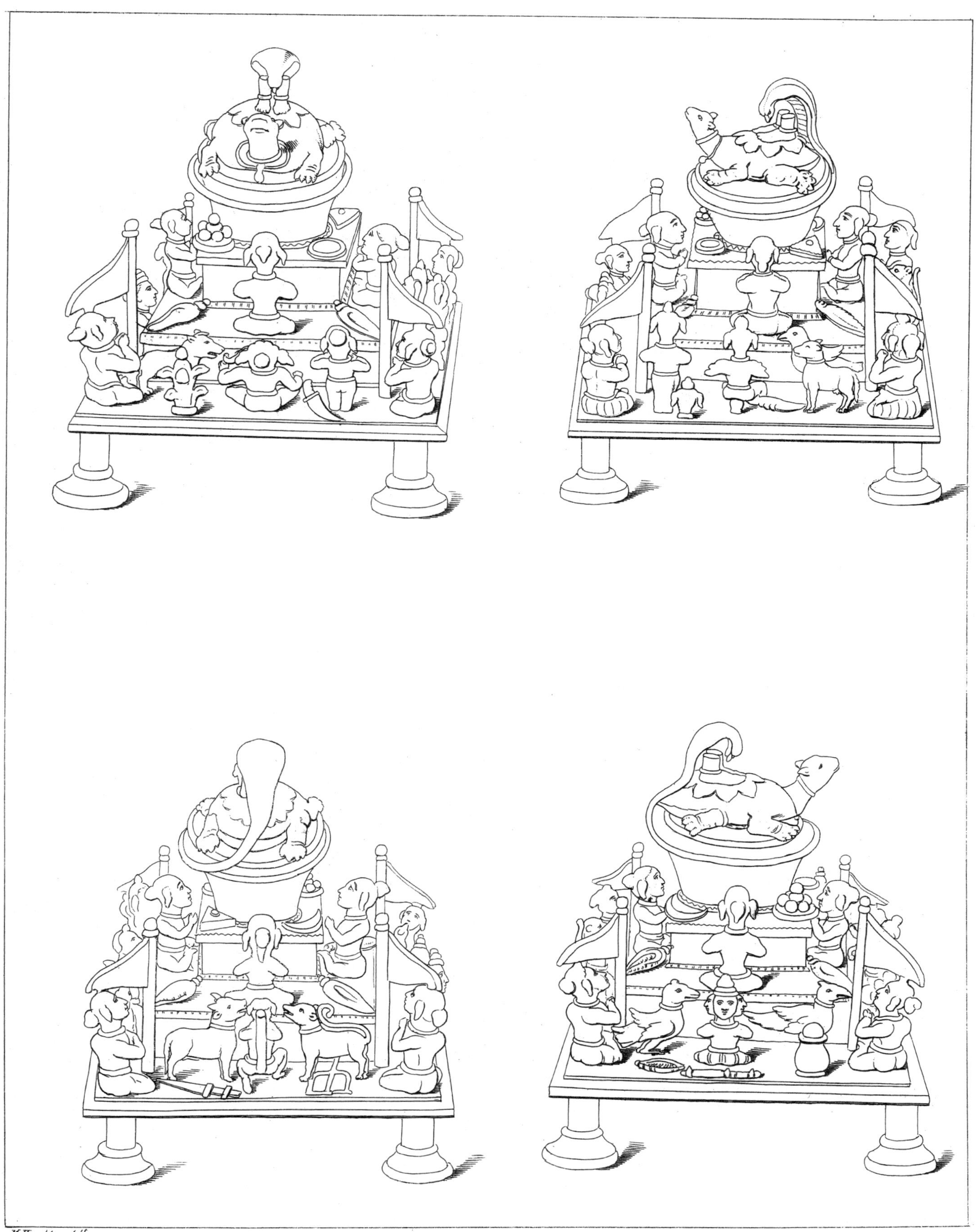

From a four-sided Cast in Brass. In the collection of the Right Honorable Viscount Valentia.

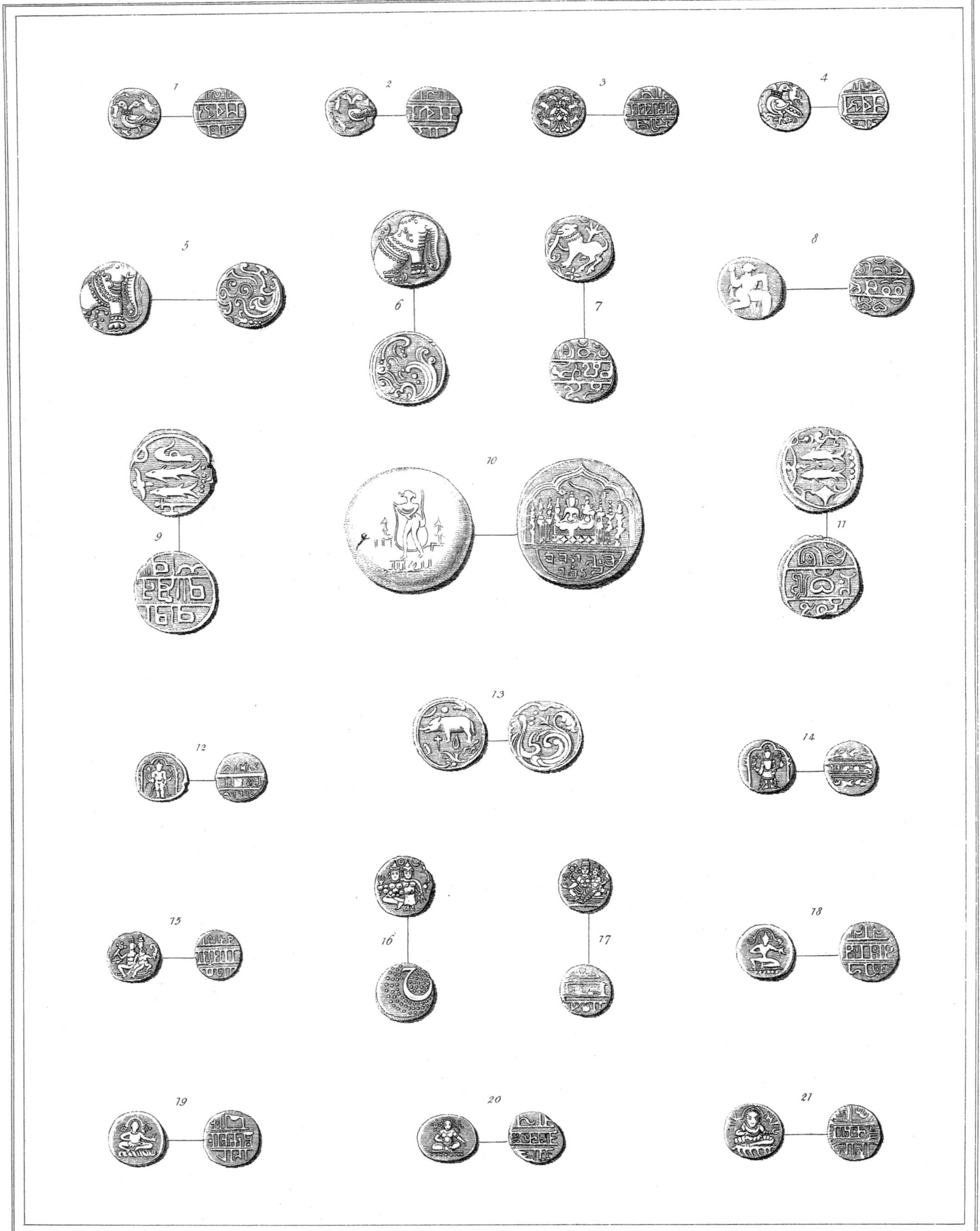

ANCIENT HINDU COINS & MEDALS.

From the CABINET of the late TIPPOO SULTAN, now in the Possession of MAJOR DAVID PRICE.

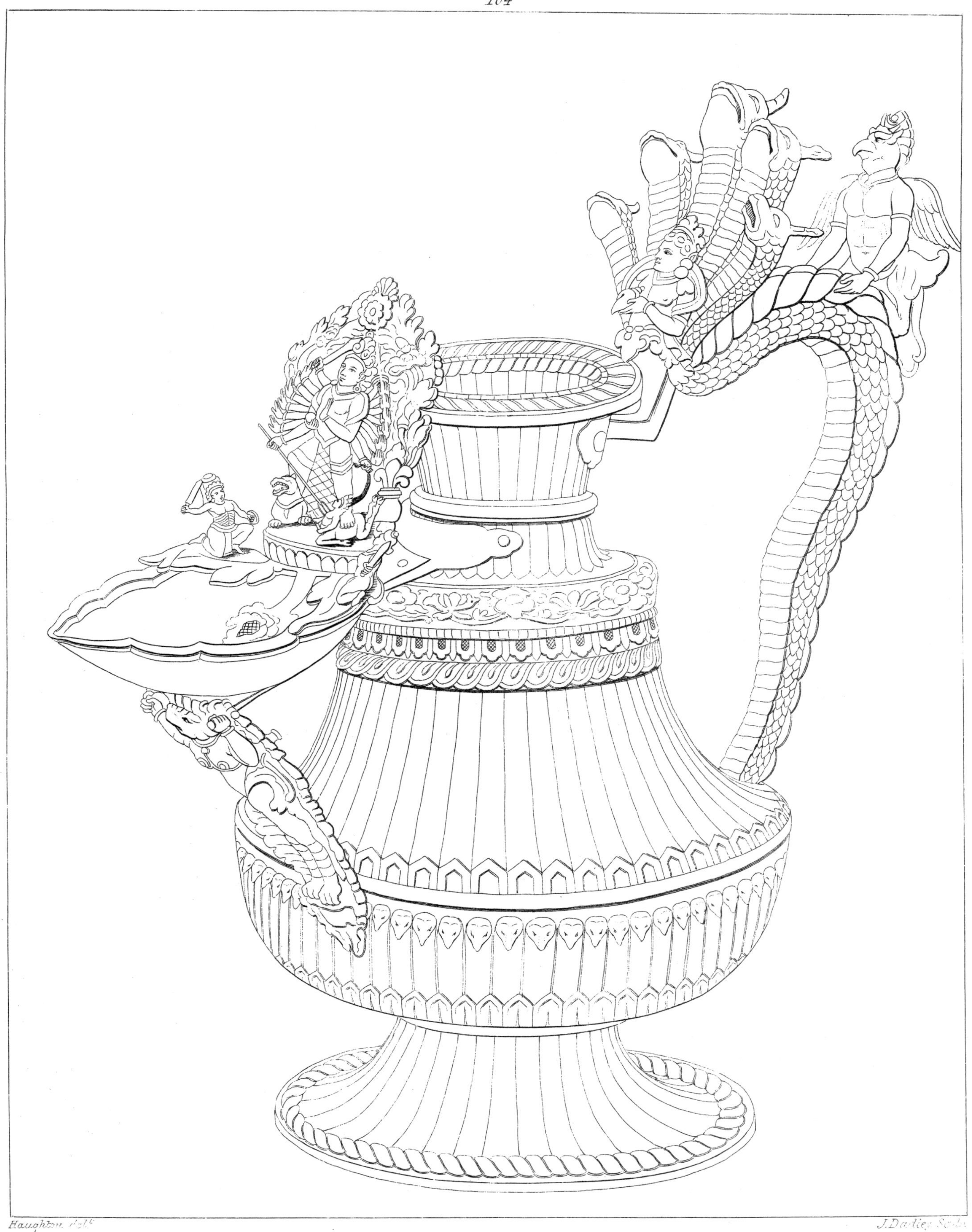

A SACRIFICIAL VASE of gilt Copper.

in the Museum at the India House.